The Management Myth

Also by Matthew Stewart

The Courtier and the Heretic:
Leibniz, Spinoza, and the Fate of God in the Modern World

Monturiol's Dream:
The Extraordinary Story of the Submarine Inventor Who Wanted to
Save the World

The Truth about Everything:
An Irreverent History of Philosophy, with Illustrations

The Management Myth

Why the Experts Keep Getting it Wrong

Matthew Stewart

W. W. NORTON & COMPANY   NEW YORK LONDON

For information about permission to reproduce
selections from this book, write to Permissions,
W. W. Norton & Company, Inc.,
500 Fifth Avenue, New York, NY 10110

For information about special discounts for bulk
purchases, please contact W. W. Norton Special Sales
at specialsales@wwnorton.com or 800-233-4830

Manufacturing by Courier Westfor
Book design by Chris Welch
Production manager: Anna Oler

Library of Congress Cataloging-in-Publication Data

Stewart, Matthew, 1963–
The management myth : why the "experts" keep getting it wrong /
Matthew Stewart.
p. cm.
Includes bibliographical references and index.
ISBN 978-0-393-06553-4 (hardcover)
1. Management—Philosophy. I. Title.
HD30.19.S74 2009
658.001—dc22

2009018464

W. W. Norton & Company, Inc.
500 Fifth Avenue, New York, N.Y. 10110
www.wwnorton.com

W. W. Norton & Company Ltd.
Castle House, 75/76 Wells Street, London W1T 3QT

1 2 3 4 5 6 7 8 9 0

For K., S., and A.

Contents

III. Thinking Ahead

IV. Striving for Excellence

The Accidental Consultant

M y entry into the field of management consulting was like one of those wrong turns that take you into a part of town you never knew existed. At the time, I was just finishing my doctoral dissertation on nineteenth-century German philosophy. My business experience consisted of a miserable summer at a fast-food restaurant, and my acquaintance with management theory was limited to a poster in the restaurant staff room celebrating the virtues of Quality! Service! Cleanliness! I had no clear idea what management consulting was, except that it sounded like the kind of thing that people like me should be prevented from doing. I had no clue what I was getting into.

The adventure began in a pub, over a game of pool. The annual recruiting season had long since come and gone. I was losing badly to a pair of undergraduates who had recently received offers from a prestigious consulting firm. There was something very wrong in the giddy way they talked about their careers in "corporate strategy," I thought. They were 22 years old or so; I was going on 26. What could they do for the corporations of the world that I couldn't do better?

The truth is that I badly needed a job. My life savings had dipped into three-digit territory. The only occupation for which I was qualified was teaching academic philosophy; but, on the basis of somewhat obscure philosophical objections, I had developed an aversion to the subject. (To be fair, the feeling appeared to be mutual.) As I gazed at the pool balls ricocheting on their predetermined but unpredictable paths, it occurred to me that, instead of spending the next year watching daytime TV, I, too, could make some ready cash by offering strategy tips to CEOs of Fortune 500 companies.

On the morning after pool night, I typed up a CV and sent copies to about ten management consulting firms. I was unaware of the custom of writing personalized notes to each firm driving home my passion to work for them and them alone, so my cover letters were limited to three curt sentences announcing my availability for employment. Nine out of ten of my envelopes met with the likely response: a swift rejection, accompanied by insincere assurances that I was bound to find suitable employment elsewhere. One CV, however, happened to intersect with a founding partner of one of the smaller, so-called boutique consulting firms just as a space opened up on his schedule in a planned visit to town. This partner, I was later informed, had embarked on an enlightened program of recruiting "experimental" hires.

That I should have been classified with the laboratory animals seems fair enough. After all, I was in the market for an "experimental" job. The plan, as I formulated it to friends, family, and skeptical professors in those heady days after winning the interview lottery, was to make a tidy sum of money for a year or two and then resume the journey toward my true calling (whatever that might turn out to be). Spinoza polished lenses for a living and Bertrand Russell wrote potboilers, I reasoned, so what could be wrong with moonlighting as a corporate adviser?

Although the probability that I would get the job was at this point vanishingly small, I nonetheless began to entertain some alarming ambitions. Academic philosophy is landlocked in a desert of pedantry and idealism, I told my friends. Management consulting represents a return to the material world from which philosophy must draw its inspiration. I pictured myself standing on the forecastle of a mighty corporation on the hunt for the great white whale of global capitalism. "To the East Asian markets, mateys!" I shouted out in my mind. "Thar blows a profit opportunity!" I was tempted to call myself Ishmael. In short, I was not only unemployable but a potential menace to the working people of the world.

In any case, my competitive instincts had already overwhelmed any merely rational deliberations about the course on which I was set. The interview might as well have been for a position as a tennis instructor; now that I was in the running, I was determined to ace it. Over the next two weeks, I read the *Financial Times* cover to cover every morning. I set aside my turgid Germans in favor of a copy of Tom Peters and Robert Waterman's breezy best seller *In Search of Excellence*, from which I learned to say things like "hands on/value-driven!" and to extol the virtues of "simultaneous loose-tight properties," whatever those were. Every night I put myself to sleep (literally) with a textbook on corporate finance.

On a drizzly spring morning in 1988, in a baroque-style hotel conference room littered with recently emptied Louis XV chairs, I squared off against Henry,* a dapper, silver-haired, 50-ish Englishman with an angular head that looked too big for his small frame. I leaned forward in my seat, tugging at the sleeves of a suit that seemed to have grown tighter since its glory days on the high school debate team and awaited the opportunity to deliver my fortnight's worth of insights on "globalization," "securitization," and the driving need of modern corporations to develop those "simultaneous loose-tight" properties in the face of relentless international competition. I was prepared, if necessary, to expound my theory that management consulting is a lot like whale hunting.

After the briefest of greetings, Henry smiled, or perhaps smirked, rubbed his chin, and cocked his head a little sideways. Then he looked straight at me and asked, as though the question had just occurred to him, "How many pubs are there in Great Britain?"

Life is full of surprises. And that's mostly a good thing. Every surprise is an opportunity for learning. My career as a management consultant was a long list of learning opportunities. Like all other consultants, I owe my education to the extraordinary generosity of clients. With their

---

* The characters and scenes taken from my life in this book refer to real people and actual events. However, in order not to violate needlessly the privacy of the individuals involved, and in recognition of the fact that they feature here merely because they had the misfortune of encountering me, I have changed all of their names. In the case of clients and client individuals, I have gone further and altered incidental identifying details.

assistance, I traveled the world and became an expert in several dozen subjects. I helped found a new consulting firm. It shot up like a rocket and then exploded in a fireball of recriminations and lawsuits. Then the stock market, in its inscrutable wisdom, scattered rewards and punishments with benign indifference among the merely undeserving and the viciously incompetent. The experiment that began in my interview with Henry lasted ten years. Frankly, it got a little out of hand. At times it got ugly. But in the end it did yield some interesting and unexpected results.

My experience posed a series of disturbing questions—questions that eventually prompted me to write this book. The trouble began even before my interview on pub life in Great Britain, with a particularly nagging question: Why on earth would anybody hire me as a management consultant? Shortly after receiving my one and only offer, I rephrased the question: Why would anybody hire a firm that would hire me? I squandered quite a bit of mental energy batting away the suspicion that maybe the firm had made an embarrassing mistake. Were its partners smacking themselves on the forehead, wondering what had possessed them to conduct such a hazardous experiment? In truth, however, the most remarkable aspect of my entry into the field of consulting was just how *un*remarkable it was. At the time (and even now), firms just like mine were manically hiring all kinds of people—some of whom, if it is possible to imagine, were even less qualified than me.

Beginning in the early 1980s, a giant sucking sound could be heard on elite university campuses. It was coming from what one recent author aptly calls "the world's newest profession."[1] Although management consulting dates from the early decades of the twentieth century, it had been for much of its existence something of a gentlemen's club. In 1980, the consulting industry, in the broadest definition, employed about 18,000 professionals worldwide.[2] Twenty-five years later, it employed about 10 times as many. (The exact numbers depend significantly on how the boundaries of the industry are defined.) In the top-tier firms, furthermore, the typical young associate flames out less than 2 years on the job. As a result, the consulting industry developed a fearsome appetite for fresh recruits. Roughly one-quarter of graduates at top business schools and up to one-sixth of undergraduates at elite universities now begin their careers by advising other people how to manage their businesses.

It's all about the money, of course. I was taken aback when my prospective employers offered me a starting salary of $75,000. It seemed like an injudicious amount for an unemployable philosopher. It made me question the financial savvy of the firm's partners. Yet shortly I had cause to wonder who was fooling whom. Like any other average consultant at a top-tier firm, I was soon being billed out to clients at the rate of about half a million dollars per year.

The numbers thickened the mystery around my newly discovered vocation. As I was leaving graduate school, an old professor summed up the enigma in the form of a question for which I had no good answer at the time. Over a last lunch of fish and chips, he put on a good-natured frown and asked me, "How can so many who know so little make so much by telling other people how to do the jobs they are paid to know how to do?"

As I prepared to take up my new job, I felt somewhat insecure about the evident deficiencies in my business training. I called my brother (who has an MBA) and asked him to give me some pointers in the language of business. He just laughed, adding that his classmates would be pretty annoyed to hear that I'd picked up the job without having to pass through business school. At the department store where I bought a dark gray suit, I practiced making businesslike expressions in the full-length mirror. On my first day of work, as I approached the firm's Fifth Avenue office in my somber new duds, I felt like a snake oil salesman without snake oil. I was sure I'd get busted for impersonating an MBA.

Over the past century, the MBA has evolved from a handy accessory to a virtual necessity for entry into the upper ranks of the corporate world. In 1968, the nation's universities awarded fewer than 18,000 master's degrees in business subjects.[3] In 1988, the year I started work, that number had grown to 70,000. As of 2008, it has passed 140,000, representing one out of four master's degrees of all types. Sometime in the next decade, the population of living MBAs will exceed the population of Chicago. There will be, literally, millions of people trained to speak in the language of business, all presumably prepared to jump "outside the box" together.

For the sake of avoiding ugly stereotypes, I hasten to add that I count the people I met as one of the pleasant surprises in my experiment in business living. The gray-flannel set turn out to be far more colorful and humane than my ornery professors or the popular novels about callow yuppies getting lost on the wrong side of town had led me to expect. The organization man today might very well be a frustrated baritone, a nighttime novelist, or a world-class hunter. In the course of my career, I visited hundreds of workplaces in over a dozen countries, and I came away with the impression that every corner in every office in every firm is as different from the rest as one family is from another. Plus, some of my best friends (not to mention relatives) are MBAs. When I hear easy generalizations about "corporate types" now, I usually find myself think-ing of a dozen counterexamples.

At the same time—here was the surprise—it soon became clear that my lack of a business education just didn't matter. My business career was far from all glory (to put it mildly); but neither the highs nor the lows had anything to do with the fact that I had no business degree. More important, it turned out that my case was nothing special. I had the good fortune to work with consultants from an exotic variety of educational backgrounds: lawyers, doctors, chemical engineers, astrophysicists, and historians, as well as MBAs. In formal evaluations, as well as in my own estimation, those who did not have MBAs performed *better*, on average, than those who had MBAs.

Others in the consulting industry have made the same observation. A member of the London office of the Boston Consulting Group told the *New York Times* that "non-MBAs were receiving better evaluations, on average, than their peers who had gone to business school."[4] McKinsey & Company decided to perform an internal study of the matter, reviewing the performance of associates at the one-, three-, and seven-year marks. "At all three points," the firm's chief recruiter told the *Times*, "the folks who don't have a business degree are at least as successful."

The pattern extends beyond the peculiar occupation of management consulting. In a review of the evidence on the performance of MBAs across the board, business school professors Jeffrey Pfeffer and Christina Fong concluded that "neither possessing an MBA degree nor grades earned in [MBA] courses correlate with career success."[5] Henry Mintzberg, perhaps the most able contemporary critic of business school curricula, observed that none of the four most widely celebrated CEOs has an MBA, whereas 40% of the CEOs cited in a *Fortune* article, "Why CEOs Fail," do have MBAs.[6] Jack Welch, one of the fantastic four, who happens to hold a PhD in chemical engineering, recently advised students at MIT's Sloan School of Management to concentrate on networking. "Everything else you need to know you can learn on the job," he said. The school's dean reportedly went slack-jawed as he picked up the scandalous implication that the degree itself is "a waste of time."[7]

There is also good reason to doubt whether the research material that the business schools supply to the world is any more useful than the credentials they offer their students. A 1988 study sponsored by the business schools themselves stated the obvious when it concluded that "key managers pay little or no attention to [academic business] research or its findings."[8] A study from 2003 confirmed that "most business schools . . . have not been very effective in the creation of *useful* business ideas."[9] Among the colleagues and clients with whom I worked, I cannot recall a single individual who relied on the academic literature on management in a serious or systematic way.

Yet the enrollments keep growing, and the fundamental idea behind business education remains widely accepted, even among its critics. Warren Bennis and James O'Toole, a pair of well-known professors from the University of Southern California, for example, open a much-discussed 2005 article in the *Harvard Business Review* with the frank declaration that "business schools are on the wrong track."[10] But then they turn around and assert that "business is a profession, akin to medicine and the law, and business schools are professional schools—or should be."[11]

This very premise of business education, however, stands in need of some uninhibited questioning. After all, if it turned out that having an MD bore no relation to an individual's performance as a doctor, or that doctors routinely ignored the research supplied by medical schools, questions would have to be asked. My experience certainly left me scratching my head. Is business a profession? Do business managers need to be trained in a discipline of business management? Why do business schools exist?

In those fretful weeks before taking up my new job, I decided to turn for help to the local bookstore. There are, in fact, two kinds of books on management: the kind that the business school professors inflict on their students, and the kind that people actually buy—the works of so-called "management gurus." I gifted a large part of my hard-earned sign-on bonus to the gurus. As soon as I started work, however, I found myself too busy to open the books in my stash. Only after my consulting career had come to its ignominious conclusion was I at last able to catch up with the gurus. The experience was, to speak frankly, shocking.

To look on the bright side, the gurus can seriously enhance your fantasy life. While reading their books, I find that I am often overcome by the urge to become a CEO. I really like the idea of making heroic decisions to sell off underperforming divisions, conquer new markets, and unleash the creative genius of "my people"—especially if it means receiving millions in stock options from grateful shareholders and getting my face on the cover of *Fast Company* as a "VISIONARY MAVERICK!!" "Get 30 or 40 of your colleagues together and divide them into four or five teams" in order to review your corporation's management processes, says guru Gary Hamel in a typical passage.[12] Sure, I think, and then maybe I'll order the corporate jet to take me and my admiring underlings to Aspen.

Upon putting the gurus' books down, however, I find that I get the same feeling I get after reaching the bottom of a supersize bag of tortilla chips. They taste great while they last, but in the end, what am I left with? I reopen Jim Collins' *Good to Great* to a random page and find, for example, that "all good-to-great companies began the process of finding a path to greatness by confronting the brutal facts of their current reality."[13] So true! But then, what is the alternative? Achieving greatness by clinging to fanciful delusions about current reality? Peters and Waterman themselves acknowledge that the eight lessons of *In Search of Excellence* are "motherhoods" and "platitudes"—and then they turn around and suggest that the "intensity" with which these commonplaces are believed can miraculously transform them into something more.[14] Peters and Austin devote chapter 1 of the sequel, *A Passion for Excellence*, to a vindication of the claim that their work amounts to "a blinding flash of the obvious."[15] But, in that case, is there really a need for a chapter 2?

The strangest thing about the guru business, however, is not its questionable content but its incredible size. You might think that the market for advice on how to manage a multibillion-dollar conglomerate would be comparable to the market for, say, the interior design of corporate jets. Given that most of the people offering the advice haven't run big businesses themselves and seem content to smother their readers with truisms, you'd think the market would be smaller still. But in fact, telling people how (not) to run big businesses is itself a big business. It's as if a band of unemployed corporate-jet decorators had found a following with the minivan crowd. As I plowed through my shelf full of management advice, I could not avoid contemplating an impolite question: How can so many bad books sell so well?

Not long after I started consulting, I made the humiliating discovery that my grand salary and even my exorbitant billing rate were just so much corporate chicken feed. It turns out that management consultants are able to bill themselves out at half a million dollars per year in part because they work for people who think that half a million dollars isn't a lot of money.

In 2006, the CEOs of the Fortune 500 averaged $15 million in compensation;[16] and in 2007, median CEO pay continued to rise, despite the onset of an economic downturn.[17] CEOs now take home an average of about 400 times the salary of the typical worker, up from a multiple of about 40 three decades ago.[18] Along with the money has come a whole lot of admiration for the great leaders of the corporate world. University leaders, philanthropists, hospital administrators, and politicians promise to manage their fiefdoms like CEOs manage their companies. George W. Bush, the first MBA to become president of the United States, promoted himself in the 2000 election as a "CEO-president." When Jesus is compared with a CEO, it is Jesus who is thought to gain by the comparison. Whether the problem is a soul in search of salvation, a relationship on the rocks, or a superpower in trouble, according to the received wisdom the answer is to turn it into a private corporation and then manage it like a CEO.

Many have rightly questioned whether the performance of today's corporate superstars justifies so much money and love. When a CEO such as Robert Nardelli of Home Depot is paid hundreds of millions to *stop* working, for example, or when Angelo Mozilo of Countrywide Financial earns hundreds of millions for building a business that doles out mortgages to people who can't afford to pay them back, after all, people are bound to ask questions. In its 2007 survey of executive compensation, the Associated Press observed that "CEO pay rose and fell regardless of the direction of a company's stock price or profits."[19] American CEOs make on average two to three times as much as their European counterparts do, but, as Northwest Airlines Chairman Gary Wilson noted in the *Wall Street Journal*, "there is no evidence that American CEOs perform any better for their shareholders."[20]

The most important question about today's managerial superheroes, however, is not whether they are "worth it." It's about who works for whom. Do managers exist to serve their corporations, or is it the other way around?[21] In a world where board members tend to be the CEO's dearest friends, where the chairman of the board is often the CEO, and where shareholders are in and out of their positions in the company before lunchtime, this is not an idle question. It is the same one that the Romans asked themselves when their empire began to get unruly: *Quis custodiet ipsos custodes?* Loosely translated: Who will manage the managers?

Maybe the biggest surprise I encountered in my trip through the material world was the feeling of déjà vu it inspired. The experts who aren't really experts, the degrees that certify ignorance, the atrociously written books, and the troubling questions about who is really in charge—where had I seen it all before? In its best and its worst moments, management reminded me of the subject I thought I had left behind—philosophy. When, upon my early retirement, I finally had the opportunity to examine the management literature in depth, it felt as though I had stumbled into a familiar, untidy backyard. I found a discipline that isn't a discipline so much as a collection of unsolved problems and hidden agendas—where asking the right questions is much more important than finding the right answers, where issues are not resolved so much as temporarily placated, and where the biggest rewards go to those who can stay focused on the one big thing that really matters.

Gradually it dawned on me that management is indeed a neglected branch of the humanities, and that the study of management belongs, if anywhere, to the history of philosophy. Management theorists lack depth, I realized, because they have been doing for only a century what philosophers and creative thinkers have been doing for millennia. This explains why future business leaders are better off reading histories, philosophical essays, or just a good novel than pursuing degrees in business. Indeed, it explains why we'd all be better off if businesspeople eased off of their business degrees. (Which is not to say that the humanities as currently practiced—with their phobias about numbers and basic economics and their proclivity for pseudotechnical jargon—couldn't stand for some improvement.)

Unfortunately, the true nature of management as a humanity is not yet widely understood. For almost a century, a very different view of the nature of management has held sway in business schools and among management theorists and consultants. The paradoxes that I encountered in my detour through the business world, I now think, arise from this widely shared but ultimately mistaken idea about the nature of management. My aim in this book is to trace the genealogy of this idea, to expose its flaws, and to replace it.

The conventional view holds that management is a kind of technology—a bundle of techniques, based on scientific observation, tended by experts, and transferable to students. "If you have two cars in the garage, a television in every room, and a digital device in every pocket, it is thanks to the inventors of modern management," declares Gary Hamel.[22] He goes on to draw an extended analogy between the invention of management and the invention of the gas-powered automobile. Peter Drucker takes for granted the same basic idea of management when he argues that "management has transformed the social and economic fabric of the world's developed countries."[23] The idea that management is a technical discipline can be traced to a number of earlier, seminal thinkers—notably Henri Fayol, Mary Parker Follett, and, above all, Frederick Winslow Taylor, the so-called father of scientific management.

This idea of management has its roots firmly planted in the American experience. It represents a worthwhile effort to understand economic authority and cooperation in a manner suitable for a democracy. It draws its power from the most fundamental tension in American society: the unsettled conflict between the egalitarian instincts of a democracy and the hierarchical requirements of modern nation building. In this respect, it straddles the debate that first emerged in the late eighteenth century between Thomas Jefferson and Alexander Hamilton. It currently plays a crucial role in supporting the ideal of meritocracy that guides the modern university system. It will continue to feature in American thought as long as the underlying contradictions that give rise to it persist.

But the modern idea of management is right enough to be dangerously wrong and it has led us seriously astray. It has sent us on a mistaken quest to seek scientific answers to unscientific questions. It offers pretended technological solutions to what are, at bottom, moral and political problems. It conjures an illusion—easily exploited—about the nature and value of management expertise. It induces us to devote formative years to training in subjects that do not exist. It favors a naïve view of the sources of mismanagement, making it harder to check abuses of corporate power. Above all, it contributes to a misunderstanding about the sources of our prosperity, leading us to neglect the social, moral, and political infrastructure on which our well-being depends.

The sixteenth-century English philosopher Francis Bacon defined an idol as a phantasm of the mind—sometimes founded in the limitations of our rational faculties, often furthered by the misuse of language and the sophistry of false teachers—that leads to a pattern of misunderstanding of the world and sustains irrational practices. By that definition, the idea of management is an idol of our times. It is a fat word over a lot of thin question marks. It is an edifice of grammatical errors, misperceptions, and superstitions that keeps in business much that should be put out of business. In his *Twilight of the Idols*, Nietzsche vowed to test the idols of his time "with a hammer and perhaps to hear for an answer that famous hollow sound that speaks of inflated bowels."[24] The management idol, I hope to show, stands in need of a good, hard knock.

So, how many pubs are there in Great Britain?

"I dunno, a lot?" I blurted out.

"Why don't you just have a guess?" Henry said. The smile was now definitely a smirk.

"How about 200,000?"

After a few moments of embarrassing silence, I understood. He was testing me. I was supposed to show how I could reason my way to a credible answer. My pool buddies hadn't bothered to warn me about the "case interview" technique, which is now so much the standard among consultants that business schools run training sessions to prepare students for it.

The only relevant facts I could summon were the approximate population of Great Britain and the price of a pint at the local pub. I took in a deep breath and on the exhale blasted out a long series of arithmetical operations involving many other numbers pulled right out of the hot air in my head. With the benefit of aggressive rounding and convenient fudge factors, I eventually settled on the claim that there were 100,000 pubs in Great Britain. The correct number, Henry said at the time, was 76,000.

Of course, accuracy wasn't the point. The purpose of the exercise was to see how easily I could talk about a subject about which I knew almost nothing on the basis of facts that were almost entirely fictional. It was, I realized in retrospect, an excellent introduction to management consulting.

"Winging it" would be one way to describe the most important skill required of a management consultant—though other, less polite terms come to mind too. Throughout the years I spent consulting, I never lost the sensation that I was just making it all up as I went along. My career, such as it was, sometimes felt like a cabaret of one-act plays, each more preposterous than the last.

We are all limited by experience, and my experience was in some ways more limited than that of most members of the management classes. Some of the episodes I recount in this book are not exactly models of good behavior. In fact, the history of the firm I helped to found has much more to say about what is wrong in the world of management today than about what is right. As I offer up a few scenes from my working life in this book, in any case, I hope it will be understood that I do so not because my story is special, but precisely because, on the whole, it is not.

I. Doing Things with Numbers

The Whale

The Whale is a kind of graph. Its official title is usually something like "Cumulative Customer Profitability," and it also goes by the generic name of the "skew chart." Various other kinds of graphs occupied my days and nights during my first years as a consultant, but it is the Whale that captures the spirit of the whole experience. The Whale is my madeleine. One glance at its distinctive curves and in my mind I'm back, cutting and pasting charts and text (with real scissors and tape, the way we did it then), running through airports, hovering over a transparency projector in front of skeptical men in suits, and trading boozy fish stories with teammates in an overpriced hotel restaurant. Somewhere in the belly of the Whale lies the essence of consulting wisdom—a surprisingly deep insight into the power of numbers over life. At the same time, I can't help but see in the graph a kind of frustrated promise, like a window onto a brick wall, or an expressionless face in an old photograph.

The Whale is always part of a story. Every whale story takes place in its own setting, and each is shaped to fit the needs of its audience and the ambitions of the speaker; but all the stories are at some level the same. They all feature the same plot and characters: the hapless client, the fiercely intelligent consultant, the unexpected insight, and the mutually profitable ending. I must have heard my first whale story in New York, sometime in the month or two I spent "on the beach" between the day I started and the day I was first unleashed on paying clients. I remember taking my place among a group of young associates in a windowless conference room, relaxing as a series of the firm's leaders recounted their latest seafaring adventures over brief slide show presentations.

The best of the storytellers was a senior partner named Roland, the individual who would have more influence on my subsequent career than any other. If Henry, the partner who had hired me, was a thin, cool line, like a human razor blade, Roland was a jolly, well-rounded figure—the kind who makes the people he meets feel unexpectedly good about life. He had a face like a pink bowling ball and a belly to match. With just a few wisps of red hair circling his permanently ruddy complexion, it was hard to say if he looked more like a bulldog or a newborn baby. He had a thick French accent and drew heavily on a limited stockpile of American colloquialisms, cheerfully painting the world in the bold strokes and primary colors that are typically the lot of those who live their lives in a foreign language.

He was, literally, a hunter. I often caught sight of him in corduroy trousers and jacket—the kind with leather patches on the elbow—on his way to some lodge, where he would undoubtedly have a cigar and cognac by the fireplace before heading out early in the morning to endanger a local animal species. At his home deep in the forests of middle Europe, where we often met while stalking prospective clients, I slept in a guest cottage that served as a kind of zoological mausoleum, under the glassy gaze of dozens of stuffed animal heads from Africa, Asia, and the Americas. There was something innocent and appealing about Roland, in a rascally sort of way. I figured he always let his quarry get a head start before blasting them into oblivion with his high-powered rifle.

"I asked Joe (or whoever it was)," Roland would have said (or words to that effect), "Joe, how well do you really know what your people are doing in the corporate business? Can your people tell you, right now, which of your customers are profitable?" (It always sounded like he was calling them "profiteroles.") Joe would have been the clueless client, a senior manager of a large bank or something like that. According to the conventions of the genre, he would have had no idea how his profiteroles were doing.

In the economy of the firm, Roland was the harpooner. His specialty was sinking the barbed hook of our services deep within the flesh of unsuspecting clients. He had an uncanny ability to home in on the things that really mattered to clients. "It's really important to have a client who understands the way it works," Roland once explained to me. "It's like you're riding in parallel elevators. You help me up, I help you up." Roland didn't just sell something to Joe. He became Joe, inhabiting all the hopes, fears, and insecurities that beset Joe in his struggle up the slippery slopes of a large organization. He learned to think like his quarry. Like the cave painters of ancient times, Roland revered his prey.

"Joe showed me the reports he was getting," Roland would go on, snorting emphatically as though he'd just had a whiff of some inferior cheese. "He knew it was all accounting bullshit! I said to him, how can you put up with this?"

In most business enterprises, financial data is captured for accounting and operational purposes: to keep track of how much cash goes in and out, to figure out how much tax to pay, and so on. For the purpose of analyzing business activities, however, such information is often incomplete or even misleading.

"So how old do you think he is?" one of my new colleagues whispered to me in the back of the room. I glanced at Roland's well-weathered face and generous paunch and hazarded a guess: "Early fifties?" In fact, he was 37 at the time.

The same conversation took place many times among the new members of the firm. Roland stood as a morbid cautionary example—our living portrait of Dorian Gray. This is what you, too, will look like if you stay in consulting for 10 years, we'd say to each other. On the other hand, we shared a kind of fascination with his "better to burn out" way of life. Many of us soon found ourselves trying to keep pace with Roland in smoking cigars, downing rare vintages, and engaging in other extreme sports.

The analysis Roland and his team performed for Joe would have followed a prescribed course. First they construct a database of the client's customers, detailing each customer's product and transaction activity over the preceding year. Next they establish a clean profit and loss statement for the whole business, including all overheads but excluding extraordinary items. Then, to allocate the revenues and costs of the business to each customer, they devise algorithms based on detailed models of each kind of product and transaction. The complexity of these algorithms, naturally, is such that they are far beyond the powers of ordinary clients to comprehend. The result is an analysis of the exact revenue, expense, and profit to the client attributable to each of its customers. Finally, the team lines up the customers according to their profitability, thus allowing the client to see how much of its profits can be attributed to its most profitable customers, and how much to the least profitable.

"Et voilà!" Roland would say, at the climax of the presentation, slamming down the transparency of his graph "Cumulative Customer Profitability, Revenue, and Expenses." It was the leviathan. He would trace his felt tip over the all-important top side of the Whale, which tracked the cumulative profitability of customers. "Look at this skew! It's terrific!"

The Whale

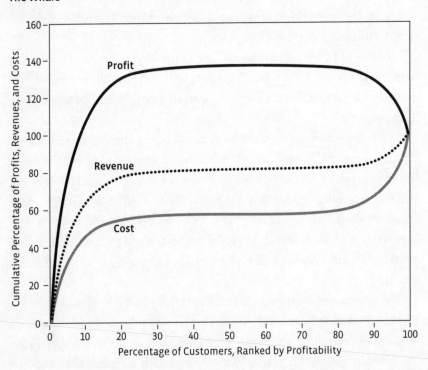

The typical graph showed that the top 20% of the client's customers generated so much business that they accounted for significantly more than 100% of its profits. That is to say, if the client had served only these customers, it would have made much more money than it did. For the next 70% or so of the customers, the line went flat, indicating that they made little additional contribution to the bottom line. For the final 10% of customers, the line took a nosedive, meaning that these customers were subtracting from the client's profits. Roland liked to slap big fat capital letters over each of the groups: the star customers were As, the space wasters were Bs, and the dogs were Cs.

The lower two lines on the graph added some explanatory flesh to the results. The middle line tracked the cumulative share of revenues for the same customers. Not surprisingly, it leapt up at the start and then flattened out, showing that the As, representing only 20% of the customers, accounted for 80% of the revenues, while the Bs and Cs, representing 80% of the customers, accounted for only 20% of the revenues. The lower line tracked expenses. Here one could see that, though there was a big rise at the start, indicating that the As also represented a large part of the expenses, there was also an appreciable upturn at the end, registering the fact that the Cs were running up significant expenses. Thus, the "dogs" were chewing up the client's precious resources, while offering no revenues in return.

"Joe peed his pants!" Roland would say exultantly. Faced with such a devastating analysis of his core business—what on earth were his people thinking, doing all that work on behalf of unprofitable customers?!—Joe had no choice but to hire us to sort out the mess. This was the moment that consultants lived for: the triumph of brains over bureaucratic miasma.

I don't remember if it was my idea or someone else's to call it the Whale. At some point, in any case, there was a keen discussion about the nature of the beast.

"Our whale was fatter," one veteran said. A fat whale, he pointed out, was a serious problem, because it indicated that the Cs were running up big expenses and big losses.

"It's more complicated if it has a grin at the end," someone else chimed in. A grin meant an upward slope in the revenue line toward the end, showing that the Cs were generating significant revenue even if they were losing money overall.

Someone else suggested it was important to look for "humpback" whales. A humpback, or sudden change in the slope of the profitability line, could mark a break point among qualitatively different kinds of customers.

"Anybody ever seen a dolphin?" A dolphin would have been the ideal shape—profits, revenues, and expenses all sloping gently upward.

In short, I had fallen in with a group of very uncommon people. One of my colleagues was a talented musician who did a poor job of concealing the fact that he would rather have been composing symphonies than fiddling with spreadsheets. Another colleague, an Englishman, seemed as if he had just stepped out of an Evelyn Waugh novel. He was a master of irony who rarely said anything that did not allow a second, less kind interpretation. Then there was the Euro stud, a financial whiz and sports car fanatic who went all gooey when chatting up his various girlfriends on the phone. The younger associates seemed as if they'd been plucked straight from the front row of a college classroom, like the brilliant science major who made a honking sound when he laughed and regularly applied abstruse statistical concepts in deciding where to have lunch. The more mature associates, mostly MBAs, were almost 30 years old and already married. They wore serious-looking eyeglasses and talked a lot about the babies they saw only in the screaming hours of the night. It was a thoroughly international group, with representatives from every major European country, as well as South and East Asia.

What we had in common—aside from the fact that we were blatantly young and male (with a few exceptions)—was that we were geeks. Propeller-heads. Henry had assembled a firm out of what he thought were the pointiest people he could find. He also seemed to like them a little insecure. The result was a roomful of people trying to prove that they were the smartest in the room. It was an intensely competitive environment, a place for preening with numerical feathers. The mathematical posturing became especially aggressive when a partner was present.

All good whale stories came to an end in the same way: with a Gantt chart showing how our work on behalf of the beleaguered Joe would proceed over the next year, with dotted lines extending hopefully into the indefinite future beyond. I can picture Roland winding up dozens of presentations in this way, straightening up in the glow of the overhead projector and looking around the room. When he spoke at internal meetings about his recent kills, he beamed like a fur-clad tribal leader, surrounded by an enthusiastic band of warrior-huntsmen.

The Whale made a deep impression on me. I found it remarkable that Roland and his band of warrior-geeks could step into a hoary bank and expose the innards of its business. I instinctively felt contempt for Joe and his ilk of corporate apparatchiks. Didn't they see that their livelihood revolved around a fraction of crucial customers, and that they were squandering precious resources on the rest? It was worrisome to think that so much economic power was tied up in the hands of such fools. In every business, I began to think, a handful of customers—or of products or stores or employees—*are* the business, and everything else is just a bucket of red herrings. Armed with this insight, I imagined that I could walk into any corporation and tell its managers something they didn't know.

As a matter of fact, Roland and team had stumbled onto something close to a universal law. It is sometimes called the "80/20 Principle" or "Pareto's Law," although I prefer to think of it as the Great Whale Principle. Vilfredo Pareto, an Italian sociologist of the late nineteenth century, noticed that in many countries the distribution of income and wealth follows a particular mathematical pattern.[1] According to the formula he devised,* if 80% of the wealth is in the hands of 20% of the population (or some similar combination of percentages; the formula allows for variation in the skew), then it is possible to predict how much wealth belongs to, say, the top 10% or the bottom 50%.

The Pareto distribution has since emerged with remarkable consistency in hundreds of studies of wealth and income distributions around the world. Joseph Juran (1904–2008), a Romanian-born American engineer and consultant who championed quality control, showed that Pareto's insight has wide application in industrial and manufacturing settings. He called it the principle of "the vital few and the trivial many."[2]

And yet the Great Whale Principle is about much more than money. At work in Roland's graph, just as in Pareto's equation, is an elemental

---

* For the mathematically inclined, the formula is generally rendered as follows: $\log N = \log A - m \log x$, where N is the number of people with income or wealth higher than x, and A and m are constants.

truth: Whales exist—and they dominate our lives. They are the 20% of your record collection that you listen to 80% of the time; the two hours of fruitful effort that compensate for eight hours of unrewarding toil; the couple dozen pages of a lengthy book that say just about everything it has to say; the three simple words that establish the meaning of an afternoon's conversation; the rare, serendipitous encounters that lead to lifelong relationships; and the handful of memories that make up almost all of what we imagine to be the past. The Great Whale Principle is about focusing on the things that really make a difference. It is the number one item on every management guru's to-do list. It's about the big break, the main chance, the sweet spot, the Big Kahuna. It is the secret of success.

Even better, or so I imagined at the time, I had been handed a tool that would make the whale hunting a cinch, at least in business situations: the spreadsheet. Odd though it may seem now, as a graduate student in philosophy in the mid-1980s—and even though I had initially majored in physics as an undergraduate—I had never seen a spreadsheet. Fortunately, during my time "on the beach" when I started work, the firm organized a three-week "mini-MBA" program for the likes of me—the main outcome of which was that I experienced for the first time the joys of spreadsheet math.

With the help of my able teachers, I, who had previously thought of regression mainly as a bad thing that happened to coddled children, could now perform multiple regressions and other simple statistical analyses with a handful of keystrokes. I was and still am amazed, in the same way that it continues to surprise me that one can walk into a whirring metal tube full of hazardous materials and end up on the other side of the earth just hours later. Before the spreadsheet age, producing a proper skew chart was rarely attempted and undoubtedly required hours of laborious calculations. In my three weeks of training, I learned how to produce one in minutes. Like most consultants today, I soon found that I could not leave home without a spreadsheet. It was the indispensable tool for bringing the secrets of business into the hard light of scientific analysis.

The data-driven approach to life stayed with me long after I left the consulting business and is something that I think I have in common with almost everyone who has experienced the joy of consulting. Henry once told me that he defined consulting as "doing things with numbers that clients would not have imagined possible." Mitt Romney, that erstwhile Bainie, said pretty much the same thing in describing his experience as a consultant: "You're going to get data that they have but have never analyzed in the proper way, and then you're going to tear it apart—and find new and bold answers."[3] Management consulting, in its best moments, is a recognition of the quantitative nature of our reality—of the fact, too easily overlooked by innumerate liberal arts graduates, that a hard look at the numbers can explain much of the structure of the world around us. Those early days in my consulting career were in some ways the most formative of my life. They were the part of my education that went missing at university. Herman Melville wrote, in the voice of Ishmael, that "A whale-ship was my Yale College and my Harvard." Except that my whales were made of numbers, I could have said the same.

In the somewhat exaggerated form with which it gripped me in those early days of my consulting career, this faith in quantitative solutions was very much a feature of the times. Like a whole generation of MBAs, I had assimilated the belief that the most important problems in management are about numbers, and that management itself is an applied science of sorts. In retrospect, my first experiences as a consultant begged a lot of questions: Is management all about numbers? Is it a science? If so, what are the implications for life, work, and education? If not, what are consultants doing?

Had I been a little better informed, I might have known that this idea of management, along with all the questions to which it gives rise, has been around for more than a century. I might have guessed that the insights we modern consultants had, the tricks we played, and the mistakes we made had all been seen before—that they had a pedigree stretching at least as far back as Frederick Winslow Taylor, the so-called father of scientific management. When I started work, however, I knew almost nothing about Taylor, except vaguely that he was a strange man with a stopwatch fetish; and I knew still less about the tradition he had originated. I slipped into the history in relative ignorance, quite uninformed about the origin and development of the ideas that now structured my working life.

"You know, I once told my philosophy prof that I thought he was splitting hairs," Roland later said to me, holding up an imaginary hair. "He told me, 'No, where you see one hair, I see four!'" He guffawed. I appreciated his effort to make me feel comfortable about my suspiciously academic past.

"You know, Mathieu, this is a fantastic opportunity for you," he continued, sotto voce, as though we were entering into a conspiracy. He had just sold another project, this time to a large European bank. A certain senior manager at the bank named Lorenzo or something like that was now his favorite person in the world. "It fits you to a tree!"

He didn't need to sell me on the project. In my mind, I was ready for the hunt.

The Pig-Iron Tale

Frederick Winslow Taylor had a talent for telling stories. His favorite was the one about the 92-pound pig-iron bars. Sitting by the fireplace at the home he called Boxly, with his pet cat Put Mut perched on his shoulder, in front of small audiences of admiring business executives, he must have told the pig-iron tale dozens of times—improving the performance until it became as familiar as an old school cheer, with every gesture and laugh line committed to memory.[4] On one occasion he was able to raise some chuckles by saying, in a tone of mock concern, "Most people think scientific management is chiefly handling pig iron. I do not know why."[5] The pig-iron tale was the first in a long line of what we now call *business case studies*. It was the centerpiece of the "Boxly Talks," which in turn became the basis for Taylor's 1911 book, *The Principles of Scientific Management*, which launched the revolution that created scientific management and the management consulting industry as we now know it.

Boxly was a 12,000-square-foot southern colonial affair lined with century-old boxwood hedges from which it took its name. It sat high in the Philadelphia suburb of Chestnut Hill, overlooking the beautiful Wissahickon Valley. The neighbors included distinguished families such as the Disstons, of the Disston Saw fortune, and the Wanamakers, of the department store.[6] When in 1904, at the age of 48, Taylor arrived at Chestnut Hill, it represented a kind of closure in the circular path of his life. Following a career that had taken him across the country and into the depths of the industrial economy, he had finally settled four miles from Germantown, the elegant Philadelphia suburb where he was raised.

Taylor's father was a prosperous man of leisure, the kind of Philadelphia gentleman of whom it might have been said he was "born retired." His mother belonged to the Winslows, a New England family that had made its fortune in whaling and could trace its ancestry to the Pilgrims. Frederick, born in 1856, showed at an early age that he was different. "It did not seem absolutely necessary that the rectangle of our rounders court should be scientifically accurate, and the whole of a fine sunny morning should be wasted in measuring it off," said one old playmate, reminiscing about Fred's distinctive approach to playground sports.[7] To the delight of future detractors, 12-year-old Fred's first invention was a special sleep harness fitted with nails to prick him awake whenever he turned over in bed. Its purpose was to prevent the nightmares that were thought to strike whenever he slept on his stomach.

As a young man from the right family and with an able mind, Frederick easily secured a place at Harvard. A lifetime of minimal exertion beckoned like a wide-open sea; but following a nervous breakdown of some sort, he took a job as an apprentice in a machine shop instead. To the consternation of family and friends, he put on overalls, took up swearing, and learned how to cut metal. The noisy lathes and drills of Taylor's first working days left a deep impression on his ideas about management. In his first workplace experiments, Taylor aimed to establish the optimum speed for operating lathes. It was in the course of seeking these mechanical improvements that he came to see the human component on the factory floor as something comparable to the machines, with properties that could be manipulated in the same way as those of a lathe. Scientific management as he presented it in the Boxly years was the extension of the logic of the machine shop into the human world. It rested on a freighted analogy between the technology of machines and the technology of human organization.

After completing his four-year apprenticeship at the Enterprise Hydraulic Works with honors, Taylor moved to Midvale Steel, where he worked his way up the ranks from common laborer to chief engineer in six years. In 1893, after blazing a trail through Midvale and then another manufacturing company, he set himself up as an independent "consulting engineer for management"—in a sense, the world's first management consultant. He spent much of the following decade on trains and in hotels, moving around the industrial landscape like an errant storm system. By the time he arrived at Boxly, he had reached the point in his career where it was his right to speak, and others' duty to listen.

The performances at Boxly followed a fixed routine. As guests filed into the elegantly furnished living room, they were handed paper and pencil to jot down questions—interruptions were forbidden during the two-hour monologue. At the appropriate moment, the trim, jaunty, and 50-ish Taylor would take his seat by the fireplace, under the painting of the *Winslow*—the erstwhile flagship of his mother's family's whaling fleet—and, following some introductory remarks, he would launch into the tale of how he had made a science out of loading 92-pound pig-iron bars onto railroad wagons in the yards of the Bethlehem Steel Company.

It all began in the spring of 1899, said Taylor, when the Bethlehem Steel Company had too many "pigs" on its hands. With 6,000 employees, five blast furnaces, and a machine shop that stretched for a quarter of a mile on the rolling banks of the Lehigh River in central Pennsylvania, Bethlehem was a colossus of the American economy. It produced, among other things, thousands of tons of raw, high-carbon iron, or "pig iron," in the form of 92-pound rectangular bars with notches at the ends that, to some eyes, gave them a vaguely porcine look. On a patch of land just beyond the main yard known as "the farm" lay a stash of 80,000 tons of the stuff, Taylor claimed—or approximately 2 million pigs—which had accumulated over the preceding years, when the price of iron had been depressed. Now, as the price rose to meet the demand sparked by the brief but glorious Spanish-American War of the previous fall, the bars were to be loaded on to railroad wagons and sent off to market.

A gang of 75 workmen was responsible for loading the metal onto the wagons, Taylor told his audiences. It was heavy, sweaty, and seemingly unintelligent labor: a man hefts a 92-pound bar from a pile on the ground, carries it up a ramp, thumps it onto a stack in a railroad car, huffs back down the ramp, and then repeats the process hundreds of times a day. But in Taylor's mind it was a science waiting to be discovered. Thus he formulated what may be considered the inaugural question of modern management science: How many tons of pig-iron bars can a laborer load onto a wagon in the course of a working day?

At Bethlehem's headquarters, Taylor examined the company books and calculated that the gang had been loading pig iron at the rate of 12½ tons per man per day. Was this the best they could do? In the old days, Taylor said, shaking his head, one might have simply asked the foreman if they could do more, or perhaps one might have made some kind of rough estimate based on intuition or "shop lore." The question would thus have been decided by the "rule of thumb." The first step in making a science out of pig-iron handling was to replace the tyranny of the thumb with precise analysis based on quantitative observation and controlled experiments.

At the core of Taylor's new thinking about management was the notion that all human activities, however humble, can be improved through rigorous analysis. His aim, he said, was always to find "the one best way" to perform any given task. In another case, where he sought to increase the efficiency of shoveling operations, he laid out a proof that the optimum shovel for moving any particular stuff is one that lifts 21½ pounds. (More than that, and the laborer tires too quickly; less, and he can't shovel fast enough to tire himself out at all.) On the grave topic of moving dirt by wheelbarrow, Taylor's analysis was punctuated with equations such as this:[8]

$$B = (p + [a + b + d + f + \text{distancehauled}/100 \times (c + e)]27/L)(1 + P)^{\star}$$

In all of his work, it was a matter of taking math where it had never gone before. The essence of his new philosophy could be condensed in the following formula: *Work smarter, not harder.*

Implicit in Taylor's drive for quantitative analysis is a fundamental shift in management focus from *accounting* to *accountability*. A central purpose

---

* The variables in the equation are as follows: B = time per cubic yard picking, loading, wheeling any given kind of earth to any given distance when the wheeler loads his own barrow; p = time loosening 1 cubic foot with pick; a = time to fill wheelbarrow; b = time preparing to wheel; d = time dumping and turning; f = time dropping barrow and starting to shovel; c = time wheeling 100 feet; e = time returning 100 feet empty; L = load of a barrow in cubic feet; P = percentage of day for rest and delays.

of analysis, as managers have since grasped, is to be able to understand and control performance. At least as useful as, if not more so than, the time-and-motion studies for which he became famous—especially to latter-day consultants charged with producing skew charts and the like—are the cost-accounting methods Taylor developed in order to parse the financials of a firm down to its lowliest product. Capital budgets, financial controls, profit analyses, and many of the other wonders of modern management information systems can be traced to Taylor's practice. He was the original advocate of what should be called the first maxim of management consulting: *If you can't measure it, you can't manage it.*

Faced now with the challenge of managing the pig-iron business, Taylor gathered up a team of assistants—"college men," he called them—equipped them with special-order decimal stopwatches, and sent them down to "the farm" to conduct some experiments on the pig-iron gang. Their task was to determine how much pig iron could be loaded in a day. Soon enough, science came back with an exact answer. Under proper supervision, the analysis demonstrated, a laborer can load 47½ tons of pig-iron bars per day. It was, he acknowledged, an astonishing number—nearly four times the achieved rate—but there was no arguing with science. (In his published accounts and in transcripts from Boxly, incidentally, Taylor did not provide further details on the method by which his associates arrived at the 47½ ton number, though his audiences apparently did not evince much concern over the omission.)

The second step in the effort to shine the light of reason on the pig-iron trade was "the scientific selection of the workman." In the old days, Taylor said, managers had tended to assign a job to whoever happened to be walking by at the time. They had grouped laborers within broad classes, and had treated everyone in the same class exactly the same way. But such practices were scientifically indefensible. For each distinct job, Taylor insisted, there is a type of man who is best able to perform it—a "first-class man" for that particular line of work. The difference between first-class men and the rest, he said, "is quite as great as that between fine dray horses and donkeys";[9] it is therefore absurd to put them "all in the same stable." Inasmuch as he maintained that there is a science in recruiting, training, and compensating individual workers, Taylor was the spiritual ancestor of the modern human resources department.

Under his guidance, Taylor reported, Bethlehem had launched a scientific recruitment effort for "first-class pig-iron handlers." The local press, he said, had gotten wind of his plans, and the effort had become the subject of much excitement in the community. From a list of enthusiastic volunteers on the existing gang of 75, he had made a preliminary selection of four men and then had undertaken a detailed investigation of the history, habits, character, and ambition of each man. He had finally settled on one individual to serve as the world's first scientifically trained pig-iron loader—a "very quick and wiry" Pennsylvania Dutchman (of German extraction). "This man we will call Schmidt," Taylor writes in *The Principles of Scientific Management* (though transcripts from Boxly indicate that there he used a real man's name, Henry Noll or Nolle).

Aside from his physical stamina, Schmidt had two virtues that made him a good fit for the pig-iron project. The first was that he was eager to earn extra cash. "A penny looks about the size of a cart-wheel to him," one of his co-workers reportedly joked. Taylor noted that Schmidt was in the habit of trotting home after work to build his own house in his spare time. The second was that Schmidt was, in Taylor's words, "mentally sluggish," "very stupid," or about as intelligent as an "ox." The man best suited for loading pig iron on wagons all day, he explained, was not one with an active mind: "No one would think of using a fine trotter to draw a grocery wagon, nor a Percheron to do the work of a little mule."[10]

The third step in the program amounted, in effect, to a solution of what might be called the "labor problem." That is, Taylor claimed that scientific management would provide a basis for ensuring "hearty brotherly cooperation" between labor and management in pursuit of the common goal of increased productivity. In the typical workplace of old, Taylor lamented, workers had had little incentive to collaborate with management to increase productivity. Indeed, they had typically believed that it was in their interest to limit their own effort. It was not just that they were lazy; it was that they had mistakenly subscribed to a "lump" theory of labor—the false notion that there is only so much work to go around, and therefore that working at top speed means working oneself or others out of a job. Taylor used the term "soldiering" to refer to the resulting practice of willful underproduction, and he argued passionately that it was one of the gravest menaces confronting the industrial world.

The program to eliminate soldiering involved the forthright communication of goals to the workers coupled with a scheme of scientifically determined financial incentives. The basic idea was to share some of the gains from increased productivity with the workers by compensating them with an appropriately calibrated piece rate instead of the usual hourly rate. Scientific management would thus please everybody, in Taylor's mind. It would deliver both higher wages for workers and lower unit costs for capital. Indeed, when describing a future world under scientific management, he sounded like a utopian socialist. "Scientific management ceases to exist when injustice knowingly exists," he said. The essence of scientific management is "the substitution of peace for war; the substitution of hearty brotherly cooperation for contention and strife; of both pulling in the same direction instead of pulling apart; of replacing suspicious watchfulness with mutual confidence; of becoming friends instead of enemies."[11] He was the first in a very long line of management thinkers to champion the "win-win" solution to problems in the workplace.

To make clear to his audience the nature of his utopian scheme and the best way of communicating the vision to laborers with skill sets like Schmidt's, Taylor helpfully rehearsed his own exchange with this fine specimen of Pennsylvania working stock. For live audiences at Boxly, Taylor undoubtedly deployed his theatrical flair and talent for mimicry in relating the conversation. In *The Principles of Scientific Management*, he had to content himself by rendering Schmidt's accent through variant spellings:

"Schmidt, are you a high-priced man?"

"Vell, I don't know vat you mean."

"Oh yes you do. What I want to know is whether you are a high-priced man or not."

"Vell, I don't know vat you mean."

"Oh, come now, you answer my questions . . . What I want to find out is whether you want to earn $1.85 a day or whether you are satisfied with $1.15, just the same as all those cheap fellows are getting."

"Did I vant $1.85 a day? Vas dat a high-priced man? Vell, yes, I vas a high-priced man."

"Oh, you are aggravating me. Of course you want $1.85 a day—
everyone wants it! You know perfectly well that has little to do with
your being a high-priced man. For goodness' sake answer my questions, and don't waste any more of my time. Now come over here.
Do you see that pile of pig iron?"

"Yes."

"You see that car?"

"Yes."

"Well, if you are a high-priced man, you will load that pig iron
on that car tomorrow for $1.85. Now do wake up and answer my
question. Tell me whether you are a high-priced man or not."

After a few more iterations, Schmidt got the idea. Instead of receiving
the usual daily wage, he would be paid by the ton, with the rate set so that
he would earn a 60% premium over his normal daily pay if he managed
to load the 47½ tons—and proportionally less, naturally, if he failed to do
the scientifically allotted tonnage.

But there was one more thing. Taylor pointed to one of the college
men who had been running the experiments and asked Schmidt,

"You have seen this man here before, haven't you?"

"No, I never saw him."

"Well, if you are a high-priced man, you will do exactly as this
man tells you tomorrow, from morning til night. When he tells you
to pick up a pig and walk, you pick it up and you walk, and when
he tells you to sit down and rest, you sit down . . . And what's more,
no back talk. Now a high-priced man does just what he's told to do,
and no back talk."

The management style evinced in this dialogue, it is worth noting, is
quite representative of Taylor's approach throughout his career. Taylor
put the freak in *control freak*. When he wanted workers to clean a boiler,
he didn't just hand them a rag; he gave them several sheets of fanatically
detailed instructions. He positively abhorred the idea that workers might
have to think for themselves. "Our scheme does not ask for any initiative
in a man," he told his Boxly listeners. "We do not care for his initiative."[12]
He also didn't care for his workers' ability to speak. "It is up to us to do
all the talking," he said, "and John all the listening."

Schmidt apparently found Taylor's proposal attractive. Early the following morning he reportedly faced off against his assigned pile of pig bars. He picked up when he was told to pick up, sat down when told to sit, and presumably kept his mouth shut. By half past five in the afternoon he had loaded his 47½ tons. Taylor presented the event to his audiences as a terrific victory for science. In the subsequent days at Bethlehem, he added, many more men had been recruited and trained as first-class pig-iron handlers, and they, too, had achieved the scientifically established mark of 47½ tons per day.

The fourth and final step in the program was to embed the science of pig-iron handling in a new kind of organization, based on a very clear division of functions. "Planning" and "doing" are the two elemental functions of industry, Taylor argued, and they are best performed by two very different kinds of people. The actual labor of pig-iron handling "is so crude and elementary in its nature . . . that it would be possible to train an intelligent gorilla so as to become a more efficient pig-iron handler than any man can be." But the same is not true of the science of pig-iron handling. This science "is so great and amounts to so much that it is impossible for the man who is best suited to this type of work to understand the principles of this science, or even to work in accord with these principles without the aid of a man better educated than he is."[13]

Even as he (theoretically) reduced the number of pig-iron workers and diminished the range of their responsibilities, Taylor defined into existence a brand-new job category: the scientific pig-iron manager. In all the other activities he tackled, from shoveling to wheelbarrowing, the effect was the same: to divide the work between a class of purely physical laborers and a new class of purely mental managers. He was unambiguously a workplace "dualist," to use the jargon of modern philosophy: laborers are bodies without minds; managers are minds without bodies.

In Taylor's telling, the pig-iron story came to an end with smiles all around. Once Bethlehem Steel had adopted the new approach to pig-iron handling, its rolling green yard teemed with first-class workmen collaborating eagerly with scientific managers, and the 80,000 tons of pig-iron bars were enthusiastically whisked off to market. Had the point of the Boxly talks been to report such a splendid outcome for the Pennsylvania metals business, of course, Taylor might well have receded into the history of obscure trades. His name would have endured as a curious and perhaps troubling memory for subsequent generations of pig-iron handlers and Bethlehem employees. But in fact the whole point of the tale and the several other stories with which he entertained his Boxly audiences lay in the universals, not the particulars.

Taylor's greatest gift was for generalization, and his grandest generalization was the leap from his particular experiences as a consultant in the yards of Bethlehem to the idea of a universal science of management. What was true for pig-iron handling, he announced, was true for all management. His intention was to prove that management is "a true science" with "laws as exact, and as clearly defined . . . as the fundamental principles of engineering."[14] He began with the pig-iron case only because he wanted to start at the bottom.[15] Here, better than anywhere else, he could show that there were no limits to this new science of management. "The same principles," he declared, "can be applied with equal force to all social activities: to the management of our homes; the management of our farms; the management of the business of our tradesmen, large and small; of our churches, our philanthropic institutions, our universities, and our governmental departments."[16]

Taylor's grand generalization played a crucial part in the creation of a new discipline. The *practice* of management undoubtedly preceded him; but the *idea* of management was something new. Without management of some sort, the pyramids of Egypt would never have been built, the Great Wall of China would have failed to keep out the Mongols, and the tracks for a North American transcontinental railroad would never have been laid. Taylor's contribution was to insist that all of these and many other activities should be thought of as a single thing. Although others among Taylor's contemporaries (notably Henri Fayol, a French mining executive and author of an insightful monograph titled *General and Industrial Management*) also took up this new idea of management, Taylor was among the first—and by far the most successful—of its champions. In a sense, he gave management a name. And in giving it a name, he also announced what kind of thing it is. Management, he said, is a body of technical expertise. It is an applied science, much like engineering or medicine. And it ought to be the purview of a distinct class of specially trained professionals.

Taylor wasn't peddling a better mousetrap; he was preaching a new way of thinking about work, perhaps even a new way of life. Scientific management, he insisted, requires "a complete mental revolution."[17] Many commentators have concurred in this assessment. The management guru Peter Drucker says that "Scientific Management . . . may well be the most powerful as well as the most lasting contribution America has made to Western thought since the Federalist Papers."[18] Gary Hamel, discussing the work of Taylor and his peers, adds that "it was the invention of industrial management at the dawn of the twentieth century that turned enlightened policy and scientific discovery into global prosperity."[19] Harry Braverman says that "it is impossible to overestimate the importance of the scientific management movement in the shaping of the modern corporation and indeed all institutions of capitalist society."[20]

Like any good revolution, Taylor's had its vanguard, made up of the associates and acolytes who worked alongside him and gathered at Boxly. In the first years of the new century, the group on Chestnut Hill might easily have been mistaken for a religious cult. Some observers compared Taylor with Luther; one suggested he was "the messiah"; and another went so far as to say that "Taylor in this movement is comparable to the Almighty."[21] All agreed that he was "the father of scientific management," as his gravestone eventually proclaimed. The tales about pigs and the rest of the Bethlehem stories were transfigured into a kind of holy writ. Taylor's followers—who came to be called his "disciples" and "apostles"—issued forth from Boxly and even after his death continued to spread the gospel of scientific management far and wide.

Perhaps because he was later so effectively demonized by labor leaders, or perhaps on account of his rebarbative personal style, it is often forgotten that Taylor's most ardent initial supporters, outside his circle of advisers and clients, were the stars of the progressive movement of the day. Ida Tarbell, the muckraking journalist famous for her courageous investigative assault on John D. Rockefeller, declared that "no man in the history of American industry has made a larger contribution to genuine cooperation and juster human relations than did Frederick Winslow Taylor. He is one of the few—very few—creative geniuses of our time."[22] The columnist Walter Lippmann praised Taylorism in the pages of the *New Republic* as a means of improving society. President Theodore Roosevelt called on Congress to confront "the question of national efficiency."[23]

Morris L. Cooke, a noted reformer who helped turn Taylor's Boxly talks into a properly written book and who disseminated the liturgy of the stopwatch in the field of education, argued that neither the "visions of Christianity [n]or the dreams of democracy" will be fully realized until "the principles of scientific management have permeated every nook and cranny of the working world."[24]

In 1910, Taylor at last hit the front pages of the nation's newspapers—thanks to one of his new friends in the progressive movement. At the time, Louis Brandeis—an up-and-coming activist lawyer, defender of the people, and eventual Supreme Court justice—was engaged in a court battle against a collection of railroad companies in the "Eastern Rate Case." The railroads had petitioned the government to allow a large increase in freight rates, and Brandeis had taken up the fight against them on behalf of consumers. After interviewing Taylor and some of the apostles, Brandeis concluded that the father of scientific management was "a really great man—great not only in mental capacity, but in character."[25] Brandeis decided to base his opposition to the price hike on the argument that the railroads could get the money they craved—a million dollars a day, he claimed—by adopting the Taylor system instead. In a flash, scientific management became the talk of the nation. "A MILLION DOLLARS A DAY!" the headlines screamed.

It was in the course of the conversations between Brandeis and the disciples, incidentally, that the term *scientific management* emerged as the preferred label for Taylor's work. What appealed to the progressives was precisely the notion that science could be brought to the management of human affairs and so be placed in the service of social justice. The preceding half century of industrialization, they believed, had created a crisis of legitimacy in the modern world. New corporations of hitherto unimaginable size and complexity now dominated the economy, and yet these behemoths seemed accountable to no one. As these corporations sought to advance their interests, they created enormous conflicts with the working classes, giving rise to the so-called labor problem. In a turn of thought that had ample precedent in social movements extending back to the French Revolution, the progressives hoped that science would supply a neutral standard with which to adjudicate and resolve social conflict. They sincerely believed Taylor when he vowed that scientific management would ensure that workers would finally get their due.

In 1911, to satisfy the growing public curiosity about scientific management, Taylor and the apostles rushed out *The Principles of Scientific Management*—essentially a version of the "Boxly Talks" cleansed of the salty language that Taylor had picked up on the shop floor. The book became a phenomenon. Self-help gurus such as Elbert Hubbard immediately seized on the efficiency doctrine and showed how it could be applied to personal life. In France, Germany, and Japan, politicians and business leaders held up their translations of Taylor's book like flashing signposts on the path to national greatness. Some of the most enthusiastic supporters of scientific management, interestingly, turned out to be communists. In 1918, on the pages of *Pravda*, Vladimir Lenin declared, "We must arrange in Russia the study and teaching of the Taylor system and systematically try it out and adapt it to our own ends."[26] The Soviet five-year planning process—surely the ultimate management challenge—took its inspiration directly from the work of one of Taylor's most successful disciples, Henry L. Gantt.

The efficiency craze that Taylor spawned reached its nuttiest extreme in the life and work of Frank Gilbreth, an early admirer who made groundbreaking discoveries in the noble science of bricklaying. Gilbreth's work receives warm praise in *The Principles of Scientific Management*; he and his wife, Lillian Gilbreth, a pioneer in the field of industrial psychology, returned the compliment by raising their 12 children according to Taylor's principles. The results are recorded in the charming novel (and later more than one film) *Cheaper by the Dozen*, penned by two of the 12. In that book one can learn about the various devices Dad developed in order to rear children in the most efficient way possible—the special whistle for calling emergency family meetings, for example, or the semi-personalized gift-giving routines. The book also includes self-help for harried parents. Dad discovered, for example, that shaving with razors in both hands sliced 44 seconds off his morning toilette. He abandoned the practice, however, after calculating that bandaging the resulting facial wounds added back a full two minutes.

The most important audience for Taylor's idea of scientific management would turn out to be the one represented by two men who made their first pilgrimage to Boxly in May 1908. Wallace Sabine, already a

Taylor enthusiast, was the dean of Harvard's recently created Graduate School of Applied Science. At his side was Edwin Gay, a wiry and energetic professor of economics who had just accepted the responsibility for opening the Graduate School of Business at Harvard, which was to be the first such school in the nation dedicated exclusively to graduate students. With his pig-iron story and the rest of his talk about scientific management, it seems, Taylor told these two Harvard men exactly what they wanted to hear.

The intense interest at Harvard and other universities in the subject of management education was an inevitable consequence of the massive industrialization and economic consolidation of the final decades of the nineteenth century. The robber barons who had built the giant new enterprises—such as the militantly ignorant railroad magnate Cornelius Vanderbilt or the self-taught steel man Andrew Carnegie—could afford to disdain academic learning, just as Taylor himself did, at first. But the huge organizations they established could not. Inside a large corporation, success no longer required inhaling large amounts of smoke from blast furnaces. A business career was a bureaucratic career, and like all such careers it evinced an inevitable proclivity for titles and degrees. At about the same time, universities like Harvard were debating the need for specialized degrees for diplomats and public servants.

So the question naturally arose: should there be a degree aimed specifically at preparing students for careers in business management? Inspired to some extent by Prussia's efforts to establish schools to train administrators for its militaristic state, American universities launched an experiment that arguably has not yet come to its conclusion.[27] In 1881, Joseph Wharton provided a grant to establish the Wharton School at the University of Pennsylvania, the first college-level program in business. Dartmouth followed in 1900 with the Amos Tuck School of Business, and another dozen or so universities joined the ranks over the next two decades.

By 1908, however, the prospects for the business school experiment were looking decidedly shaky. In what must surely count as a very bad sign of things to come, Harvard had made its decision to offer an MBA before figuring out what exactly it would teach its students. Gay was caught between an academic establishment that recoiled in disgust at the thought of hosting a vulgar trade school on campus and a business establishment that didn't see the need for all that fancy "larnin'." "I am constantly being told by businessmen that we cannot teach business," Gay writes in an exasperated letter to a fellow economist.[28] He arrived at Chestnut Hill desperately in need of a curriculum.

There, seated before the fireplace at Boxly, Gay heard the answer to his prayers. "I am convinced that there is a scientific method involved in and underlying the art of business," he later told his economist friend. "There is at present little available . . . I shall be glad, however, to send you an article by Mr. Taylor."[29] The idea of scientific management offered the ideal blend of academic respectability (it was a science, after all) and vocational satisfaction (it taught seemingly practical skills, like how to manage a pig-iron business).

After much cajoling (Taylor, essentially a Harvard dropout, was one of those who did not see the need for fancy larnin'), the father of scientific management was at last persuaded to endorse a plan to use his work as the basis for the first year of the MBA program. From 1909 to 1914, Taylor visited Cambridge every winter to deliver a series of lectures for students—inspirational discourses marred only by his habit of swearing at inappropriate moments. The Harvard men, no less than the progressives, thrilled as much at Taylor's social message as at his science. Gay's colleague Sabine wrote back to Taylor to congratulate him for being "on the track of the only reasonable solution of a great sociological problem."[30]

Over at the Amos Tuck School of Business at Dartmouth, Dean Harlow Person likewise found in scientific management just the kind of doctrine that his school needed to justify its existence. He argued that Taylorism was "the only system of management which was coherent and logical, and therefore was teachable."[31] Person organized the world's first conference on scientific management in 1911 and became the president of the Taylor Society.

In 1913, Gay asked Taylor to join the faculty of the Harvard Business School. Taylor received the request as a pope might an impertinent invitation to dinner from a cardinal: "I am conducting in Philadelphia here an even larger school for scientific management than the one which you have in Cambridge," he replied.[32] And indeed, high up on Chestnut Hill, the father of scientific management continued to regale his many visitors with the pig-iron tale and other stories, all recounted with such an air of conviction that no one doubted but that they were true.

When he finished the last of his stories, before taking his guests on a trip to a local factory that employed the Taylor system, the gracious host typically invited all to join him on a tour of the house. The climax of the tour took place on the upstairs balcony in the back of the house. As the assembled company paused to take in the grand scene of landscaped gardens and valley beyond, a flock of pigeons invariably swooped down over the house as if by magic and dispersed among the hedges.

One of Taylor's acolytes, a frequent visitor, marveling at the ornithological serendipity of it all, decided to investigate the miracle of the pigeons. He discovered that there was a line of bird cages on the other side of the house. When Taylor arrived on the balcony with guests, it seems, he issued a secret signal to one of his housemaids, who ran to the gardener, who released the birds in time to fly right over the visitors' heads.[33]

College Man

In the 1910s, the engineering consulting firm of Arthur D. Little, which had hitherto concentrated on offering its clients solutions to chemical and civil engineering problems, crossed the metaphorical bridge laid down by Taylor and began to supply advice to CEOs on problems in "management engineering." In the 1950s, the elders at A. D. Little schooled a young Harvard MBA named Bruce Henderson in the arcane art of management consulting. In 1963, Henderson struck out on his own to establish the Boston Consulting Group. One of Henderson's wards in the 1970s was Henry, the man who eventually hired me. In 1984, after a detour through the large consulting firm of Booz, Allen, & Hamilton, Henry and his friends broke away to found the firm I later joined. Henry passed his knowledge along to his junior colleague Roland, and Roland passed it along to me. In a sense, I had joined an ancient fraternity that handed down its secrets from generation to generation. I could trace my lineage back to the father of scientific management himself. In my first assignments, I was, in effect, one of Taylor's "college men"—except that my pig-iron yards were the back offices of large corporations, mostly banks.

I soon felt more like a dentist. I inflicted a lot of pain, and nobody seemed very glad to see me. Instead of pulling teeth, however, I was trying to extract data from visibly agitated people. There was much hostility down there in the yard, and, to my surprise, it often seemed to pre-date our appearance. On my first project for Roland, our only friend upon arrival was Lorenzo, the man who had hired us. He was a lanky, taciturn fellow with dark circles under his eyes—and even he seemed to regard us with suspicion through his bottle-bottom glasses.

Most of my conversations took place two or three levels down the corporate hierarchy from managers like Lorenzo. A typical exchange between me and a minion of the planning department of a global financial institution—let's call him Schmidt—would go something like this:

Me: "We'd like to have transaction data for three trillion customers pulled from fifty-nine departmental information systems that haven't spoken to each other since time began."

Schmidt: "Ze data is not possible."

"We need it Tuesday morning."

"It cannot be! Tuesday is National Asparagus Day. Holiday for everyone!"

"OK, then Monday afternoon."

"But tomorrow is ze veekend!"

"Great! We can meet in the office!"

"But ze data vill be unclean!"

"We'll take it dirty."

"I have not ze authority!"

"On Wednesday we're meeting with the board member who is responsible for hiring and firing your boss and your boss's boss. So what do you say?"

"Ach!"

Pretty soon, like many young consultants, I was living out of hotel rooms in faraway towns where the only locals I knew detested me. In many cases, the hostility had a specific source within the organization. In Lorenzo's bank, the evil eye belonged to a senior manager named Luigi. Luigi was responsible for a collection of operations that was warily described on hand-drawn organization charts as "Luigi's World."

"So, you are Lorenzo's boys?" Luigi said through thick rings of cigarette smoke, when at last he deigned to meet with me and the team. The contempt in his voice was as thick as cement. I guessed he was about twice my age, and he probably weighed about twice as much too. His face and his hair looked like they had been rolled around in an ashtray. He spent most of the meeting regaling us with consultant jokes.

"You know the definition of a consultant?" he said. "Someone who looks at your watch and tells you what time it is!" "Ha!" he barked, in a tone that made clear that he guessed that we had heard this particular rib tickler before.

"Do you know why consultants like to have hemorrhoids?" he asked. I looked at him with alarm. "Because it makes them look concerned!"

Luigi had more jokes—one comparing consultants unfavorably with hookers, and another one about a consultant in a hot-air balloon. I don't remember the details, except that it ended very badly for the consultant. "Ha!"

I was at a loss how to handle this rather unsympathetic man. But Roland knew exactly what to do. "We'll make him our client too!" he effused, when we discussed the results of the meeting over the phone. This struck me as an appalling idea. Only much later did I come to understand that it was a stroke of consulting genius.

Following some interventions from on high, the data at last began to trickle into our spreadsheets. I eventually collected an ocean of numbers, a chaos of frothy decimal points from which I was sure nothing meaningful would emerge. With Roland out of town and returning phone calls only with cryptic messages of encouragement, I concocted many fanciful formulas for relating the various columns of numbers to one another. When at last the data stopped pouring in and I had finished with the whimsical equations, I was able to perform my first analyses. To my astonishment, the whales surfaced immediately. Like those real leviathans suddenly surging from the deep, they were beautiful to behold. Everything was hopelessly skewed.

When Roland arrived back in town, we marched into Lorenzo's office to deliver our initial "diagnostic" presentation, bristling with shiny charts and tables. Roland put on a severe expression, like a priest confronting an adolescent caught masturbating. He offered our skew charts with a histrionic finality, as though they had been etched in stone and sent down from Mount Sinai. The news was gloomy—especially in Luigi's World. In Lorenzo's widening eyes, I saw suspicion yielding to fear. It was as if he had been stripped naked in front of his entire high school graduating class. Looking at the whale chart upside down, as Lorenzo held it in his sweaty palms, I saw that it took the shape of a hook.

In the taxi back to the airport, Roland's bad-news frown yielded to a wide grin. The client was writhing at the end of our line, the barb working its way ever deeper into its flesh. I felt the thrill of the catch. At the same time, I could not quite suppress the awareness that upon dropping Roland off at the airport, whence he undoubtedly would be heading off to some faraway continent to exterminate yet another species of fauna, I would be returning to the hotel and preparing for the descent into Luigi's World.

The Truth about the Pigs

rederick Winslow Taylor told the pig-iron story so often and so well that for more than half a century after his death, critics and sympathizers alike simply assumed it was true. But it was not.[34]

The trouble begins at the beginning. In 1899, Bethlehem Steel did not employ a gang of 75 pig-iron handlers, as Taylor had suggested, but rather kept a couple dozen or so men on hand who were periodically sent to take care of pig-iron loading and other chores. According to market records, the price of iron did not go up in the spring of that year, so it could not have motivated the grand experiment in pig-iron handling, as Taylor had claimed. Most important, Bethlehem's stores of pig-iron bars did not amount to the 80,000 tons Taylor had cited, but to a much less daunting 10,000 tons.

Although we can't know why Taylor slipped an extra 70,000 tons into the pile, it is worth pointing out that, taking his numbers as given, the maximum theoretical savings from the new pig-loading program was about 5 cents per ton, or $50 per thousand tons. Yet Taylor charged $40 per day for his time, and billed smaller (but still princely) sums for each of his associates, who numbered about half a dozen during the course of his years at Bethlehem. Had he limited his work to the actual 10,000 tons, his listeners might have come to the unfortunate conclusion that the entire savings from his efforts would have been consumed by consulting fees long before the project was over.

The really serious trouble with Taylor's pig-iron story begins with the 47½-ton benchmark he set for daily pig-iron loading. From notes left behind by his associates, it seems that the all-important time study began with a dozen workers, picked at random and assigned to load a pile of pig-irons for about an hour. Over that hour, the gang achieved a rate that worked out to 23.8 tons per man per day—on the dubious assumption that they could have kept up the same rate for the entire day. On the next day, Taylor's associates rounded up 10 "large powerful Hungarians," on the scientific grounds that they looked pretty husky, and, in exchange for a bonus, challenged them to load a stack of 16½ tons as fast as they could. Keen to impress their apparent benefactors, the burly eastern Europeans accomplished the feat in under 14 minutes. Over a 10-hour day, that worked out to 71 tons per man. For reasons unclear, Taylor decided to up the theoretical maximum to 75 tons, not 71.

To have suggested that the workers could sustain such a rate throughout the day, every day of their pig-iron lifting careers, of course, would have been about as fatuous as estimating a marathon runner's time by extrapolating from the results of a 100-meter dash. Even Taylor recognized that the men needed rest time and bathroom breaks. So he adjusted the figure approximately 40% downward. Why 40%? He made some noises about a "law of heavy laboring" that required certain ratios of rest to work. But on closer inspection, the "law" in question is transparently less germane to the pig-iron question than even the great Hungarian pig-iron race. In his congressional testimony, Taylor acknowledged that in other experiments he had made comparable adjustments ranging from 16% to 70%.[35] In other words, the 47½ ton benchmark was the result of multiplying an irrelevant and uncontrolled experimental observation with a great big blob of fudge.

It was not just Taylor's method of calculation but his very approach to the problem that was deeply unscientific. A crucial feature of any activity that aspires to the name of science is verifiability: independent observers must be able to reproduce experiments and thereby confirm results. This is why journals are such an integral feature of scientific disciplines. In his pig-iron escapades, however, Taylor never supplied the data or the methods that would have allowed others to reproduce and verify his results. Instead of science, Taylor offered a kind of parody of science. He confused the paraphernalia of research—stopwatches and long division—with actual research.

The number was the number, however—in Taylor's mind at least—so the next item on the agenda was to put it into practice. The 47½-ton piece-rate plan was first proposed not to Henry Noll—a.k.a. "Schmidt," as Taylor suggests in his published account—but to the very Hungarians who had allegedly demonstrated its feasibility. When they understood they were being asked to nearly quadruple their workload in exchange for an extra 70 cents, however, the Hungarians howled with indignation and refused the assignment. The next day, unbeknownst to Taylor, the regrettably unscientific management team at Bethlehem allowed the Hungarians to return to work under the old day-rate plan. When Taylor discovered that the men had escaped the unalterable demands of science, he became incensed and insisted that they be fired. After talking up a storm at headquarters—it was a matter of instilling proper respect for authority, he fumed—he succeeded in depriving the Hungarians of their jobs. Two weeks passed in quiet bitterness, with no progress on the science of pig-iron lifting.

With a line firmly drawn in the muddy yard of Bethlehem, Taylor's associates corralled seven men from a different gang—this one composed of Irishmen and Dutchmen who had no social ties to the peeved and unemployed Hungarians. Five of seven showed up for trials the next morning. They lifted an average of 32 tons per man from a single pile, after which "they appeared fatigued." On the following day, two of the men were too exhausted to report to work. The remaining three were set to lifting individual piles, protected from the surly eastern European crowd by 200 feet and a cordon of Taylor's associates. By early afternoon, two more of the men proved too feeble to continue and dropped out of the race. At the end of the day, Henry Noll stood alone, the sole survivor of a brutal process of natural selection. He had loaded 45¾ tons—close enough to the magic number, in Taylor's view, for the "experiment" to count as a magnificent victory for scientific management.

Taylor's much-touted "scientific selection of the workman"—the conscientious investigations of history, character, and aptitudes of which he writes so passionately in his *Principles of Scientific Management*—never happened. A search through the local press from the time provides no evidence to support Taylor's claim that the community took any interest in events in the pig-iron fields or in the search for first-class men. Although Taylor intimated in the dialogue with "Schmidt" that the workers' actions through the day were to be monitored and controlled down to the individual pig, with scientifically allocated rest breaks along the way, the notes from his associates indicate that in fact the men were simply shepherded before their piles and set to work without further guidance and without breaks. Given the sequence of events, it is all but certain that Taylor's purported dialogue with Schmidt was a fiction.

Taylor's ultimate fabrication concerns the outcome of his program. It appears that a handful of laborers were able to match Noll's prodigious output over brief periods—but always under the proviso that they could return to the old plan whenever they chose, which they did frequently. The new organization of the pig-iron industry, with its high office of "scientific pig-iron manager," existed only in Taylor's theoretical imagination. There is no evidence that Bethlehem Steel realized any significant benefit from the experience. On May 1, 1901, two years after the revolution began, Bethlehem ordered Taylor to cease all work on its behalf, and it scrapped all of his various programs. Neither Bethlehem nor any other concern has since taken up the celebrated science of pig-iron handling. Taylor, on the other hand, walked away with a total of $100,000 in consulting fees (about $2.5 million in today's money). When it came to studying other people's work, Taylor was a champion of the principle of accountability; with respect to his own, it seems, he operated entirely free from any such constraint.

Taylor's fictionalization of the pig-iron case, sad to say, was hardly an aberration. In the margins of a transcript of one of the Boxly sessions, where Taylor regaled his audiences with some of his other tales about shoveling and wheelbarrowing and the like, one of his more devout associates, Carl Barth, had scribbled, "This whole page is absolutely nothing but fiction." On another page, Barth had written, "One of the worst distortions of a story told by Mr. Taylor that I have ever come across." And then, "I am fully convinced that a lot of the foregoing is fiction, but as I was not present . . . I can't say how much . . . From here on, there is a semblance to the facts, but they are badly mixed up."[36]

There is little reason to think that Taylor's non-pig-related studies were of any greater scientific merit. To be sure, in some of his earliest research on the operation of metal-cutting lathes, in which he meticulously recorded the effects of cutting different metals under different conditions at different speeds, Taylor did provide some verifiable results concerning the use of certain kinds of machines—results that were soon rendered moot by the advance of machine technology. Taylor's invention of a new, high-speed cutting device—an invention that made him a rich man—also clearly represents a triumph of applied science. But his work on shovel size, wheelbarrows, and in general everything that involved human beings suffered from the same flaws as his work on pig-iron handling. In place of verifiable data and reproducible methodologies, he provided only anecdotes, embellished with speciously precise numbers and arcane formulas of indeterminate provenance.

When Carl Barth reviewed the range of material that Taylor had left behind at Bethlehem in hopes of incorporating it into his own projects, he found he could not reproduce the data and was forced to discard it all as unusable. In 1908, before Taylor made the front pages, a consultant and management thinker named Alexander Hamilton Church wrote an article titled "Has Scientific Management Science?" The answer he gave was a clear no. Apart from "a collection of procedures involving stopwatches," he noted, "there is nothing tangible behind it."[37]

The stunning lack of accountability evident in the finale of the pig-iron tale, too, seems to have characterized Taylor's work as a whole. Although a number of factories adopted or claimed to have adopted the "Taylor system," the advocates of the program failed to provide convincing or comprehensive evidence that it did any real good. Indeed, it was difficult even to get agreement on exactly what the system was in the first place. In a 1914 study of 35 plants said to have adopted the Taylor system, Robert Hoxie concluded that "no single shop was found which could be said to represent fully and faithfully the Taylor system as presented in the treatise on 'Shop Management' . . . and no two shops were found in which identically or even approximately the same policies and methods were established and adhered to throughout."[38] Just as the science wasn't a science, it seems, the system wasn't really a system.

Taylor's own responses to challenges concerning the scientific merit of his work, on the whole, served more to illustrate the peculiarities of his personal style than to advance the debate. When gently questioned by a factory owner who had applied some of his ideas, Taylor fired back, "It may be true, as you say, that there are one or two elements relating to scientific management which are not based on full and exact knowledge . . . The fact is, however, that 999 out of 1000 of the elements which under the old system of management were the owner's judgment and opinion are now matters of exact knowledge or science."[39]

Taylor's influence, of course, ultimately depended not on his specific results in the field of pig-iron lifting and shoveling and so forth, but on his generalizations about the science of management. He became famous for the *idea* of what he was supposed to have achieved—not for what he actually achieved. The particular cases he offered were intended as instances of a general science of management. It is in this general idea, however, that Taylor invested some of his most consequential errors. And it is to these general errors that one should ultimately attribute the many missteps and fabrications that afflicted his individual studies—and those of his successors.

Embedded in Taylor's idea of scientific management are some telling misconceptions about the nature of science and the nature of management. Taylor failed in the first instance to distinguish clearly between a scientific *attitude* and science itself. Inasmuch as we mean by a scientific attitude a disposition to test hypotheses against facts through controlled observation, then it is perfectly possible and arguably very desirable to bring such an attitude to bear on issues arising out of management, as well as on all sorts of other activities. One can go grocery shopping with a scientific attitude. But it does not follow that there is a science of grocery shopping, or, in general, that there is a body of knowledge that deserves the name of *science* associated with every possible object of a scientific attitude.

Of course, Taylor intended to do more than advocate a scientific attitude toward management. His goal was to establish a universal science of efficiency. Such a universal science would apply to businesses as diverse as making hot dogs and taming lions. In Taylor's conception, the pig-iron case stands for the universal laws of this science of management in the same way that an apple falling from the tree stands for Newton's universal law of gravity. It is this kind of science, at any rate, to which the Harvard Business School's first Dean, Edwin Gay, referred when he said, "We believe that there is science in business"—that is, a body of knowledge that will systematically relate "inputs" to "outputs."[40] But is there such a universal science? Is pig-iron lifting the same thing as hot-dog making and lion taming?

In fact, there is no such universal science of efficiency. In the absence of any specification of the kinds of activities that it will govern, any attempt at such a science will produce only platitudinous reaffirmations of the definition of efficiency. And indeed, it turns out upon inspection that the so-called laws and principles that Taylor attempts to pass off as the theories of his universal science of efficiency are for the most part nonfalsifiable propositions. In the best case, they are maxims—along the lines of, say, "work smarter, not harder!" or "a stopwatch a day keeps the banker away!" Mostly, they boil down to tautologies: "An efficient shop is more productive than an inefficient shop!" Such "principles" are unscientific not because they are false, but because they are too true. As Karl Popper points out, scientific theories are interesting because they *could* be wrong. They are falsifiable; and this is why science as a whole is corrigible and progresses. By always insisting that he was incontestably right, Taylor inadvertently acknowledged that his science isn't a science.

Taylor's idea for a science of management also involves some misconceptions about management. Most people can agree with Mary Parker Follett—one of the most thoughtful of the management theorists in the period just after Taylor—that management understood in a general sense is "the art of getting things done through people."[41] Stopwatches, incentive pay schemes, and quantitative metrics are no doubt potentially useful tools for getting things done through other people. But they hardly represent the totality of such tools, much less the entire task of management. Even in the humble business of pig-iron loading, as the sorry experience in Bethlehem shows, the challenges of management could not be reduced to a time-and-motion study. Scientific management was not a valid generalization from particular instances of management experience to universal laws, but a spectacular act of metonymy—of confusing a part for the whole of management.

More abstractly, one could say that Taylor's attempts to make general claims about the nature of management involve what the Oxford philosophers would call a "category mistake." The modern economy affords an awesome array of techniques for managing specific aspects of specific activities, from loading pig iron to producing LCD screens to organizing fast-food restaurants to overseeing a book distribution operation, as well as for managing certain functions, such as accounting, marketing, and so forth. All of these techniques together represent a large—perhaps the largest—reservoir of capital in a modern economy. Some may be studied systematically, and a few may even deserve the name of science. Most are simply embedded in the actual practice of existing firms. The word *management* stands in relation to these in the same way that *technology* stands in relation to LCDs, telephones, and inventory software. To study management in hopes of doing something immediately useful is like studying technology in hopes of building a better motorcycle. It involves a mistaken inference that the properties belonging to one category also belong to another.

In his *Critique of Pure Reason*, Immanuel Kant shows how the attempt to claim scientific certainty where none is to be had leads to unreasonable dogma. Taylor's attempt to make a general science out of management is in fact crippled with such dogma. The most important examples include the following:

1. **The Dogma of Efficiency.** Implicit in Taylor's approach is the idea that management always aims at the single goal of efficiency (understood as labor productivity). But efficiency is just one of several possible, competing goals that management might pursue. Profitability, customer satisfaction, or maintaining good community relations can always conceivably outweigh the goal of efficiency. Later management theorists have argued that Taylor's obsession with efficiency came at the expense of the goal of quality.

2. **The Dogma of the Singular Metric.** Setting aside whether efficiency is the proper goal of management, Taylor's idea for a universal science makes the assumption that there is some single metric—a scalar function—against which all activities of management should be judged. Today's business schools proffer "shareholder value" as this singular metric. But such a singular metric can sustain rational action only in extreme environments where the level of information and degree of certainty

about the future rises to an improbably high level. Because we are usually unable to know with any reasonable degree of precision how much any particular action will enhance efficiency or shareholder value, for example, we judge our decisions against a multiplicity of more accessible goals, such as serving customers well, building quality products, establishing a positive environment for workers, and so forth. Indeed, Taylor failed to appreciate that in an imperfectly knowable world, there is a latent irrationality in all metrics. That is, for any given metric, there will always arise instances when maximizing the metric is at odds with advancing the goals that the metric was designed to serve—instances in which an inherently imprecise synthetic judgment formed by balancing the many competing goals of an individual or an organization must trump the purportedly "rational" dictates of the metric. The modern-day CEOs who sacrifice the long-term viability of their corporations for the sake of short-term boosts in their quarterly earnings reports are direct descendants of the pig-iron managers who undermined their work teams' morale in order to achieve temporary productivity targets.

3. **The Dogma of Hardness.** Convinced that pig-iron management was just a matter of precision timing, Taylor overlooked the possibility that the demonstration of a little cultural and psychological sensitivity might have proved much more valuable to Bethlehem's pig-iron managers than a time-and-motion study did. A manager who spoke Hungarian and German, for example, almost certainly would have gotten more pigs loaded than one who was handy with a stopwatch. In general, Taylor contributed to the overvaluation of "hard" data and the undervaluation of unknowns that characterizes excessively analytic approaches to management. (Look up "Robert McNamara," "Vietnam," and "body counts" for an example of the damage this dogma can cause.)

4. **The Dogma of Functional Social Classes.** Taylor confused the logical proposition that planning and doing are distinct functions with the empirical claim that these two functions are always best performed by two distinct classes of people endowed with distinct educational pedigrees, clothing styles, and patterns of speech. The one is nonfalsifiable; the other is simply false. Cutting up your food and eating it are

distinct functions too, but it is not the case that they are always best performed by two different people. In manufacturing businesses, separating planners from doers sometimes makes sense; but, as Japanese carmakers proved to the dismay of their American rivals, getting the doers involved in the planning can result in higher-quality products and lower costs.

More troubling even than the many logical flaws in Taylor's conception of science is the attempt to extend scientific inquiry into areas where it clearly does not belong. At stake in the brutal "experiments" in pig-iron lifting was not just how much work a laborer *could* do, but how much he *should* do. It wasn't ultimately about the physiological capabilities of human muscle fibers; it was about the rights and responsibilities of workers and employers, the division of spoils from increases in productivity, and the obligations of an enterprise to its community. Taylor feigned research where negotiation was required. This confusion of facts and values—or, more generally, the attempt to find pseudotechnical solutions to moral and political problems—is the most consequential error in Taylor's work and is the cardinal sin of management theory to the present.

Scientific management was a rhetorical screen used to advance a distinctly political vision. The vision was an essentially utopian one, according to which all conflict would dissolve through the advance of scientific knowledge. It was also an inherently unilateral (or perhaps authoritarian) vision, in that it assigned to a new managerial elite the sole authority for accumulating and applying the new knowledge. At the same time that it advanced the idea of a managerial society, scientific management inevitably engaged in direct combat with the interests of both capital and labor.

That scientific management was an assault on the power of labor hardly needs to be stated. Scientific management was not a body of facts but a proposal about how managers should treat workers—principally, as mute, brainless bundles of animal muscles whose activities are to be subject to minute control from above. From the perspective of the laborers in Bethlehem's pig-iron yards, Taylor's "science" was just an obtuse language game whose manifest purpose was to coerce them into working harder than they had before. Taylor's insistence on making "scientific" distinctions among individual workers was in effect an attempt to atomize the working class, thus implicitly denying the very possibility of collective action based on collective interest.

Although Taylor promised that science would put the working man on equal footing with his social superiors, in fact the drive to bring science into the workplace served rather to reduce wage laborers to nearly inhuman status. Charlie Chaplin captured this tendency to great comic effect in *Modern Times*, his satire about life in a Taylorized factory. In the opening sequence of that film, the hapless star gets tangled up inside a huge apparatus of whirring gears, representing in a comic visual the fear that modern machines, far from liberating us, might ultimately reduce us all to "cogs in the wheel."

The dehumanization of labor reached its logical destination in the mass-production assembly line factory system pioneered by Henry Ford. Although Ford was dismissive of Taylor and of consultants in general, it seems that he could not stop himself from mimicking some of the more alarming aspects of Taylor's style. "The average worker," Ford averred, "wants a job . . . in which he does not have to think." To this he added the rather disturbing observations that, of the 7,882 operations required to build a model T, 2,637 could be performed by "one-legged men"; 670 by "legless men"; 715 by "one-armed men"; 2 by "armless men"; and 10 by "blind men." "Why is it that when I ask for a pair of hands," Ford once quipped, "a brain comes attached?"[42]

As the initially favorable impression created by Taylor's paeans to workplace harmony faded, organized labor in the United States grasped the threat represented by scientific management. On a second reading of *The Principles of Scientific Management*, labor leaders realized that Taylor's attitude toward Schmidt was not so friendly after all. "What happened to poor Schmidt?" became a rallying cry among sympathetic journalists, who descended on Bethlehem in search of the truth about Henry Noll. Across the country and around the world, the humble tale of a pig-iron loader's life became a kind of refracting prism through which people of all types read back their own frustrations with life in the working world.

In 1914, when Taylor's apostles bungled a time study at an armaments plant, leading to a strike in which workers refused to cooperate with the men with stopwatches, labor leaders had the incident they needed to declare Taylor an enemy of the working man. At the hearings that Congress organized in the wake of the incident, Taylor and his antagonists reached such a pitch of emotional and physical agitation that a recess was called and their indecorous altercations expunged from the record. As the controversy mounted, Harvard and the other business schools began to distance themselves from the father of scientific management, even though their commitment to the general idea of a science of management remained undiminished.

As much as it was an assault on labor, scientific management arguably represented even more of an affront to capital. In Taylor's mind, the unfettered competition and unceasing turbulence of the market economy was just as wasteful as undisciplined labor. In 1893, he quit his last full-time job out of contempt for financiers who wanted only to "make money quickly" and "took no pride in manufacture."[43] The contempt was often mutual. Taylor's merciless focus on production without regard to profit and his unalterable preference for control over risk reflected a decidedly uncapitalist disposition.

Taylor's personal aversion to capitalism became an explicit doctrine of the movement in the work of his disciple Henry L. Gantt, now remembered chiefly for his eponymous chart. In 1916, Gantt founded a society called the New Machine for the purpose of advancing the conviction that manager-engineers should rule the world in "an aristocracy of the capable."[44] During the First World War, he became incensed at the inefficiencies resulting from competition among the capitalists, and advocated a cartelization of industry. He wrote President Woodrow Wilson a slightly mad letter in which he demanded that control of "the huge and delicate apparatus" of the national economy be transferred immediately into "the hands of those who understand its operation."[45] An even loonier group, identifying itself as the American Technocratic Party, preached a gospel according to which undereducated and downwardly mobile members of the middle class could one day hope to usurp the power of the corporations over the national economy. Little wonder, then, that scientific management was enthusiastically received in the Soviet Union.

Taylor's utopian vision of a new managerial order, triumphant over both capital and labor, follows a long-established pattern in rationalist thought. Plato, like Taylor, maintained that the advance of knowledge would eliminate social conflict. He, too, envisioned a utopia in which those who possess knowledge would guide society to its irenic end. He also believed that natural-born rulers were made of different stuff than the common sort. To ease the transition to his utopia, Plato supplied a myth, to be related to the people, according to which the philosopher-rulers were said to have evolved from a superior kind of mineral deposit. Taylor, on the other hand, grounded the legitimacy of his managerial ruling class on a purported physiological distinction between people with brains and those with muscle. The main difference between the ancient philosopher and the father of scientific management, it seems, is that while Plato acknowledged that his utopia was founded on a "noble lie," Taylor insisted to the end that his was based on scientific fact.

Taylor's ultimate aim was to advance the interests not just of the managerial elite, but of an elite within the elite—the special cadre of management experts, or consultants. Self-interest was never very far from the center of his work, and therein lay the most obdurate source of its errors. Scientific management isn't a science; it's a business. The same may be said of the work of the consultants, the gurus, and even many of the professors who have followed in Taylor's lucrative footsteps. Their specialty, at the end of the day, is not the management of business, but the business of management. As in any business, what separates the winners from the also-rans isn't independently verifiable expertise; it is the ability to move product. And there is no better paragon of this particular virtue than the father of scientific management himself.

Perhaps the eeriest aspect of the pig-iron tale is the fact that Taylor repeated it so many times over so many years. To embellish a story once may be counted a minor offense; but to lie repeatedly and gleefully, and to base one's career on the lie, even while cultivating a public image as one of history's most notorious sticklers for the facts—this requires character. That Taylor was a control freak is easy enough to see; but perhaps the more consequential facet of his personality was his theatricality—his talent for mimicry, his passion for a good story, and his fanatical drive to master every detail of a performance through to the pigeons swooping across the sky in the final scene. Like a great actor, he had an uncanny ability to inhabit his tales, to visualize the truth of whatever story it was he happened to be selling. Evincing conviction with such apparent sincerity, he evoked it easily in his customers. In fewer words: he was a huckster.

Boxly turns out to have been a brilliant sales platform. It was the center of gravity in an exercise of pull marketing. "The best way [to make a sale] is to let those who want [your services] see that other people want you very badly, and that you don't particularly care about them," Taylor explained to his young associate Carl Barth. "I have found that the moment you let people have an idea that you want to secure their work, then they begin to hold off."[46] The scientific rhetoric in which he couched his work served much the same purpose as the magnificent house. It put a shine of disinterestedness and respectability on the product. Upon delivering the Boxly treatment to his eager audiences, Taylor had only to wait for inquiries from prospective clients insisting on further enlightenment. Then he would carefully steer them into the care of the "expert" associate he deemed best suited for them. It all worked like a beautiful, well-oiled machine.

The Art of Hunting Whales

Over a dinner of venison and berries of the forest, Luigi regaled me and a couple of colleagues for the fifty-third time with tales about how he had started his career in the mail room and helped the bank grow from a corner grocery store into a global powerhouse. Over the previous months, he had become more nostalgic and more reckless at the same time. After we had washed down our cheese course and profiteroles with a barrel of fine Bordeaux, he dropped us back at the hotel, skidding through a couple of red lights.

At this point in the course of our consulting engagement, our ever-expanding team had penetrated almost every operation in Lorenzo's bank. We had given a long series of "interim" presentations, whose content was generally a variation on our initial findings. As the months dragged on, Roland's visits became less and less frequent, until they amounted to little more than a ceremonial dinner, usually around the time that an invoice was to be delivered.

By the time I had produced the fifth or sixth version of the Whale, I realized that I could do the same for just about any business anywhere. It made no difference whether the business was inherently good or bad, well-managed or in the hands of chimpanzees. It didn't even have to be a business—it could be a football game or a population chart. In fact, I didn't even have to do the analysis. I could save 80% of the effort by just borrowing data from some previous analysis. There was always going to be a skew. In most cases most of the time, the skew chart merely records a curious fact of economic life. It isn't science; it's a party trick.

Nietzsche once wrote that "there are no facts; there are only interpretations."[47] He may have gotten carried away, as was his wont; but to the extent that he anticipated what management consultants can do with data from the activities of large and complex corporations, he had a point. Very little of the "hard" data in business is as hard as it's made out to be. With a few tweaks in the assumptions embedded in the spreadsheets—a change in the historical period analyzed from the past quarter to the past year, for example; a change in the definition of a "customer"; or an adjustment of various inscrutable "factors" in allocation formulas opaque to all but a few fellow geeks—one can easily turn a minnow into whale, or flip a whale on its head.

Roland understood all of this in an instinctive way. As a result, he practiced a kind of gonzo math. If you can get 80% of the result with 20% of the math, he seemed to think, why bother finishing the calculation? He became famous in the firm for his "two-handed regression" technique. When a scatter plot failed to show the significant correlation between two variables that we all knew was there, he would place a pair of meaty hands over the offending clouds of data points and thereby reveal the straight line hiding from conventional mathematics.

Roland may have gotten ahead of the facts at times, but his method wasn't all madness. As Aristotle pointed out, one should not seek more precision in a subject than it allows. In many contexts, gonzo math turns out to be more accurate than the purer forms of analysis. "Pure" analysis in most business situations tends to be conservative rather than creative. It implicitly favors optimizing the existing business rather than building a new one. It is biased toward shrinking the business, for the simple reason that figuring out how to cut costs is easier than thinking up new ways to generate revenue. It produces an irrational kind of rationality—the kind that underestimates the impact of everything that can't be measured easily, like the cost of job cuts on a company's public image and internal morale. In pretending to analyze the future with the same fanatical precision with which it parses the past, it makes the classic mistake of assuming that the future will be a dotted-line projection of the most desirable recent trends.

My fellow consultants and I often resorted to peddling analysis not because that was what the world needed, but because that was what we could do. Our motto might well have been *"If you can't manage it, measure it!"* We were too young to sell experience; even the older partners had managed little that was more complex than a Thanksgiving dinner. Our definition of management as a form of science followed from our economic interest, not from any detached consideration of the phenomena. In this we were quite representative of a generation of MBAs, who likewise prefer to define management as the thing they are trained to do—namely, analyzing fictitious cases.

None of which is to say that whales do not exist. On the contrary, the elusiveness of whales, I eventually came to understand, follows directly from the Great Whale Principle itself. Approximately 20% of supposed whales represent 80% of actual whales; the rest are red herrings that have had unfortunate encounters with a harpoon. There is no surefire method for finding whales, for the simple reason that, in virtue of the Great Whale Principle, about 80% of applications of the method in question will yield results of little interest.

I think of this corollary as the Principle of Elusiveness. And how could it be otherwise? If whales were so easy to find—if it really was just a matter of filling up a spreadsheet—then they wouldn't be whales. This is why the next big thing so often turns out to be the last little mistake, why those sunny vacations so rarely live up to postcard hopes, and why four out of five books (at least!) that promise to deliver the secret of success aren't worth the paper they are printed on. A whale might be the most important thing in your life; it might be standing right in front of your nose; but, as George Orwell might have said, recognizing it when you see it requires a constant struggle. Sometimes the very absence of whales is itself a whale. As Spinoza said—on his monomaniacal hunt for the biggest whale of all, the truth about everything—all things excellent are as difficult as they are rare.

At Lorenzo's bank, we found our whale soon enough, and it wasn't in our charts. It was our sadly dysfunctional client organization itself. At the base of the organization's problems was a question of identity, or perhaps self-esteem. Viewed as a machine for making money, the bank was a simple thing. It filled its vaults with money that belonged to rich people, many of whom it had known for a long time, and skimmed a few pennies off the top for the service. It was a 24-carat piggy bank. Viewed in terms of its top managers' aspirations, on the other hand, the bank was a universal zoo in the making. It was going to offer something for everyone. The result was that the bank in fact consisted of one bright, shiny pig and a rapidly multiplying pack of scruffy dogs.

In an indirect way, this situation had resulted in our presence as consultants. The specific cause of our existence, as I learned after spending some more time with Luigi and his gang of nicotine addicts, had to do with the circumstances surrounding Lorenzo's arrival as the new head of a large part of the bank's scrofulous menagerie. Through the efforts of his expansion-minded bosses on the board, Lorenzo had recently been catapulted from an outlying regional operation over the heads of Luigi and his friends. He had been promoted over the smokers because they had failed to transform the bank's money-losing dogs into money-making pigs. From the perspective of Luigi and friends, on the other hand, Lorenzo was an alien, assumed to be incompetent, and probably dangerous. He was also, by virtue of hiring us, a pimp. The smokers were not entirely deluded: Lorenzo did seem to act like a man promoted out of his depth, and we were there to do his dirty work. On the other hand, it seemed unlikely that Lorenzo would do any better or worse than they had in the effort at transubstantiating dogs.

In an ideal world, perhaps, we the consultants might have been hired to help the bank gain some perspective on its identity issues. But the truth is that management hired us to fulfill its dreams, not to quash them. We were more a symptom of the problem than the solution. Our task was, in essence, to try to persuade the dogs not to be dogs. Unfortunately, they responded mostly by barking back at us. It was in many ways a Sisyphean assignment. From our perspective, of course, that was no bad thing. As long as there was a ball that had to be rolled uphill, we got paid.

Late one evening, in a hotel bar not far from Lorenzo's bank, a fellow associate and I began to discuss how we should measure the contribution of our graph-making activities to the welfare of humankind. This exchange inevitably descended into a conversation about our relative share of the firm's revenues. We pushed aside the beers and pulled out our laptops. We knew what the firm charged for its work, we knew what our own salaries were, we could make reasonable guesses about salaries up to the partner level, and, after months of analyzing our clients' activities, we were masters of all the assumptions that go into estimating overhead costs.

We produced a Whale chart, of course; 80% of the firm's compensation, it showed, went to about 20% of the staff—the partners. Flipping the numbers around, we proved to our satisfaction that 80% of the firm's analytic work was done by people representing 20% of the compensation—people like us. We were clearly at the wrong end of the whale. We decided to order a pricey bottle of wine, on the expense account.

As I examined this particular skew chart, I sensed the nearness of a fundamental insight about the nature of the business in which our firm was engaged. The many graphs and other analyses that consultants pretend are the hard core of their business are sometimes insightful, often elegant, and generally quite tasteful. And yet, notwithstanding their glittering exteriors, they are, like brand-name handbags, really quite cheap to produce. After all, how much can it cost to hire a young, inexperienced, and ignorant philosophy graduate student, train him for three weeks, and then phone in a few pointers from month to month? The truth is that, just as fashion designers aren't really selling handbags, even when they're selling handbags, consultants are selling something other than pure analysis. Our graphs weren't the whales, in a sense; they were the bait.

The first step in mastering the art of hunting whales is to understand that there are indeed a number of ways in which consultants "add value" above and beyond providing analysis and advice. Contrary to what they tell their parents and friends, consultants often serve not to provide new knowledge to their clients but merely to communicate ideas already formed. In many instances, our work amounted to harnessing work performed in one part of an organization and then packaging it all as our own work for the benefit of another part of the same organization. We often served as a kind of ministry of information within the organization. We gathered messages from on high, smoothed out the dissonances and unified the rhetoric, and then repeated and amplified them ad nauseam through the rank and file.

The chief message to be communicated, in almost all situations, was that you will be expected to work much harder than you ever have before and your chances of losing your job are infinitely greater than you have ever imagined. As savvy managers understand, consultants are the cattle prods of the modern corporation. Sometimes their work is called "transformation," sometimes it's "reengineering," and often it is covered over with a three-letter acronym. But what it usually boils down to is a program of worldwide Taylorization. It's about instilling respect for authority. On overseas assignments, just being an American was sometimes enough to get the job done. To be an American, outside of America, means to sacrifice all thought of enjoying a life outside work or of advancing any cause other than next quarter's numbers.

A crucial factor affecting the ability of consultants to perform their communication and discipline functions is the widely shared conjecture that they are "experts" in something or other. Well aware of the value of such perceived expertise, consultants have attached to the word *expert* a number of properties that it does not possess in ordinary speech. As Luigi helpfully pointed out to me one day, when a consultant reboots his computer, he becomes an expert in information technology. If he bought the computer himself, he is a technology sourcing guru. And if he takes it with him on a flight, he becomes an authority on the aviation industry.

Not long after I started my brief consulting career, I discovered that I was already an expert in, among other things, the German asset management market. After all, I had studied nineteenth-century German philosophy, as the partner on the project pointed out. "Just don't mention the Nietzsche bit," he hissed under his breath, before introducing me to the client as "Herr Doktor." After a few weeks as Herr Doktor, I naturally became an expert on global asset management, and then, by homonymy, on asset and liability management (in fact, a completely different subject). From Germany, also, my area of expertise migrated eastward, to encompass the newly liberated states of eastern Europe, where I did some of my most interesting work.

There are of course many subjects on which no one is an expert. There were no experts on doing business in eastern Europe when I went there in early 1990, for example. Consultants, if they are wise, limit their claims of expertise to just these subjects in which no one else can claim to know what they are doing. Clients, if they are wise, appreciate that the perception of expertise, however unfounded, may sometimes be used to good purpose. As the shamans who poison chickens and the priests who read entrails have long known, sometimes it is more important to build a consensus around a decision than to make the right decision; sometimes it is better to believe that a decision is sanctioned by a higher authority than to know that it rests on mere conjecture; and sometimes it is better to have a truly random decision than to continue to follow the predictable inclinations of one's established prejudices. Of course, at other times it is better if you know what you are doing—but in that case why would you hire a consultant?[48]

Consultants, following in the footsteps of their pagan forebears, understand that it is important for their task to envelop their work with an aura of sacred mystery. They must adopt the holy mien of a priestly caste. The longer I spent on the job, the more I appreciated the wisdom of the style of consulting favored by McKinsey and our other top-tier competitors. Bill Bain, founder of Bain & Company, gave his consultants a clothing allowance, and they all came back from Brooks Brothers wearing the same dark suit, white shirt, and red tie that their boss wore. As the Bainies and McKinsey-ites knew, cuff links do matter. Princes and popes always dress up for the job; so should we. Flying first class and eating well, too, is part of the job.

Like shamans, consultants also know that an outrageously unjustified level of self-confidence can add several points to one's perceived expertise quotient. This may help explain the preternatural self-regard that characterizes many young MBAs, especially those who wind up at the most expensive consulting companies. The unshakable conviction in one's own rightness increases the probability that others will follow and so can sometimes make for effective leaders. (Of course, it can also make for exceptionally obnoxious people.)

On visits back to firm headquarters, I wondered if our work for other clients had the gargantuan dimension of our work for Lorenzo's bank. I was surprised to find that our firm's business was indeed at least as skewed as that of any of our clients: 20% of our customers represented 80% of our revenues and undoubtedly even more of our profits. Had a consultant come in to do a skew chart on us, we would have presented a target as big as Moby Dick.

I later discovered that the same is true of all the top-tier consulting firms. Even more remarkable is the fact that a client that counts as a whale for one consulting firm is more likely than not to be a whale for other consulting firms at the same time. In my later consulting life, I thought my new firm was doing pretty well billing one large client between $12 million and $15 million per year for several years in a row. Then I learned that, at the time, this client's total spending on strategy consultants was about $100 million per year. Between 1991 and 1994, the consulting firm Monitor took in $127 million—representing about half of its revenues in the peak year—from a single client, the notably troubled ex-monopoly (with recidivist tendencies) AT&T. And yet AT&T spent hundreds of millions more on other consultants in the same period.[49]

The typical whale-sized engagement matures according to a now well-established pattern, pictured here.

The Phases of the Whale Hunt

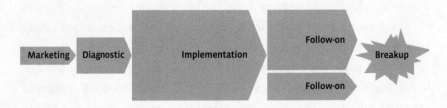

Here's how it works:

1. **Marketing (The Luring).** Fly in "experts" from around the world, never to be seen again. Hold "conferences." When that doesn't work, offer to do a quick and painless "diagnostic" at a steep discount, with a money-back guarantee. Whatever it takes.
2. **Diagnostic (Halloween).** It's trick *and* treat time. First, scare the pants off them. Crater their self-esteem. This requires what is known in the

trade as a "trick." A trick is a quick and easy analysis that will produce predictably horrifying results—predictable for you, horrifying for them. Consultants spend years honing these tricks. Second, offer to give them their self-esteem back in exchange for your treat! Choose the implementation plan that is likely to generate the largest volume of consulting fees.

3. **Implementation (Eating the Brain).** The key to establishing an enduring presence is to colonize key functions in the client's central nervous system. A good place to start is the planning function. Send the existing staff on long and impossible errands, and then steal their office space. Make it impossible for the client to think without you.

4. **Follow-ons (Metastasis).** You're already expanding deep inside the client organization, so think like a cancer. Look for subsidiaries, foreign branches, or other departments where you can replicate.

5. **The Breakup.** Yes, it's hard to do, but at some point the client either wises up to you or just gets tired of your smell. And, frankly, you're fed up with making reports that vanish into the bureaucratic ether. So try to end it gracefully.

Consultants prize their whales for much more than mere size. Large clients provide a safe haven in which to train new associates or to tuck away mediocre performers. They serve as laboratories in which to test new products. They forgive little mistakes. I once heard of a public-sector client that shrugged off a particularly pestilent consulting project as "the four-million-dollar fart." Large clients require almost no marketing expense. Better still, they often pay for the opportunity to receive marketing: Partners in consulting firms spend much of the time they bill to large clients looking for more ways to bill them.

Small clients, by contrast, are intellectually challenging, enjoyable to work for, and miserably unprofitable. They rarely repay the considerable marketing expense incurred to acquire them. They are tolerated mainly insofar as they represent prospective whales, though they may also serve to entertain staff frustrated with the monotony of blubber stripping or to embellish the image of the firm for use in recruiting and marketing activities.

The existence of whales reveals something disturbing and paradoxical about the consulting business—something that should call into question the received wisdom on the nature of the business. The conventional view holds that consultants bring value from some place outside the client organization—from some base of knowledge, some set of skills, or just a culture distinct from what the client already possesses. The conventional view also allows that consultants can serve as flexible resources, or executive "temps." But, in the case of whales, many if not all of the consultants will have acquired all of their relevant knowledge, skills, culture, or whatever it is they offer from the experience of serving that client. They are not distinguishable from members of the organization itself. In fact, they often start to look, dress, and talk like members of the client staff. After a year or more on the job, furthermore, they can hardly be called "temps"—they should really be classified as "exorbitantly expensive and structurally disloyal hires."

From the perspective of conventional economic theory, in fact, whales are inexplicable. On the basis of a two-handed regression analysis, I would estimate that the cumulative marginal contribution of a consulting engagement to client welfare grows at a healthy clip for the first three to four months of a relationship, then starts downhill and dives into negative territory at the six- to nine-month mark. For the consultant, on the other hand, the cumulative utility runs in an almost inverted path. The relationship turns positive only after six to nine months. On the assumption that the relationship between consultant and client is one of mutual utility maximization—as economists would have us suppose—this is a business that should not exist. On the assumption that the relationship is parasitic, on the other hand, it all starts to make sense. It is helpful to think of the consultant as a virus and the client as its host.

Over lunch in the giant cafeteria of one of our blubber factories, I pondered this paradox of the consulting industry with a clever fellow associate. A couple of sloppy joes into the discussion, we realized that the problem with conventional economic theory is that it makes the questionable assumption that clients are rational economic actors out to maximize their self-interest. What if we dropped such a manifestly pre-postmodern assumption? What if we analyzed the dynamics of the consulting industry from outside the limited bounds of the rationality

The Life Cycle of a Virus

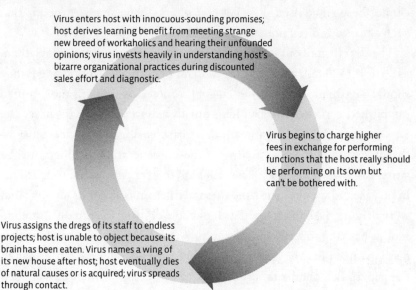

Virus enters host with innocuous-sounding promises; host derives learning benefit from meeting strange new breed of workaholics and hearing their unfounded opinions; virus invests heavily in understanding host's bizarre organizational practices during discounted sales effort and diagnostic.

Virus begins to charge higher fees in exchange for performing functions that the host really should be performing on its own but can't be bothered with.

Virus assigns the dregs of its staff to endless projects; host is unable to object because its brain has been eaten. Virus names a wing of its new house after host; host eventually dies of natural causes or is acquired; virus spreads through contact.

of its clients? On the basis of this daring insight, my friend sketched out a matrix that seemed to explain the art of hunting whales once and for all. I can't remember if he made it up or borrowed it from consulting lore. Here's my own update on the matrix:

The Consultant's Client Segmentation Matrix

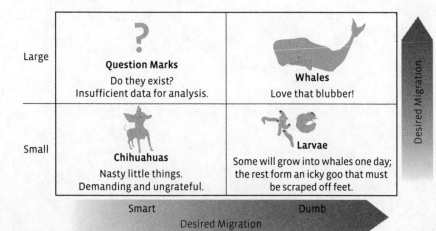

	Smart	Dumb
Large	**Question Marks** Do they exist? Insufficient data for analysis.	**Whales** Love that blubber!
Small	**Chihuahuas** Nasty little things. Demanding and ungrateful.	**Larvae** Some will grow into whales one day; the rest form an icky goo that must be scraped off feet.

Desired Migration

Desired Migration

Machiavelli once pointed out that "a prince who is not himself wise cannot be well advised."[50] What consultants have since learned is that such a prince is often nonetheless an eager customer for advice.

The net effect of our long engagement at Lorenzo's sluggish leviathan, as far as I could tell, was that Luigi and his peers made a few changes they should have made before Lorenzo got promoted over them, and Lorenzo established a truce of sorts with his unruly subordinates. In the best case, we served as a kind of organizational grease, easing the political tensions that interrupted the functioning of the bureaucratic machinery. In the worst case, we were just grease, sticking to everything that touched us. In no case did we alter the fundamental dilemmas about its identity that were driving the bank toward its inevitable destiny. Eventually, Lorenzo sent us packing, mainly in order to prove to Luigi and the smokers that he didn't need his "boys" anymore. Several years after we left, I read in the papers that the bank, after years of erratic performance, had been acquired by one of its competitors.

The Management Idol

The scientific management movement derived its passion from America's torrid love affair with science and technology. Although we tend to think that nothing can compare with the marvels of our own "information age," as the management gurus now call it, Taylor and his contemporaries had much greater cause to swoon over the technological achievements of their own age. The electric grids, the telephone networks, the internal combustion engine, the automobile, the airplane, the refrigerator car, the steamship, the motion picture, the radio, the machine gun, the tank, and the submarine—in short, the technological breakthroughs that continue to define the structure of modern life—all made their debuts in the extraordinary period between Taylor's birth in 1856 and his death in 1915. Mark Twain (a.k.a. Samuel Clemens), who in this respect was very much a man of his time, congratulated Walt Whitman for having the good sense to have been born in an age that produced "the amazing, infinitely varied, and innumerable products of coal-tar."[51]

Even grander than the actual achievements of the age of coal tar were the hopes and ambitions they excited. Twain seemed to think that, with the invention of the typesetting machine, humanity's problems could be safely consigned to the history books. William James and his coterie looked to science to shed light on the possibility of communicating with the dead.[52] Francis Galton and his friends in the eugenics movement argued that modern biology—in particular, the theory of evolution put forward by Galton's cousin, Charles Darwin—would provide irrefutable answers to problems of social and political policy.

Scientific forums at the time were given over to phrenology and even phrenological meteorology—forecasting the weather by examining the bumps on a person's head. Leaders of the "scientific eating" movement maintained that illness could be eradicated if people would eat as science dictates. Many people took to "fletcherizing" their food—chewing each bite as many as 100 times—on the basis of the scientific advice of one Horace Fletcher—a.k.a. "the Great Masticator."[53] One visionary, Frederick Augustus Baker, ardently believed that science would make headway on the problem of evil. He agitated for the construction of giant magnets that, properly situated, would diffuse the "malicious energies" that he believed radiated from the center of the earth and caused people to behave badly.[54] Some suggested that science might even prove to be of help in securing the interventions of the Almighty. "Learn to pray correctly, scientifically," Norman Vincent Peale later advised. "Employ tested and proven methods. Avoid slipshod praying."[55]

There was something very shallow in this enthusiasm for modern marvels. Americans often fell in love with the effects of science, not the method. They had little patience for the tedious work of testing hypotheses against controlled observations. They wanted fast cures to slow problems. They expected science to confirm their most pleasing convictions, not to overturn them. At bottom, their distinctly anti-intellectual fantasies rested on the facile assumption that whatever science delivered was sure to contribute to the perfection of the human race. As one commentator of the times noted, Mark Twain merely "accepted the illusion of his contemporaries" when he assumed "that the progress of machinery is identical with the progress of humanity."[56]

The claims of pseudoscience withstood common sense and the evidence of experience largely because they answered to an aching emotional need—one exacerbated by technological progress itself. Behind the euphoria about science there always lurked the suspicion that the advance of human know-how menaced the place of humankind in the order of things. Pseudoscience was intended to gain mastery of the material forces that otherwise threatened to rob the world of its sense of purpose and meaning. It reflected a strategy of returning to religion by means of science—of speaking with the dead, as James and his friends had it, with the aid of a telephone. It was an avatar not of progress but of reaction.

It is, of course, no coincidence that scientific management emerged in the same age that gave rise to scientific necromancy. Taylor's "scientific" solution to "the labor problem" was of a kind with Frederick Augustus Baker's electromagnetic solution to the problem of evil. It was a giant hope machine, a miraculous technology for bringing about moral perfection in the workplace. It wasn't science, but a simulacrum of science. It was, in short, an idol.

Voltaire once quipped that if God did not exist, he would have to be invented. The same could be said of the idol Taylor created. Considered as a science, scientific management wasn't an elaborate fraud; it was a transparent one. The most interesting question about it is how such a manifestly improbable idea survived and prospered. Why invent such an improbable thing, such a manifest contradiction in terms? The simplest answer is that scientific management fulfilled too many hopes and prayers to be ignored merely on account of its logical and factual deficiencies. Its contradictions are the contradictions of the modern workplace, magnified and exaggerated in the form of an absurd doctrine.

Scientific management achieved prominence because it embodied a number of ideals to which Americans have always been partial. Its homilies on the virtue of efficiency resonated in a nation first settled by Puritans and raised on Ben Franklin's "early to bed" wisdom, and whose marquee philosophical tradition goes under the name of "pragmatism." Its insistence that knowledge—and not birth, social class, or arbitrary favoritism—should serve as the foundation for economic power flattered America's belief in its own classlessness. When he put on his overalls and descended into the machine shops, Taylor struck a metaphorical blow for equality everywhere.

The optimistic aspect of scientific management—its view that conflict in the workplace would dissipate with the advance of science—mirrored America's utopian conviction that progress would soon make happiness into a universal law. Ultimately, the appeal of scientific management rested on its promise to supply a triumphant finale to the ongoing conflict between America's democratic values and its drive for economic modernization—between the Jeffersonian and Hamiltonian visions of America. It was quite understandable that Taylor's earliest supporters in the progressive movement hailed his work as a shining example of "science in the service of democracy."

Often, however, it is only a short step from ideals to deluded self-regard—from seeing what one wants to be to not seeing what one is—and Taylor was generally one for giant leaps. "Practical vigor is a virtue," the historian Richard Hofstadter writes. "What has been spiritually crippling in our history is the tendency to make a mystique of practicality."[57] With his time-wasting stopwatch rituals and other grossly inefficient sacraments to the god of production, Taylor embodied the subtle madness of a new and profoundly unbalanced religion of practicality.

Even his private life offered no release. When Taylor took to the links for some relaxation, he brought with him a putter of his own invention, featuring a Y-shaped handle scientifically calculated to maximize putting accuracy. He also invented a new tennis racket, with the head inclined 15 degrees from the shaft—good for scooping up the low balls, he claimed. In Taylor's world, there were plenty of opportunities to save time, but there was no such thing as free time. In a scathing minibiography of the father of scientific management included in his rambling novel *U.S.A.*, John Dos Passos has Taylor winding his watch as his last act on his deathbed. What good does it do to keep such close track of time, the novelist wants us to ask, if there is no time left to live?

The ideal of classlessness championed by scientific management, too, became a device for ignoring the reality of social class in America—and even in the scientific management movement itself. Notwithstanding the camaraderie he claimed to have established with his friends in overalls, Taylor did not for a moment entertain the notion that he was one of those "little mules." His rise from the shop floor to the commanding heights of the consulting profession would never have happened without the benefit of his excellent pedigree. In *The Principles of Scientific Management*, he matter-of-factly acknowledges that he was often able to bring about changes in the workplace precisely because he, unlike his workfellows, had the "trust" and "understanding" of management. He might as well have pointed out that he and his managers belonged to the same country clubs and went to the same dinner parties. Much of his work amounted to a hostile raid on the working class. It was an effort to gather up the information previously guarded by workers and their shop foremen and bring it back to their superiors.

Joseph Wharton, a robust scion of a prominent Quaker family who was as comfortable riding horses and sailing the New England coast as he was overseeing his empire of zinc and nickel mines, understood better than Taylor the class dynamics at play in the emergence of the new profession of business. Wharton was a member of the "high society" that his distant relation by marriage Edith Wharton so ruthlessly dissected in her novels. In the Whartons' world, the upper class traditionally parked its offspring in the polite (but not terribly profitable) professions of law or the ministry. Newland Archer, the central character and paragon of "old New York" in Edith's *Age of Innocence*, pursues a career in law neither by vocation nor by avocation, but because it is "the thing to do." As Edith sensed and Joseph knew damn well, such a lackadaisical approach to affairs could lead only to decadent irrelevance for "the people of worth." In the future, the power and the glory would be found in business. In his prospectus for the business school that he founded and that still bears his name, Joseph Wharton specifically identified his target as young men of right "inheritance" and "wealth" who might otherwise consider it beneath themselves to pursue a business career.[58]

At the bottom of all the contradictions in the idol of management lay a fundamental refusal to acknowledge the reality of economic power. By reducing management to a form of knowledge, Taylor represented management power as something that is always only good. As he said in his testimony before Congress, "It ceases to be scientific management the moment it is used for bad."[59] But the truth is that management has power not because it is particularly knowledgeable or virtuous, but because without power nothing gets done. And this power can always be used for good or bad. Just like any other form of power, it will always try to extend itself; and it will inevitably be abused at some point, unless it is checked.

Scientific management's delusions about power follow from a contradiction that is deeply rooted in American history. On the one hand,

Americans have tended to favor the idea that their country represents an exception to the rules of history. It is a land where the problems of human cooperation have been solved and power is always used for good. In its more self-indulgent moments, this optimistic self-regard can amount to what Philip Roth calls "the sincerity that is worse than falseness, and the innocence that is worse than corruption."[60]

On the other hand, the American political system in fact draws its strength from an older and darker understanding of human nature. The framers of the United States Constitution understood very well that power invariably tends toward abuse, and they set about to design a system whose chief virtue was to place checks on power. In the *Federalist Papers*, James Madison famously argued that "if men were angels, no government would be necessary. If angels were to govern men, neither external nor internal controls on government would be necessary."[61] Scientific management, like the utopian tradition to which it belonged, marked a departure from the sober wisdom of America's founders.[62]

Some historical figures are remembered for the answers they gave—an equation in physics, for example, or a mechanical invention. But others are remembered for the questions they raised. As with Marx or Freud, the fact that they are wrong in almost every detail of their alleged discoveries does little to diminish their influence. They never quite go away, because they sit atop some unavoidable contradiction. Like burrs caught in our socks, they keep scratching the same wound. Taylor belongs unambiguously to the latter group. With the management idol, he did not find a technological solution to the problem of reconciling democratic ideals with the realities of life in a modern economy. He simply restated the problem, and then etched it in giant letters across the landscape.

"The machinery of management—which encompasses variance analysis, capital budgeting, project management, pay-for-performance, strategic planning, and the like—amounts to one of humanity's greatest inventions," writes Gary Hamel in his 2007 effort.[63] He goes on to suggest that Taylor in particular should be ranked as one of the great benefactors of humanity. Peter Drucker thought that the invention of management was such a heroic achievement that he sought to take credit for it himself. In the 1993 preface to his 1946 book *Concept of the Corporation*, he asserts that his book "is credited with having established management as a discipline and a field of study."[64] These two and most other management thinkers assume that management is an invention in the same sense that the telephone is an invention. According to their way of thinking, Taylor was a hardy pioneer whose work has been surpassed in the same way that, say, the rotary-dial phone has been superseded by touch-tone.

But this is false. Taylor did not invent a machine, but a religion—one that remains exactly where Taylor left it. Management theory today, as the technological rhetoric of gurus like Hamel and Drucker makes clear, answers to the same hopes and contradictions that gave rise to scientific management, and so it continues to worship at the feet of the idol Taylor created.

To be sure, specific elements of management theory and practice have evolved and improved in a variety of ways since Taylor's day. The cost-accounting methods that Taylor first developed, for example, gave rise to the sophisticated menu of analyses available in today's management information systems. In the subdiscipline of operations management, which represents the practical core of Taylor's legacy, significant advances have been made in the study of planning, scheduling, and control of production, supply, and distribution activities. Operations researchers have arguably corrected for Taylor's methodological errors and produced nontrivial, scientifically meaningful results.

The new accounting methods, however, are in essence merely new tools for managers—in the same sense that a word processor is a new tool for writers. The telephone, for that matter, is a useful tool for managers—indeed, more useful than most cost-accounting systems. The achievements of operations research, however notable, apply to only a limited range of activities in a limited range of businesses (principally, manufacturing and distribution businesses). Operations management is at best a small part of the subject of business management in general, and indeed it represents only a fraction of what Taylor had in mind when he promised his "complete mental revolution."

Taylor's most general insight—that rigorous, quantitative analysis of even mundane tasks can help us reach our goals more efficiently—remains as true as it ever was. But the premise that all conflict in the workplace is the result of mere lack of knowledge was and is utopian. In modern management theory, just as in scientific management, this premise invariably leads to the assignment of unilateral responsibility for resolving the problems of management to management itself. It reduces the abuse of management power to bad technique rather than bad ends, and so it opens the door to an unchecked power in the workplace.

The management idol continues to exert its most direct effect on business education. Although Taylor and his doctrine fell from favor at the business schools as his name became associated with public controversy, his fundamental idea that business management is an applied science remained cemented in the foundations of the business schools. In 1959, for example, the highly influential Gordon and Howell report on the state of business education called for a reinvigoration of the scientific foundations of business education.[65] Upon discovering that the miracle of science failed to solve the problem of human cooperation, Taylor's successors took it upon themselves to call for more miracles.

Return to Shore

"It's blue sky for you, Mathieu," Roland said through puffs of thick gray cigar smoke. "I'm going to give you all the rope you can handle."

Across a table of bread crumbs and tiny droplets of lobster bouillabaisse, Roland laid out some great expectations for my future career. He described an ocean of clients swarming with giant prospects, and new lines of attack that were sure to bring in fresh blubber. Right at the moment, in fact, he had a new favorite person in the world, another Joe, whom he thought I should meet.

I puffed back awkwardly and talked tactics between coughs of foul cigar smoke. I speculated on what might be going through Joe's mind, what sort of tricks might catch his eye, and which experts to call in for the pitch. Talking in this way had become easy for me. As a consultant, I'd picked up the habit of talking—just talking, endlessly, from whatever point of view would keep the conversation going. The longer we talked, the more we billed. Sometimes when I talked it felt like an out-of-body experience, as if someone else were doing the talking. It was as if my mind had turned into a blow-dryer: with a flip of the switch, hot air and noise spewed out of my mouth, while the rest of me walked away.

I had been a consultant for more than three years now. I had taken the job with the idea that it would be a one- or, at most, two-year sabbatical before pursuing my destiny, whatever that was. But as the months had gone by, I had kept postponing my return to dry land. Partly this hesitation was because, at least by the standard measure, I had done well: I had doubled my starting salary, and in my third year my raise had tied for the highest in the firm, or so I was told. And despite my skepticism about many of our activities, I couldn't say that the work we did was entirely without economic value. Sure, we were mainly a form of bureaucratic lubricant; but someone has to keep the machine running, I reasoned. Sometimes, it was the very preposterousness of the job that kept me going. Trying to help someone twice your age grapple with a problem that you just read about on the flight over can be quite challenging.

I also had developed a fondness for my colleagues, many of whom were just as disoriented as I was by the consulting experience. They were, on the whole, some of the most curious and most interesting people I've met, and I learned a lot from watching them change and grow. The music man I'd worked with used his consulting-gotten gains to buy a state-of-the-art recording system. He eventually got up the nerve to abandon the temple of Mammon in order to devote himself full-time to the pursuit of the orphic mysteries. The sports car fanatic settled on a German girlfriend and moved to Germany, where he could race his fleet on the autobahns without fear of speeding tickets. The precocious science major turned out to be one of the more successful businessmen of the group.

Still, the more Roland and I talked, the more uneasy I became. I peered into the future and foresaw an endless parade of steak and lobster dishes alongside rows of wine bottles with fine French labels marching off into the distance. In my graduate student days, I had lived on the kind of English food that makes people long for gruel. Now I had fallen into the addictive and debilitating condition of an expense account junkie, with a credit card good at the finest hotels and restaurants in the world. In the back of my mind, I knew that someone was paying the bill, but it felt free.

At the time, I was homeless, in a literal sense. After my lease ran out on my apartment in New York, I didn't bother finding a new one. I stowed my belongings with friends and relatives and flew from hotel to hotel. For more than a year, I paid no rent anywhere. I had no home, of course, because I had no life. Except for phone calls to estranged friends, almost all of my interactions with people were connected to work in some way. Even my holidays were seamlessly integrated into the working life. If I spent a weekend in Venice, it was because I had combined the trip with a business meeting in Milan. I had evolved into a kind of Taylorist ideal, a pure economic machine—except that with my overpriced advisory services and profligate spending on luxury travel, I was a grossly inefficient efficiency expert, a parody of economic virtue.

My job as a consultant was to impose this bizarre and unbalanced way of life on Schmidt and his fellows in our client organizations. I wasn't asking client staff to do anything I wasn't doing myself—although I did expect them to do it for less money. Consultants are the janissaries of the corporate world. The Ottoman emperors used to snatch young boys from the homes of their enemies, then raise them together in isolation from the rest of society and grant them extraordinary compensation in exchange for absolute loyalty to the throne. It turns out that this is a great way to breed consultants too.

I realized I had stepped into the virtuous (or perhaps vicious) circle of the consulting life. Consulting-client organizations are, by process of self-selection, more dysfunctional than the typical corporation (which is saying something). As a result, consultants' recommendations and plans fail with more than the usual frequency. The repeated expenditure of pointless effort breeds a nasty cynicism among consultants about the human condition. This cynicism, combined with the ongoing program of deracination, in turn makes consultants particularly adept at their principal task, which is to scarify people within dysfunctional organizations.

Roland understood all of this. He was a tribal leader, comfortable in his own skin, and I respected him for that. He understood that the climax of a whale story was always the kill. Some of our young recruits were different, though, and they began to grate on me. When they parroted some fairy tale they'd heard or cooed over a clever feat of analysis, I had the urge to kick them down the stairs, make them sit with the rowers for a while, and breathe in the sweat. Their pretty stories seemed like a willful refusal to acknowledge the predatory foundations of our success. They were irritatingly oblivious to their own privilege, as if they had mistaken the luck of their own birth for the perfection of the world.

"You have a great opportunity to grow in the firm," Roland assured me. "You've got an eye for the big picture." He opened his arms wide, as though outlining a larger version of his ever-expanding midriff.

I glanced down at my midsection and once again I felt the horror. My belly was evolving into a miniature bowling ball. For the first time in my life, I—once a proud member of the third-string rowing crew in graduate school—was fat. My personal portrait of Dorian Gray was coming to life. In seven more years, I realized, I would become Roland. I would turn into a pumpkin-sized blow-dryer. And I wouldn't be able to find the off switch.

I knew then that the moment had come.

When he reached the mature age of 33, Andrew Carnegie wrote a letter to himself in which he declared, "To continue much longer overwhelmed by business cares and with most of my thoughts wholly upon the way to make more money in the shortest time, must degrade me beyond the hope of permanent recovery. I will resign business at thirty-five."[66] Of course, Andrew Carnegie went on to become a zillionaire tycoon in steel. I was 28, feeling rather degraded, with little prospect of accumulating a zillion dollars, but nonetheless eager to give up the opportunity to become a well-paid corporate appliance in exchange for an early retirement.

A few months after my dinner with Roland, I turned in my resignation, glad for the experience and confident that I would never work as a management consultant again.

II. Putting People First

Independence Day

W e are a new life-form!" Jim shouted in my ear. "We left the mother ship behind! Now it's time to leave the host vessel! We have evolved! Fuck the machine!"

A cacophony of conversations filled the humid evening air. It was late in the summer of 1994, two and a half years after I'd supposedly given up management consulting for good. About two dozen of my new consulting colleagues and I were crowded in the under-air-conditioned boardroom of a Wall Street law firm, surrounded by elaborately framed portraits of the firm's eighteenth-century founders. Jim was wearing a white T-shirt—not the expensive kind, but a Fruit of the Loom variety—and his thin, strawberry blond hair was flying around his freckled face in its usual imitation of a small brush fire. At his side lay a soft leather briefcase that looked like it had been put through a laundry machine.

Jim was shockingly old for a consultant—definitely over 50. He often spoke in the semi-intelligible way that suggests a higher form of consciousness, or possibly a misspent youth. He exuded an air of haplessness that could bring out the maternal instinct in a stone—or, more to the point, a fresh young college graduate. He was like a cross between a basketball coach and a yogi. As the firm's chief recruiter, he was the first partner that just about every one of the hundreds who eventually joined the firm would meet. He invariably struck newcomers as the most uncorporate human being ever, and the antithesis of what a management consultant is supposed to be.

"I hate to think what would happen if he ever got in front of a client," Roland mused. "But he's fantastic with the kids."

The "mother ship" was McKinsey & Company. With the exception of Roland and me and a few others, the 35 leaders of our division had begun their consulting careers at McKinsey, and they often talked about "The Firm" as though they had never really left it. The "host vessel" was A. T. Kearney. We, the "new life-form," were the leadership of the financial institutions division within A. T. Kearney. Our division had been formed two years earlier, when a core group had departed the "mother ship" aboard a "space pod" bound for our current home. We were now assembled to debate a declaration of independence. Before us was the resolution that we the people who ran our division in New York should break the ties that bound us to our employer in Chicago and take to the galaxies on our own.

Jim showed off a slide on the history of consulting that he would later present hundreds of times to prospective recruits. It was a time line of the noble profession of consulting, from which one could trace the genealogy of existing firms back to ancient times. It showed, for example, that in 1946 A. T. Kearney himself, then a partner at McKinsey & Company, was the first to depart the mother ship and set up his own firm in Chicago. Almost all of the major consulting firms, in fact, had budded from one another in similar fashion. With his grand historical narrative, Jim gave prospective recruits a sense that they were participating in a movement much larger than themselves. They usually left feeling very good about the progress of humankind.

"We are *responsible individuals*," I heard Richard saying across the room. In any group like ours, there is usually a man with a bowtie, specs, and silver hair who looks like he has stepped out of a black-and-white film about small-town bankers; and for us, Richard was that man. Along with Jim and one or two others, he was one of our senior citizens. He was an academic manqué in the field of amateur military history, and he could talk about the most obscure battles of World War II as if he had really been there.

Richard was the author of a five-page pamphlet titled "The Book of Common Prayer," in which he articulated the doctrine of "responsible individualism," the phrase that had become our mantra. "We deemphasize hierarchy and control structures as far as practical necessities allow," he wrote. The gist of his screed was that all individuals (or, more precisely, all individuals who have achieved the exalted status of a partner in a consulting firm) are created equal and endowed with certain inalienable rights, such as the right to pursue profits without having to fill out bullshit reports and show up at pointless staff meetings. Our group mantra was that work is fun, dissent is good, and authority is evil. We believed that an innovative people can prosper only in freedom.

The source of all evil, we maintained, is the Taylorist bureaucracy of the old corporate world, and the scariest words in the English language are, to paraphrase Ronald Reagan, "I'm from headquarters and I'm here to help." "It's medieval!" I remember Richard saying, or words to that effect, about life under the yoke of Chicago's bureaucratic overlords. "It's like being stuck in a dungeon with a bunch of rats and a giant block of cheese. All the rats keep climbing the cheese, two years at level one, two years at level two. The threes shit on the twos and the twos shit on the ones, and everyone shits all the time on the rats at the bottom. All they care about is rat-face-time. As in, please-sir-would-you-stick-your-rodent-butt-closer-to-my-face time. You keep going up until one of the other rats bites your ass off."

One after another, the partners rose to speak in favor of independence and against feudalism. Charles, an Englishman, emphasized the virtue of our global approach to the business. Charles was the Aston Martin of consultants—classy, expensive, and the embodiment of the value system of a bygone era. A tall, blond-haired man named Barry spoke at length about the importance of breaking free from the culture of control of our oppressors in Chicago. A married couple (both of whom were partners) took turns discussing the finer details of the democratic organization of our proposed new firm.

Our effort to break free from our faraway masters, we knew, would inevitably entail legal warfare, significant expense, and considerable professional risks. Our unborn firm at this point did not even have a name. Most consulting firms take their names from their founders. But to us that smacked of the aristocratic ways of the Old World. (And besides, most of the older partners had really ugly surnames.) We wanted a democratic name—an abstraction like "The United States"—that would stand for an idea and not a hereditary title. (My favorite was "The Athena Group"; but the others objected that we'd be confused with a female choir or that we'd end up being tagged as TAG.)

"You can't govern us!" Jim shouted, with his famous genealogical slide up on the projector. "We come from 32 different countries! We're fluent in 47 languages! We've got people from every side of every major war in human history! We've all taken our own path here, over mountains in Nepal and prairies in Kansas and freshwater lakes in South America! We are unique! We are bizarre! We're not yuppies—we're Global Urban Professionals, a bunch of guppies, we swim around the world, like it's our fishbowl, a fishbowl full of neurons and hormones, hey, wear a bathing suit to work every day, I don't care, man! If you don't get it, step aside! Fuck it, man!"

My own path to "Independence Day" did not involve mountains or prairies, though it did certainly count as unique and bizarre. It had begun nearly a year earlier, with a phone call from Roland and a plan to make some spare change.

"Hey, Mathieu, how is that book going?"

"Great!" I preferred not to burden him with the information that, after two years of work, I had finished a draft of an irreverent history of philosophy, and it had been rejected by every publishing company in the phone book.

"Fantastic! Glad to hear you're doing so well."

"Oh yeah!" My savings were rapidly disappearing and, the market for irreverent histories of philosophy being what it was, my financial future was looking very bleak.

"So I have this project. It is the perfect catch for you. A diagnostic. Four weeks. In Mexico. I'm putting together a team of five. I'd like you to manage it for me. What do you think?"

"Mexico?"

"Beautiful country! I can pay you by the day, as a freelance consultant. How much do you want to get paid?"

"Yeah, well, I don't know." I really had no idea what unemployed writers should say under such circumstances.

"I can do $1,500 a day. How does that sound?"

"Yeah!" It was all starting to sound very good to me. After two years of rarely leaving my own head, a brief consulting adventure in Mexico seemed like a good way to relax. In four weeks, or 20 working days, I figured, I'd have a nice little refill for my savings account. I was not at all concerned by the fact that, as I guessed at the time, this meant that the client would be paying close to $4,000 a day for my valuable time.

"Excellent!"

"So, what's the project about?"

"It's a fantastic project. It's for a bank, and it's about risk management. They need a lot of help. It's pretty scary down there. I'm going to position you as a risk management expert."

"You know I never did any work in the risk management area, right?" Our old firm had done much work in the area, but for one reason or another I had never been involved in any such projects.

"Relax! We have three weeks before the project starts. I'll send you some reading material. Hey, did I tell you I'm working with a new group?"

"A new group?"

"They're a terrific bunch. I've learned so much from them. They're really focused on people. It's amazing. They don't care about all that technical bullshit we used to do. They just want to get the best people, and let them figure out what to do. It's a 'supply-side' strategy—the supply of top quality consultants. It's all about giving people the right motivation!"

I took this to mean that he'd been lured over from our old firm by a hefty compensation package.

"I want to introduce you to Owen. He's the one who started the group, brought them over from McKinsey. He's been really great at putting together the team. He's a big-picture guy, very entrepreneurial, too creative for McKinsey. At company parties he used to dance on the tables and stuff. Wild man. You're really gonna like him."

That was the first I heard of Owen. Quite some time passed before we actually met.

A couple of months later, I landed in Mexico. The four-week diagnostic lasted seven weeks and led to a yearlong implementation phase, one client led to a second one, and pretty soon I was running a small business, with 10 consultants, a personal assistant, and more than $300,000 a month in revenue. It was hardly the way I imagined I would spend the year, but it was nonetheless a very pleasant time on the whole. My teammates were an adventurous bunch, mostly fresh recruits from the United States and Europe, and, in the time-honored tradition of management consultants everywhere, we built up our expertise on the spot, with the generous support of our local clients. We spent weekends exploring the country-side and climbing the many pyramids left behind by the Mesoamerican civilizations. I had almost complete independence in running the business. Roland came down on occasion to shoot an unusual species of bird and share meals of fried caterpillars, rose-petal pie, and other local delicacies, but he was otherwise occupied with four or five similar projects for European clients. As a freelance consultant with no long-term career interest, I had little need or desire to spend time at the headquarters of the financial division, which was in New York, or at the firm's general headquarters in Chicago.

Only in the few months preceding Independence Day did I discover that New York was engaged in an undeclared war with Chicago. From the associates who came down to work on my projects, I heard rumors about a "Battle of the Beer Carts." Apparently, New York had started up a tradition of funding a beer cart on Thursday afternoons. Chicago had nixed it. The New York partners had fought back, buying six-packs with their own money and slamming them down on their desks. The freedom to bear drinks, they seemed to think, was part of their bill of rights.

More serious conflicts arose as our group attempted to expand, especially into countries and territories where the parent firm already had operations. In one instance, New York made an offer to a prospective partner in one such territory; Chicago retroactively rescinded the offer, on the grounds that it already occupied that territory; and the jilted recruit sued Chicago, for he had already left his previous job and taken out a lease on office space. Behind the disagreements, I discovered, there was a surprising degree of personal animosity. The New Yorkers seethed at the mention of Chicago. They relished playing the part of the rule breakers. To the Chicagoans, the New Yorkers probably seemed like juvenile delinquents; they were always dancing on the tables.

Much of the controversy centered around one individual in particular: Owen Chase, the nominal leader of the New York tribe. Owen had spent many years at McKinsey, where he had cut either a prominent or a notorious figure, depending on whom you asked. There was some mystery about the circumstances in which he had left the firm. His supporters assured me that he had become a director—the highest-ranking kind of partner. But others claimed that he had always remained a lower-ranking principal, repeatedly passed over in favor of those around him, and that he had departed in deep frustration as one of the oldest principals in the firm.

A midwesterner by birth, Owen had acquired two advanced degrees from Harvard. Apparently he had discovered a loophole in university regulations that allowed him to pursue a JD and an MBA at the same time. As I later understood, Owen was always looking for a rule to bend or a system to game. If you happened to be one of the many people who fell into his orbit, he'd try to bring you in on the deal. If you weren't on the team, you were well advised to read the fine print.

Roland had an almost childlike fascination with Owen. "Owen doesn't focus on what you're saying," he marveled one day in Mexico, over a dinner of fried crickets and ant eggs. "He tries to figure out what you want to get by saying it. And then he tries to figure out *why* you think you want what you want. And then he tries to figure out what he can do about the things that make you think you want it." He gestured with a circle around his forehead and then held up three fingers. "It's third-order conversation," he said, nodding gravely. "He's unbelievably smart. He's always three steps ahead of you."

After Owen started peppering his conversation with one of those psychological frameworks that slots all the billions of people on earth into four or so handy categories, Roland eagerly tried to master the new syntax. So-and-so is "left brain–external" or whatever it was, and the other guy is "right brain–internal," he began to tell me. Hearing Roland use this kind of psychological language was a little bit like hearing your grandmother sing along with gangsta rap. I was never quite sure whether he didn't entirely believe what he was saying or he just didn't really understand it.

Sometimes he seemed to be fishing for an opinion. "You know what

Owen used to do to clients?" he said one day, sounding excited and yet a little uncertain, as though he'd chanced upon a new, secret harpoon but he wasn't sure if it would blow up in his face. "He'd show up to important meetings with three invoices in his briefcase and then, depending on how the meeting went, he would deliver the highest invoice he thought he could get away with!"

In New York, on our way into the meeting of our "Continental Congress," Roland whispered to me in his conspiratorial voice, "You know, Owen and some of the guys are seeing a shrink."

"Well, I guess this transaction is pretty stressful," I replied, trying my best to adopt an enlightened tone of voice.

"No, I mean, they've been seeing the *same* shrink . . ."

I didn't know what he meant. Had Owen and friends undertaken some kind of program in industrial psychology, a plan to alleviate the anomie and fatigue arising from the stressful life in a modern office? Roland shrugged. I knew for sure that *he* at least would draw the line well before sharing a shrink with his co-workers.

On Independence Day, Owen gave the final presentation. I had previously seen him only to shake hands or say hello in the hallways. He was the tallest man in the room, the loudest, and, at 50-something, among the oldest. He had gray hair, watery eyes, and a face that seemed creased with wrinkles well beyond his years. His thick lips and slight buckteeth made him look like a cross between a wolf and an old woman. As he paced in front of the slide projector, throwing his intense gaze at individuals around the room, he had everybody's attention.

"At McK," he said, "I learned about teamwork . . ." ("McK" was the way he usually said "McKinsey," when he wasn't calling it "The Firm.")

"Teamwork means we work together. We are a team. If we stick together, we can pull this off . . ."

If Jim was the outside face of our humanistic management culture, then Owen was the inward-looking side of it. He paid closest attention not to the feelings of clients or recruits, or to the billions of human beings outside the firm, but to the emotional needs of our own people, and especially the partnership. He had bestowed on many of the partners present a nickname ending in *ie*. What the "ie" people had in common, I eventually determined, was that they had worked for Owen in one capacity or another at "McK" or at one of its clients and had formed a bond of fierce mutual loyalty with him. There was, for example, "Robbie"—a small, stooped man with a mustache who hovered behind Owen and kept slipping him papers and passing him messages. I thought he was a secretary, until it became clear that he was a partner too. There was "Trickie," for Patrick—a former banker and Boston Irish type who looked like the kind of policeman who looks like a thug. He, too, turned out to be a partner, although, like "Jimmie," he had been deemed unsuitable for client viewing. So Trickie handled purely internal matters, such as, mainly, our massive dealings with law firms.

Owen began his presentation with a chart showing three bars. The first was a minuscule bar representing the size of our group *ab initio*, two years previously. A circle above with a lonely "$ –" indicated that revenues at the time were negligible. The second was a larger bar, showing the size of the group at present. We now employed 180 professionals, and the circle over the bar showed that our revenue had reached an impressive level of $70 million per year.

"That is the reward for putting people first!" Owen exclaimed.

"Let freedom reign!" shouted Richard.

The third bar, which towered over the other two, showed how big we would become in five years, if all went according to plan. We were going to employ more than 500 professionals and generate more than $200 million annually.

"We're going into orbit!" Jim cried out from the back.

It was an exciting proposition. I felt very fortunate to have the opportunity to participate in the project. Together we had the chance to build an organization from the ground up according to sensible, humane, and democratic principles. We were going to establish a new kind of economic entity, a postindustrial organization free from the burden of yesterday's management dogma, grounded in a psychological understanding of people. Like the heroes of the American Revolution, we were going to make the world anew—and we were going to make a lot of money doing so.

"And that is just the beginning," Owen continued. From the bottom of his deck of slides, he pulled out a new chart as if he were revealing for the first time a secret cargo. The chart this time matched up our tiny firm with gigantic bars representing the number of professionals at the world's most elite consulting firms. At the front of the line stood McKinsey, with a staff that numbered in the several thousands. An almost imperceptible pause interrupted the noise of ongoing whispered conversations in the room. It seemed outlandish, maybe even unhinged, to compare our puny group to such powerful, long-established firms.

"What's going to happen once we get clear of this transaction?!" Owen boomed, his voice filling the room. The partners leaned forward in anticipation.

"We're going right up McK's tailpipe!"

The crowd loved it. I, too, found myself swept up in the passion of the moment. From the raucous aye-ayes around the room, I gathered that all the sailors were on board with the plan. It felt as if we had taken a blood oath. We were going to hunt down the great white whale of the consulting industry. Owen tapped on the bright screen with an air of grim satisfaction. He might as well have been Captain Ahab nailing his ounce of Spanish gold to the mast.

The Ideological Origins of the Humanist Revolution

E lton Mayo disembarked in the harbor of San Francisco on August 1, 1922, at the age of 42, with $250 in his pocket and some deep convictions about how to rescue Western civilization from imminent catastrophe. Back at the University of Queensland, his fellow members of the philosophy department were under the impression that his sabbatical would last one year. But he was determined never to return to Australia, a land he deemed unforgivably provincial. His plan was to earn some money on the lecture circuit in Berkeley, then press on through the United States to London—the capital of Western civilization. It is safe to say that no one at the time would have guessed that this wandering philosopher would very soon occupy a coveted post at the Harvard Business School, where he would be hailed as the mastermind of "the single most important social science research project ever conducted in industry"[1] and the intellectual leader of a revolution that promised to replace Taylorism with a more humane approach to management.

Mayo arrived in San Francisco with a long history of underachievement under his belt. Born to a prominent family in Adelaide, he had spent the first half of his life establishing himself as its most troublesome child. His parents had enrolled him in a prestigious secondary school, but he came home with few friends and only mediocre grades. He had drifted into the local medical school but soon failed out. While his siblings had climbed to positions of leadership in Adelaide's professional communities, Elton had sailed off to seek his fortune in Great Britain, where he failed out of two more medical schools. In London he had proved unable to find paying work. The cousins with whom he resided had grown to detest him. His family had called him home to Australia and set him up with a job in a printing shop. He had quit. He at last had found something worthy of his interest in the courses on philosophy and psychology at the local University of Adelaide. He had picked up his bachelor's degree just as he was rounding 30.

Even as he left behind a trail of disappointments, Mayo somehow conveyed to those around him the sense that he was a man with a brilliant future. He acquired his reputation not by dint of his writings—which, throughout his career, conspicuously lacked in vigor and volume—but by virtue of his talent for conversation and extemporaneous speaking. Gallivanting effortlessly across disciplinary boundaries, tossing out perfectly timed vignettes, turning a sympathetic ear at the appropriate moment, and sprinkling his replies with just the right number of puns, jokes, and literary allusions, he left his interlocutors with the exhilarating feeling of having exchanged ideas with a great mind. Wherever he sat was the head of the table. "How good it was to hear English spoken so well," they said in Philadelphia.[2] Sometimes, to be sure, Mayo's English sounded just a little too smooth. "What does it all mean?" wondered one student in Boston, reviewing his lectures notes in the cold light of day.[3] Another student, later a prominent sociologist, remarked that Mayo's stories from his clinical experience would unfailingly "enliven the conversation"; but upon reflection they seemed "so bizarre that I was sure he had made them up."[4]

Mayo was a short, bald man, worrisomely thin, with an impressively protuberant dome, and prone to fits of depression, which, according to his self-diagnosis, arose from "the superstitions of an obsessive."[5] He sported a cane, favored colorful bands on his hats and socks to match, and smoked his cigarettes through a long filter, useful for punctuating his utterances.[6] He drank tea religiously, rarely allowed lunch to pass without a good sherry, could speak at length about red wines from France, and maintained, when asked, that even the politicians were better in England. In this respect he remained true to his hometown. Having been settled by proper gentlemen—as opposed to convicts—Adelaide was a city that often suspected it was too good for Australia.

The shortage of funds notwithstanding, Mayo promptly took lodgings at the opulent Palace Hotel in downtown San Francisco. In his first days there, he succeeded in attracting attention from some reporters, who wanted him to elaborate on comments he had made to the Honolulu press concerning the psychology of flappers. He obliged them with a discussion of his view that flapperism represents a "nervous breakdown" of society, as neurotic young women, goaded by popular music and literature, seek release by throwing themselves into an unreal social whirl.[7] But the interest in the provocative Australian philosopher quickly faded, and—very bad news indeed—the lecture assignment at Berkeley fell through. With his $250 stash disappearing at an alarming rate in room service bills, Mayo began casting around for jobs—in the magazine world, for Standard Oil, elsewhere on the lecture circuit.

The old feelings of futility and worthlessness came back. He took to wandering the hilly streets, his face clouded with gloomy forebodings, overcome by anomie. Even the prostitutes, he lamented to his wife, failed to return his gaze. His last card was a letter in his pocket that he had finagled from the office of the prime minister of Queensland, in which he had permitted himself to be identified, quite falsely, as a "Professor of Psychology and Physiology." (He was a lecturer in philosophy and had taken to offering psychiatric counseling to shell-shocked war veterans on the side, without any formal qualification.) But he had no place to send his embellished résumé. He contemplated the dreadful prospect of a return to southern Australia but was short of money for the fare home.

In the second month after his arrival in San Francisco, Mayo's luck turned. At the Bohemian Club, while lunching with a doctor who had come to him through Australian connections, he met Vernon Kellogg, a leader of the National Research Council, a powerful entity established by the National Academy of Sciences during the Great War that served to coordinate and promote research in universities and industry. Mayo told Kellogg of his plan for saving Western civilization from imminent collapse. Kellogg seemed to think it was a good plan and suggested they meet again, in Washington DC. Ecstatic over his career prospects now, Mayo forgot all about London, cadged another $1,000 from family in Australia, and hopped aboard a train heading east. In Washington he conferred with some of the nation's most influential science administrators, all of whom responded favorably to the winning conversationalist from the Antipodes. Riding a crest of enthusiasm for his cause, he journeyed to New York, where he met with representatives of the Rockefellers. There he hit the jackpot.

Mayo's message about the future of civilization was one that America's business and scientific leaders were ready to hear. The essence of that message was already quite plainly stated in a handful of writings he had published before and just after his arrival in San Francisco. In a 70-page booklet titled *Democracy and Freedom: An Essay in Social Logic*, published in 1919, Mayo warned of the danger of ever-increasing conflict between labor and capital, whose catastrophic consequences had been all too clearly telegraphed in the events of 1917. "A worldwide revolution of the Russian type," he later whispered to a friend, "would completely destroy civilization."[8] In Australia, it all came very close to home with the rancorous New South Wales railway strike that took place in the same year that the Bolsheviks mounted their coup in Moscow. According to Mayo's account, the railway strike was the result of the workers' "irrational" response to a single word: *Taylorism*.

Mayo's position involved more than the usual Red scare. The novelty in his message lay in his analysis of the remote cause—and hence the treatment—of the revolutionary threat. Others might have laid the blame for strife between workers and owners on bad working conditions, low pay, or similar conflicts of interest. But Mayo had a different idea. "To any working psychologist," he declared in one of his early writings, "it is at once evident that the general theories of Socialism, Guild Socialism, Anarchism, and the like are very largely the phantasy constructions of the neurotic."[9] That is to say, the revolutionary ideologies that portend the demise of civilization are psychopathological in origin. In simpler terms, the workers of the world are nuts.

Life in the modern world, Mayo elaborated, is hard on the psyche. The masses labor in monotonous jobs that induce fatigue, or "organic disability." They find it impossible to understand how their specialized, routinized, and impermanent employments perform meaningful func-

tions for the social whole. So they succumb to "reveries," or passive obsessions, and to a sense of futility or disconnectedness called *anomie.* Mayo
contrasted the modern condition with the happier life of the medieval
era and of primitive societies, in which everyone knew his place and all
collaborated spontaneously for the good of the whole. (Many indigenous
cultures, incidentally, were just beginning to receive attention from
anthropologists, such as Mayo's good friend and companion in Australia, Bronislaw Malinowski.) The damage done to the soul by industrial
working conditions, he further insisted, is buried in the subconscious
mind—or what he sometimes called "the night mind of the child"[10]—and
is largely hidden even from the workers themselves. "Industrial unrest,"
he wrote in the same year he landed in America, "is not caused by mere
dissatisfaction with wages and working conditions but by the fact that a
conscious dissatisfaction serves to 'light up' as it were the hidden fires of
mental uncontrol."[11]

To illustrate his thesis about working-class psychopathology, Mayo
regularly drew on a small portfolio of case histories, many of them
involving individuals who had been referred to him in his capacity as
a common-law psychiatrist. He was particularly fond of the case of a
young "agitator." The man in question was a known troublemaker in the
workplace. He refused to accept orders and was interminably organizing
strikes and other disturbances. Upon clinical examination, the young
man revealed that his father was an alcoholic and had beaten him regularly. Thus, the agitated young man's "'response situation,' we learned,
was determined by the facts of his early childhood"—and not, presumably, by any legitimate grievances against his employers. Upon receiving proper psychiatric care, Mayo crowed, the young man underwent a
"complete change of attitude to authority" and became a well-adjusted
factory worker.[12]

Others might have argued that the way to improve working conditions would be to empower workers to negotiate the terms of their
employment—that is, to support unions and, in general, to promote
democracy. Mayo's analysis impelled him to the opposite conclusion.
Relying on worker assemblies to solve the problems of industrialization,
he said, made about as much sense as calling a meeting of the neighbors
to decide how to treat a case of typhoid.[13] In collective bargaining, he

wrote not long after landing in America, "the principle of the primitive squabble has been accorded a pseudo-scientific rank."[14] Democracy, in general, he saw as a means of empowering those who had no idea whence their problems came. Far from solving anything, it plays upon the psychopathological conditions of the masses. "Democracy, as at present constituted," he announced, "exaggerates the irrational in man and is therefore an anti-social and decivilizing force."[15] In his sour moments he referred to democracy as "ignorant ochlocracy"—the rule of the mob.

The solution to the psychopathological condition of modernity, Mayo argued, must be located at the source of the problem—in the industrial workplace itself. Thus, he had a stern (and yet perhaps not altogether disagreeable) message for employers: "So long as . . . business methods . . . take no account of human nature and social motives, so long may we expect strikes and sabotage to be the ordinary accompaniment of industry."[16] Equipped with the right business methods, on the other hand, industry can tame the unruly psyches of the workers and establish peace in our time. In Mayo's view, large corporations would play the central role in bringing about a more harmonious future. By assimilating and implementing the correct psychological methods, large corporations would do for Mayo's vaguely imagined future what the church and trade guilds had done for the medieval world. And the larger the corporations, the better. Mayo favored monopolies on the grounds that competition only added to the horrible sense of strife pervading modern society.

In order for the monopolistic corporations of the world to treat the working masses with the psychiatric consideration they deserved, Mayo cautioned, society would require an as-yet undeveloped science—a proper psychology of the workplace. This is where Mayo himself fit in, with his well-polished curriculum vitae. As a "Professor of Physiology and Psychology," he proposed to undertake a program of research in industrial psychology, whereby he would contribute to "humanity's knowledge of itself." The stakes, he argued, could not be higher. "Out of this research," he promised the readers of *Harper's* in 1924, "will come the power to amend and advance civilization, to defy the possibility of decadence. This is not one way but the only way to save society."[17] From the time he left Australia until he finally made his way out of America 25 years after landing in San Francisco, Mayo would adhere to his doctrines concerning industrial psychology and the fate of civilization with a kind of unalterable, perhaps even fanatical conviction that could not but recall the psychology of the very revolutionaries he studied.

In forming his rather apocalyptic philosophy of management, Mayo drew heavily on intellectual currents that were fashionable at the time. Gloomy global forecasts had come into vogue with amateur historian Oswald Spengler's publication of *The Decline of the West* in 1917. The analysis of the psychological ills of modern society and the term *anomie* itself Mayo borrowed directly from Émile Durkheim (1858–1917), the pioneering sociologist who had developed the concept in the context of his 1897 analysis of suicide rates in modern societies. The celebration of an integrated social whole, characterized by unforced and spontaneous collaboration, echoed the thoughts of the idealist philosophers popular in Britain around the turn of the century—notably the neo-Hegelian Thomas Hill Green and the German philosopher Johann Gottlieb Fichte. Mayo's contempt for the herd and his concern over the crisis of nihilism may have owed something to Friedrich Nietzsche, the philosopher of "the over-man." His concept of the unconscious mind marked a heavy debt to Sigmund Freud, of course, and his theories about reveries, or passive obsessions, came from Pierre Janet, an early practitioner of psychoanalysis in France. The fascination with the vexatious mind of the workingman (and woman) was also a feature of the times, as is evident in contemporary titles such as *What's on the Worker's Mind by One Who Put on Overalls to Find Out*, by Whiting Williams, a theologian, university administrator, and personnel manager.

Perhaps the most important influence on Mayo was Vilfredo Pareto, the French-Italian sociologist and grandfather of the skew chart. From Pareto, Mayo borrowed the idea that human beings are motivated in their political and economic life not by reason but by sentiments, which they defend with pseudo-logical belief systems. Of particular interest for Mayo was Pareto's idea that elites serve to maintain an equilibrium among all these irrational forces in society, and that when they fail to do so, society succumbs to revolution. (Some commentators suggest that Pareto was for the bourgeoisie what Karl Marx was for the proletariat.) Gathering signs everywhere of what he took to be the weakness of the existing elites in the face of the unruly working mob, Mayo fretted over Pareto's teaching that "history is the graveyard of aristocracies."[18]

For all the sophistication of his intellectual pedigree, Mayo was not above indulging in some of the crudest pseudohistorical narratives. Like many of modernity's discontents, his rage settled at least some of the time on the usual scapegoat. "One is staggered by the effective destruction that the Jew is accomplishing," he once wrote to his wife. "One cannot talk about this topic because one is instantly classified with the 'antis.'"[19]

It is likely, in any case, that Mayo did not burden his well-heeled listeners with the intellectual genealogy of his positions, for he had already developed some skill in handling Americans. He later confided to Peter Drucker, the Austrian-born management guru who would lay claim to his legacy, "One must be exceedingly careful in the display of intelligent capacity before Anglo-Saxon audiences. I am sure that your Continental training will enable you to understand what I am talking about."[20]

Evidently, the Rockefeller people, along with the rest of the establishment types Mayo encountered in his travels up the northeastern corridor, liked what they heard. Which is perhaps not so surprising: they were at least as keen as Mayo on avoiding industrial unrest, they undoubtedly shared his low opinion of the Bolsheviks, and they had every reason to think that *monopoly* wasn't quite the bad word it was made out to be. To put the matter in the crude language that Americans are presumed to understand, when the self-credentialed professor spoke, what they heard was a plan to reduce strikes, thwart unionization, and establish peace in our factories, without having to make substantive changes in working conditions, all for the price of a professor and a few research assistants.

The Laura Spelman Rockefeller Memorial agreed to fund a position for Mayo, first at the University of Pennsylvania and then, starting in 1926, at the Harvard Business School. The foundation also promised to underwrite Mayo's research expenses. Just four years off the boat in San Francisco, Mayo had achieved what academics dream about when they dream about heaven: no real teaching responsibilities, and all the research assistants money can buy. Over the next 20 years, Mayo would channel $1.5 million in Rockefeller cash for himself and his favorite research projects—an awesome figure in an age when the typical Australian professor of philosophy received less than $3,000 in annual compensation.

The only complaint from the Rockefellers was that he couldn't spend the money fast enough, leaving portions of his grants unclaimed.

The business school crowd was no less enthusiastic about Mayo than the money men. At the Harvard Business School, Taylorism had lost its luster. Thanks both to the very unpleasant public controversies surrounding scientific management and to increasing concerns about its narrow focus on manufacturing efficiency, Taylorism no longer seemed an adequate justification for the existence of the school. The new dean, Wallace Donham, saw in Mayo's proposals just the kind of program that would lend business education the scientific credibility it still lacked. In the same way that medical schools rely on basic research in biology and chemistry, he reasoned, the business school would depend on basic research in the social sciences, such as that provided by "Professor" Mayo. Thus was born on the south side of the Charles River the Harvard Fatigue Laboratory, or "human biology program," as Mayo preferred to call it.

Mayo's program implied a heroic future for the Harvard Business School and like-minded institutions. Emboldened by the new science emerging from his laboratory, according to Mayo, the business schools would spawn an invigorated cadre of graduates who would shake off the decadent tendencies Pareto warned about and rescue the world from the peril of a workers' revolution. "The world over we are greatly in need of an administrative *élite* who can assess and handle the concrete difficulties of human collaboration," he wrote. "As we lose the non-logic of a social code, we must substitute a logic of the understanding."[21] The Harvard Business School, the presumptive cradle of this "administrative elite" would thus serve to develop the "logic of the understanding" that would save civilization from itself.

In the interest of lending the program an air of clinical seriousness, Mayo allowed himself to be styled "Doctor Mayo." University authorities only later discovered, to their consternation, that this title, like that of his earlier professorship, was a response to the needs of the situation rather than a factual representation of his educational credentials. Mayo defended himself by saying that he often let the honorific slide because to have explained that he was not in fact a doctor would have "interrupted the flow of conversation."

Although he constructed his professional life around the study of workplace conventions, Mayo soon made clear to his Harvard fellows that he was not the sort of man who wished to live by the rules. "He never conformed to a convention he did not find congenial,"[22] observed one of his fellow professors. Authentic scholars and scientists, like the aristocrats of old, he once explained to a friend, are by nature agnostic, fearless, and exempt from the very moral codes it is their job to create and enforce.[23] "Education should be the prelude to adventure," he told the readers of *Harper's Monthly Magazine*, "and life the adventure."[24] True to his creed, he would roll into his faculty office at around 11:00 a.m., hold court for his students, then retreat to St. Clair's restaurant for a wet lunch before returning home. He eventually decided that his colleagues at Harvard epitomized the "bourgeois." They returned the compliment, hinting posthumously that he was aloof, arrogant, "a bit of the juvenile delinquent," and "perhaps . . . fundamentally a lazy man."[25] He was a man with a mysterious past, observed one, "some of which he had reason to keep mysterious."[26]

In the spring of 1928, two years into his Harvard posting, "Doctor" Mayo began to feel the downward tug of anomie all over again. On paper, his ascent from penniless Australian philosopher to Ivy League pontiff read like a great American success story. On the ground, his forays into industrial research had thus far produced little of substance. In one factory, he'd offered his services as the workingman's psychologist—but only a handful of workers had opted to avail themselves of his therapeutic services. He'd been hounded off the project when, in hopes of relieving a female employee of her ignorance about her own physiology, he loaned her a book on sex. In another factory, he had just begun some promising work on the use of rest periods when disputes with senior management made him unwelcome. The "human biology program" thus far consisted of a pool of workers' blood pressure data that appeared to prove nothing at all. Of more immediate concern, the Rockefeller money still had to be renewed on a year-to-year basis, so the prospect of an ignominious return to South Australia could not be ruled out.

In a letter of April 11, 1928, to the Rockefeller officials, Mayo put a brave face on the situation.[27] The program in industrial research was progressing well, he averred; he lacked only a secure niche in industry to carry it to its conclusion. The truth was that he had a grand theoretical artifice, and no data to fill it. He was a researcher without research.

Two weeks after writing the letter, Mayo at last responded to an invitation to visit the Hawthorne Works, a colossal factory belonging to the Western Electric Company located in the flat, grim land on the west side of Chicago. There, he had learned through his Rockefeller and Harvard connections, an industrial research program had run into trouble, producing intriguing yet inexplicable results. If Mayo was a theory desperately seeking data, Hawthorne would soon prove to be a trove of data in dire need of a theory. The "researcher" and his "research" would soon be united in mutual and enduring fame.

Western Electric was a company that cared. For the benefit of its 22,000 employees—mostly first- and second-generation immigrants from Chicago's various ethnic communities—the company provided a hospital, a savings and loan, and a company store. On land abutting the factory site, among the low-rises where Poles and Italians eyed each other suspiciously across the cracked sidewalks, it had cleared space for six baseball diamonds, thirteen tennis courts, a running track, and a giant gymnasium. The company also organized dances, parties, vacations, and beauty contests. It offered courses of evening study, including classes on health and hygiene, which the female employees in particular were strongly encouraged to take.

It wasn't all about fun and fitness. Internal company memoranda listed "freedom from Labor Unions" as a principal justification for the generous benefits program, and the plan appears to have worked for a time.[28] The constant threat of congressional investigation, too, made the profusion of indulgences seem like wise policy. As the chief manufacturing subsidiary of AT&T, the Western Electric Company was an integral part of the Bell System, which under J. Pierpont Morgan's guidance had established itself as the monopoly provider of telephone services to the nation. The Bell companies were eager to be perceived as good corporate citizens, quite capable of taking care of the needs of their stakeholders without the burden of excessive government oversight.

If there was anything that the Bell companies valued more than peace in the workplace, it was the very idea of science. Their leaders understood quite well that scientific research was the foundation of the Bell System's past fortune and of its future prospects. So it was perhaps inevitable that Frederick Winslow Taylor's idea of scientific management should have awakened lively interest at Western Electric. By the early 1920s, the company employed a staff of piece-rate analyzers and researchers tasked with shining the light of science on its manufacturing processes.

In November 1924, three and a half years before Elton Mayo set foot on the west side of Chicago, the researchers at Western Electric began a series of experiments to test the hypothesis that increases in workplace illumination would lead to increases in worker productivity. The official sponsor of the research was the National Research Council, but that august body in fact served chiefly as a front for the major companies and utilities in the electricity sector. The electric companies were understandably enthusiastic about a line of scientific research that seemed to augur so well the future sales of lightbulbs.

Over the next three years, under the day-to-day supervision of a piece-rate analyst named Homer Hibarger, the illumination in various sections of the Hawthorne facility waxed and waned. At one point, Hibarger persuaded a pair of female employees to carry out their tasks in a closetlike space, with the lights turned down to about the level of moonlight. Productivity drifted upward modestly and unevenly throughout the trials, but without any significant correlation to lighting levels. Even the ladies in the moonlit closet managed to keep up the pace. The experimenters sensibly concluded that extraneous factors—changes in supervision or possibly the experimental protocol itself—had outweighed the effects of changes in illumination.

The electric companies, not surprisingly, lost their enthusiasm for the research. But Hibarger and his supervisors, in hopes of taming some of the uncontrolled variables that had spoiled their illumination experiment, decided to continue the program anyway. They wanted to find out why worker productivity seemed to fluctuate through the day; whether the work resulted in excessive fatigue; how the attitude of the workers might affect their output; and, most important, whether the introduction of rest periods and other changes in working hours might improve productivity.

In April 1927, with an eye on the last question in particular, they set up the soon-to-become-famous Relay Assembly Test.

Relays are small electric switches. They are used for, among other things, routing telephone calls in automated exchanges. As AT&T expanded its telephone network across the country, it developed a stupendous appetite for relays. The relays came in several varieties and were made up of over 30 parts, including coils, armature, springs, pins, insulating material, and screws. An average worker could assemble a typical relay in about one minute. He or she was then expected to repeat the process about 50 times an hour, every hour over an 8¾ hour workday, 5½ days a week, for as many weeks as he or she could stand it. During the 1920s, the main relay assembly floor at the Hawthorne Works housed several hundred employees who sat four to a bench under an echoing roof and produced 7 million relays every year.

The Relay Assembly Test took place in a room separated from the main floor and equipped with a single workbench, temperature and humidity monitors, and a device for recording the output of each worker throughout the day. Hibarger assigned six women to the project: Anna Haug, Beatrice Stedry, Wanda ("Lottie") Blazejak, Adeline Bogatowicz, Theresa Layman, and Irene Rybacki. Anna was 28 and of Norwegian descent, Beatrice was a 24-year-old Czech. The others were all under 20 and the children of Polish immigrant families. Theresa was only 15, though the company believed her to be 18.

The women immediately had a number of reasons to feel good about the move. Walled off from the cavernous main floor, they had a chance to chat and get to know one another as they worked. Hibarger, who sat in the room to observe them every day, encouraged an informal atmosphere, and they took to calling him "Hi." They began to hold parties to mark birthdays and other events, and took turns bringing in cookies and cakes. When the workers on the main floor heard about the tea parties—during working hours!—they dubbed it "the T Room." In addition, to make measurement easier Hibarger limited the variety of relays assembled, sticking with the simplest types. Most important of all, the T Room ladies were put on a new compensation arrangement, whereby they would receive substantial extra pay as a function of their group productivity. The only negative, as far as the women were concerned, was a certain loss of privacy. Every month Hi sent them off to see a doctor, who took their blood pressure, probed and prodded them, and asked indelicate questions about their menstrual cycles.

After a three-month warm-up period, Hibarger began to introduce rest breaks. At first it was two 5-minute breaks; then two for 10 minutes each; then six for 5. Over the first eight months of the experiment, productivity drifted upward a modest 9% to 13%, depending on how "base"-level productivity was defined. Total production was up only 4% to 7%, however, because the total number of hours that were worked declined with the rest breaks.[29] Statistically speaking, given the very small sample size and the lack of clarity about the base level of productivity, the experimenters had very little to hold on to.

As the summer of 1927 turned to fall, sadly it became apparent that Adeline and Irene were bad apples. Intoxicated with their newfound status as members of the T Room, the two young women began to make demands. They asked for screens to be placed in front of the workbench to protect their legs from Hi's gaze. (The request was granted when they pointed out that constantly pulling down their skirts ate into their productivity.) They complained that the lights in the room were much brighter than on the main floor. (A test confirmed that they were right, and the lights were dimmed.) They kicked up a fuss about the visits to the doctor. (Hibarger arranged to have the doctor come to them; they retaliated by turning doctor day into an excuse for more cake and cookies.) They expressed the suspicion that Hi was monitoring their conversations with each other (he was), and they simply refused to stop chatting.

"We do what we want, we work how we feel and we say what we know!" Irene chanted. She had become a poster child for worker empowerment run amok.[30]

Irene and Adeline's fatal mistake, it seems, was to convey the impression that they were restricting their production. Managers took Irene aside and "reproved" her for her "low output and behavior." They told her that she "did not have the right mental attitude."

"For the love of Mike!" she responded. "They tell you to work how you feel, and when you do, it isn't good enough!"[31]

She had a point. By goading her to work harder, the experimenters had, in fact, undermined the very foundation of the experiment, which was to see how rest periods, not pressure tactics, would affect her level of productivity.

One fine morning, Irene bragged about how many relays she could make in a day. Adeline was heard to say, "Don't do it! Don't be a fool!" Shortly thereafter, on January 25, 1928, Irene and Adeline were removed from the T Room and replaced with two new women: Mary Vorango, an 18-year-old daughter of Polish immigrants; and Jennie Sirchio, a 20-year-old Italian-American.

It was manifestly a case, to use modern managerial language, of getting rid of deadwood, bringing in fresh blood, and instilling a fear of God in the survivors. The remaining women evidently got the message. Hi recorded in his notebook that Theresa, now 16 years old, was observed to be showing signs of "resentment" in the wake of Adeline and Irene's dismissals.

Jennie, it appears, was made of tough stuff. In the three months before joining the test, her mother and sister had passed away, and her father and brother had lost their jobs. She had become the chief breadwinner in a traumatized household. She came into the test room with records in productivity already under her belt and a reputation as a rate buster. She rapidly became the informal leader of the group.

She also had a clear grasp of the unique T Room compensation arrangement, according to which the women were paid a substantial premium above their normal wages as a function of their group output. When she saw the lackluster production figures for the existing test room women, she blurted out, "Oh! What's the matter with those other girls? I'll kill them!" She began to goad the other workers to increase their efforts. She took to rushing them back from breaks in order not to lose production time, and even persuaded them to forgo some of their tea parties.

Not surprisingly, the arrival of the new girls coincided with a surge in productivity. From the moment she started, Jennie was almost 20% more productive than Irene had been; and Mary, herself no slouch, was 16% more productive than Adeline. Right after the dynamic duo joined, furthermore, the other women turned in their biggest individual leaps in productivity, which in turn gave the group its single biggest period-to-period increase in productivity: 11%. By the middle of 1928, the women were producing about 25% more relays per hour than they had been when they started. From the end of 1928 to the end of the experiments in early 1932, the team's productivity averaged 35% or so higher than the base level (and peaked at 45% or so, depending on how one chooses to measure). Owing to significant reductions in the number of hours worked, however, total production was up a more modest average of 13%.

The experimenters continued with new variations in the T Room regime, providing the ladies with snacks and even allowing Saturdays off. During one three-month period in late 1928—the soon-to-be-famous "Period 12"—Hibarger eliminated all the breaks and snacks and resumed work on Saturdays. The women kicked up a fuss and were quieted only when Hi assured them that at the end of the period the breaks would be reinstated. Productivity fell 3%, but, with Saturdays back on, total production increased 11%.

Approaching the end of 1928, the Hawthorne experimenters appreciated that they had a great big bowl of spaghetti on their hands. They had plenty of leads to follow, but no way to untangle a reasonable explanation for the increase in productivity in the T Room. Was the increase due to the rest breaks, the intense supervision, the decrease in relay types, the accumulated experience of the workers, statistical noise, the special compensation arrangement, Jennie and Mary, or what? Elton Mayo, who was something of a specialist in the "or what" category, soon gave them an answer.

At first, Mayo took pleasure in the visits to the Hawthorne Works. The company put him up at the fabulous Palmer House Hotel in Chicago and treated him as they would a senior manager. In a letter to his wife he describes the scene: "Every morning at 8:30 the doorman clears the taxis away . . . and a large limousine with a uniformed chauffeur slides noiselessly in. The door is opened and Elton Mayo, formerly of South Australia, gets in and glides off to his alleged industrial researches."[32]

Mayo's second visit was delayed by summer. He was already booked to spend the hot months with his wife and children in Europe, where he had settled them, having decided that America was no country in which to raise a family. During his first year on the project, Mayo managed a record of five visits to Hawthorne, each lasting a few days to a week.

After that, his enthusiasm flagged, and he brought it down to two courtesy calls per year. At no point did he direct the research program at Hawthorne; his role was always more that of an involved commentator and mentor to the researchers.

It took some time for Mayo to appreciate that interpreting the Hawthorne results was his destiny. His first step upon getting out of the limo was to review the medical data on the women of the T Room and elsewhere at the Works. As a founder of Harvard's Fatigue Laboratory, "Doctor" Mayo was keen to establish an "objective" correlation between a worker's productive capacity and her blood pressure and pulse rate. Upon first glancing at the data, he noted with jubilation that the most productive worker was the one "who [had] achieved an organic equilibrium—and kept it."[33] Unfortunately, a second glance at the data didn't back up the first glance.

Next, in the story about Adeline and Irene, Mayo thought he saw a more promising opportunity to confirm his hypothesis about the connection between blood and toil. He noticed that Irene's hemoglobin count had come back low, indicating anemia. Here, surely, he exclaimed triumphantly, was the scientific explanation of why she "became paranoid and 'turned Bolshevik.'" Unfortunately, this theory failed to explain why Adeline, too, had joined with the Reds; her hemoglobin count was normal.[34]

After discarding the blood data, Mayo poked around some of the other research activities under way at the Works. As part of their effort to understand workers' attitudes toward their jobs and the company, the Hawthorne researchers had decided to conduct fact-finding interviews of each of the plant's tens of thousands of employees. Mayo had no use for the fact-finding questions; they were all obviously addressed to the conscious mind of the worker, when the problems, as he knew, originated in the night mind. "The idea that one might construct from interview material an accurate picture of situations in the Works was frankly abandoned," he writes, graciously disguising his influence behind the passive voice.[35] He recommended instead that the researchers undertake much longer, open-ended interviews, in which workers would be encouraged to talk about whatever was on their minds. The purpose of the program, as Mayo saw it, was not just informational, but therapeutic: the interviews would serve as a means for workers to "get things off their chest."

As a further service to the program, incidentally, Mayo had the
interviewers practice their skills by donning white coats and posing as
doctors while interviewing actual patients in a conveniently located
Boston psychopathological clinic.[36] There is no better snapshot of Mayo's
philosophy of management in action. Workers were directly analogous
to psychiatric-ward patients, in his mind, while he and his team were
obliged, for the sake of the common good, to put on the costumes of
learned authority and claim credentials they didn't have.

The interview program at Hawthorne soon turned up just the kind
of data Mayo expected to find. He was particularly delighted by the case
of a woman who complained that her new supervisor was tyrannical,
unlike her previous bosses. In a lengthy, free-association interview, she
mentioned that the new boss reminded her of her stepfather, who had
badly mistreated her mother. Immediately the diagnosis was clear: there
was nothing wrong with the new boss; the source of the woman's dissatisfaction at work was a lamentable "home environment."[37]

The interview program, however, soon encountered turbulence.
Arthur Kornhauser, an industrial psychologist at the University of Chicago, reviewed some of Mayo's material and noted that the absence of
meaningful scientific controls rendered the program "rather fruitless."[38]
Proving that he could turn his clinical eye on professional rivals just
as easily as on workers, Mayo countered that Kornhauser's comments
were "negative" and therefore "unhelpful," and further suggested that
they arose from Kornhauser's personal "neuroses." He promised the
Hawthorne managers that he would "cram the methods of the Western
Electric Company down the throats of researchers like Kornhauser and
his tribe."[39] (Kornhauser, incidentally, was Jewish.)

Not until more than a year after his first visit did Mayo realize that the
thing he had been looking for all his life was now staring him in the face.
"We are 'sitting in' at a major revolution in industrial method—a revolution that will probably be as far reaching in its ultimate effect as the so-
called industrial revolution of the latter eighteenth century," he wrote to
his wife.[40] With the benefit of the Hawthorne researches, he announced
to his colleagues, "industry will enter upon a new and undreamed of
era of active collaboration that will make possible an almost incredible
human advance."[41] In November 1929, Mayo published an article in which

he revealed to the public the earth-shattering findings of the Hawthorne experiments. This was followed by a series of articles—which, as with his earlier writings, tend to read more like the same article published a series of times—as well as books and radio talks.

At the center of Mayo's revolution was a particular interpretation of events in the T Room. According to Mayo, the phenomenal rise in productivity among the relay assembly workers could be explained only by the occurrence of a transcendental, almost mystical transformation in the psychology of the group. In his telling, the six women had entered the room as ordinary workers, lost in their dissociated reveries and presumably every bit as psychologically disturbed as their fellow workers on the main relay assembly floor. Yet, in the course of the experiment, they had fused into an organic whole. Upon receiving recognition for their work from the company and from each other, they had gladly given their all to the project. "What actually happened was that the six individuals became a team and the team gave itself wholeheartedly and spontaneously to cooperation in the experiment. The consequence was that they felt themselves to be participating freely and without afterthought, and were happy in the knowledge that they were working without coercion from above or limitation from below."[42]

The T Room operators had effectively succeeded in re-creating the Middle Ages, at least in Mayo's interpretation. That is, they had achieved, in microcosm, the kind of highly integrated society in which each individual understands and affirms her social function and cooperates without the slightest pressure from above or below for the sake of the common good. Like Taoist sages, one could say, the women had aligned themselves with the forces in their universe and thus reached a state of "action without effort," or work without work. "Their own self-determination and their social well-being ranked first and the work was incidental," Mayo gushed.[43] Thus, the T Room experience demonstrated the central tenets of a new, humanistic philosophy of management: that a happy worker is a good worker, that the road to happiness passes through the satisfaction of the worker's psychological and social (as opposed to material) needs, and that the "informal" or "human" side of an organization—its culture and values—is far more important than its formal hierarchy.

The obvious difference between the T Room and the primitive societies that Mayo had idealized in his Australian writings was that the little Eden outside Chicago had been created in a modern, laboratory environment. Therein, said Mayo, lay the hope of future generations. The new knowledge derived from the test-tube utopia at Hawthorne would allow scientists and managers to gain control over the all-important human side of the enterprise. Creating idyllic workplaces could be rendered just as routine as manufacturing bicycles. "With the institution of adequate researches, physiological, psychological, and social," Mayo grandly concluded, "society has nothing to fear from industrial mechanization."[44]

Mayo made his interpretation of the test all the more powerful by accompanying it with a gripping narrative of scientific discovery. His articles for the wider public sparkle with cognates of the word *surprising*. In Mayo's version of events, the twelfth period in the Relay Assembly Test (when the rest breaks for the T Room workers were withdrawn) was to the Hawthorne research team what the apple tree was to Isaac Newton. Before Period 12, researchers had clung to the notion that some straightforward material condition—such as rest breaks—might explain increases in productivity. After Period 12, Mayo reported breathlessly, it hit researchers like the force of gravity that human factors—notably, the psychology of the group—matter much more than working conditions. Mayo's assistants—all young Harvard men—described this as "the great *éclaircissement*, the new illumination, that came from the research."[45]

Mayo's story about the enchanted life in the T Room was a beautiful one, and it undoubtedly expressed an important insight into human behavior. But it proved quite a burden for him to maintain it as a "scientific" interpretation of actual events in the face of so much contrary evidence. As researchers at the time and later pointed out, any explanation of the rise in productivity would have to consider the possible influences of, among other factors, the reduction in the variety of relay types that the women assembled, their accumulation of experience, and sheer statistical noise. Mayo adopted the expedient of ignoring these possible alternative explanations.

The replacement of the slackers Adeline and Irene with the dynamic duo of Jennie and Mary, one would think, would have been harder to ignore. After all, one-third of the total productivity gain took place the moment the two pairs switched places, and another third followed shortly thereafter. Mayo was compelled to airbrush Adeline and Irene from the history. In his first book on the subject, he notes in passing that two of the women "dropped out."[46] In his second book, he says they "retired."[47] "At no time in the [whole period of the study]," he sweetly insists, "did the girls feel that they were working under pressure." Evidently, neither the firing of two women for failing to produce nor the hiring of a known rate buster with serious financial needs amounted to "pressure."[48]

The most inconvenient of the facts that haunted Mayo's narrative was the money. During the course of the Relay Assembly Test, the workers netted close to double what they might otherwise have expected to earn. Aside from getting more pay for more output, they were also compensated for hours *not* worked (when their schedules were pared back for experimental purposes). One very good reason for thinking that such an attractive financial arrangement was a factor in explaining the rise in productivity is that, upon being interviewed, the T Room workers themselves invariably said it was.

The interview data, naturally, was easy enough to discard. For Mayo, it was a matter of principle that workers' observations on their own working conditions are as intelligible as the howling of primates at the zoo.[49] A much bigger headache arose when, during one of Mayo's long absences, the Hawthorne researchers recklessly launched an experiment to test the hypothesis that the financial incentives had been a factor in the T Room. In October 1929, the researchers selected a second group of five relay assemblers to receive the same special compensation arrangement provided to the T Room group. This time, though, they left the test subjects to work on the main floor, with no change in supervision, schedule, or other conditions. Productivity of the second relay gang shot up 14% in the first week and remained at that level over the next nine weeks, and total production rose by the same amount. In other words, the researchers were able to match both the productivity gain achieved in the first T Room in the period before Jennie arrived and the average total production gain throughout the experiment—all with the simple expedient of paying the workers more. When their neighbors heard about the sweet deal for the second group, however, the mood on the floor turned ugly.

The researchers hastily ended the special compensation arrangement. Productivity slumped 16%.[50]

It is easy to see that, on the basis of the parallel relay assembly tests, an outside observer might have reached the unfortunate conclusion that it was money, and not the special T Room ambience, that mattered most to workers. In a bravura performance of reinterpretation, however, Mayo put forward the view that the second relay test was marred by a pathological discord on the floor between the specially compensated group and the other workers. The temporary increase in productivity was thus merely a symptom of social neurosis, a flare-up of unhealthy competitive paranoia, and demonstrated once again the central importance of atmospherics in the workplace. Mayo's Harvard-trained epigones soon began to parrot the extraordinary claim that the second relay test *confirmed* the findings of the first.

Not content to leave well enough alone, the Hawthorne researchers set up another test, this time involving a group of workers responsible for the specialized task of splitting mica (a kind of rock used as insulating material). The mica splitters were granted a version of the special T Room environment, complete with independent supervision and rest breaks, but they were not offered the special compensation arrangement. The results were not promising. Using some statistical sleight of hand, Mayo and his team were able to conjure the illusion of a productivity gain at the start of the test. Some months later, unfortunately, even this mirage dissipated to statistical insignificance. This time, Mayo elected to ignore the results.

All of these tests took place in the years up to 1933, incidentally, in the midst of the Great Depression—when thousands of Hawthorne workers outside the sanctuary of the T Room were losing their jobs. When the economic environment at last forced Western Electric to forswear the luxury of running experiments on its rapidly declining workforce, the T Room workers, too, lost their jobs. Jennie walked the streets before finally securing a job weighing macaroni in a factory where her dad worked as night watchman. Mary eventually found work in a rubber factory at half the rate she had received as a relay assembler.[51] Theresa and two of the other women remained unemployed for some time, and in 1933 they were found to be living in poverty. But for Mayo and his followers, it nonetheless remained an article of faith that the special feeling in the T Room could not have been accounted for by "anything so naïve as economic incentive."[52] In this they had the solid backing of the higher authorities at Western Electric, along with the Rockefeller people. The whole point of the investment in psychological research, after all, was to find ways of keeping workers happy *without* having to pay them more.

Toward the end of the experiments, Homer Hibarger and Donald Chipman (a researcher who had replaced Hibarger in the T Room in 1930) participated in a review of the history of the project. With their heads no doubt still spinning around Mayo's nimble interpretations of the experimental data, they had this to say:[53]

> [Hibarger:] "Well, we know that we could take either side of any question and prove or disprove it [in] whatever [way] we want."
>
> [Chipman:] "Yes, they say that figures don't lie, but we have shown that we can take a set of figures and prove anything we want to."

Chipman's words could well serve as an epitaph for the Hawthorne experiments. The astonishing fact of the matter is that the Hawthorne story, as passed on by Mayo, is *all* interpretation. Scientifically speaking, there is no *there* there. Like Frederick Winslow Taylor with his pig-iron tale, Mayo conjured a simulacrum of scientific theorizing out of an anecdote whose details were quietly altered wherever they failed to make the right point.

Perhaps the most egregious aspect of Mayo's tale is the thrilling narrative of "surprising" scientific discovery within which he encased it. Notes taken at the time indicate that the famous Period 12 came and went without any discernible change in the researchers' state of mind; the apple did not hit them until Mayo threw it at them sometime later. Considering just how tightly the Hawthorne "results" conformed to his prior convictions, furthermore, the findings could hardly have come as a shock to Mayo himself. The subtext of his T Room interpretation—that workers are akin to psychiatric patients whose feelings should be "scientifically" manipulated by a monopolistic corporation for the sake of achieving a quasi-medieval harmony in the workplace—had been written down and published long before Mayo arrived on the west side of Chicago. The

Hawthorne "research" was simply a restatement of Mayo's ideological plan to save civilization from itself.

For two decades Mayo's interpretation received little challenge on the facts. In this it helped considerably that Mayo and his votaries controlled the facts. Of the 33 articles that appeared on the subject of Hawthorne in the decade following Mayo's first visit to the Works, 25 were penned by Mayo or members of his Harvard team. Of the three books, two issued from Mayo's pen and the third, much longer one was the work of Fritz Roethlisberger and William Dickson, his Harvard assistants. Mayo's corporate backers at Western Electric, through selective release of data and enthusiastic writing in their own research reports, also played a part in corroborating his interpretation of events. Not until independent researchers took a fresh look at the evidence did the extent of Mayo's fraud become apparent. His posthumous critics eventually described the Hawthorne work as "worthless scientifically" and "scientifically illiterate."[54] But by then it was too late to prevent the myth of Hawthorne from wreaking its profound effects on management thought and the social sciences.

Mayo reached the peak of personal fame in 1941, when he made the cover of *Fortune* magazine. Yet he remained oddly disengaged from the research that had made his career. He openly rejoiced when at last he was freed of the obligation to make the "dreadful excursions to Chicago."[55] Back at his hotel-apartment in Cambridge, he promised Harvard Business School Dean Wallace Donham that he would write up an authoritative account of the Hawthorne research. But he soon got bored with the project and passed it off to his assistants, Roethlisberger and Dickson, who published the results under the title *Management and the Worker.*

Mayo in his final years seems little different from the man who appeared in America in 1922—alone, frustrated, bitter, and disdainful of the "bourgeois" colleagues who had long ago learned to ignore him. His pronouncements about the destiny of humankind were as grandiose as they had ever been—only more apocalyptic. "The outlook for the present and future of civilization is somber," he intones in his last book, published in 1945.[56] World War II might have been averted, he adds, if only the world's administrative elite had followed his prescription to develop its "social skills"—which was not so different from the message he had published in the aftermath of World War I. He confided to his wife that, although he had reconciled himself to laboring on behalf of the "the modern world," he felt under no obligation to like it, and indeed he did not.

Twenty-five years after disembarking in San Francisco, Mayo at last resumed the journey he had begun. He resigned his professorship at Harvard and departed for London, the center of civilization, in search of a new academic posting. Two years later, in 1949, he died of a stroke without having found a job.

The Counterrevolution

On the weekend after Independence Day, while I was climbing the pyramids at Chichén Itzá, where the ancient Mayans had made ritual sacrifices of unlucky youngsters, I heard the news that four members of our group of 35 had abandoned the revolution. They had accepted new contracts to go back to work for Chicago. Each of the next several days brought news of another defection. Frantic calls, vigorous ego massages, and any number of whispered promises of extra bonuses, extra secretaries, and corner offices filled the wires around New York. Chicago knew our soft spot. They pulled out a checkbook the size of a bazooka and aimed it straight at our wallets.

The war took place in a curious legal limbo, where the boundaries of acceptable behavior seemed lost in a fog of legal disputes. The underlying situation was one that, in essence, has repeated itself hundreds of times in the history of the consulting profession. A group of rebels wants to exit from an existing firm with its clients and staff in tow, but the parent firm holds against them contracts with threateningly worded noncompete clauses. In the nastiest phase of the confrontation, the New Yorkers contemplated a "lifeboat" strategy. The partners would leave individually, each holding on to a Rolodex, and then assemble on a desert island to build a new utopia.

The two sides eventually agreed to negotiate a more reasonable plan of separation through an arbitration proceeding overseen by a nice old lady with a prominent background in labor law. The arbitrator, who seemed curiously sympathetic to the rebels, soon mediated a settlement that seemed very much to their advantage. In exchange for a small fee and a few other stipulations, partners who wished to leave with the rebels would be allowed to do so with clients and staff in tow. The only catch was that there was nothing to stop Chicago from "poaching" back its very own partners and staff.

One of the senior partners from Chicago flew down to Mexico to have dinner with me. He was a dour, lugubrious man who looked to be suffering from sleep deprivation. He flickered to life when I told him that I thought my little operation in Mexico could double its revenues in a year. Grimacing over some spicy enchiladas, he offered me a multiyear contract that would have significantly topped my income as a freelancer. When I demurred, he insisted that I follow him back to Chicago to meet some people there and discuss the matter further.

In Chicago, at a country club high up in the black Sears Tower, the old sailor and I lunched on steak and mashed potatoes. He gestured around the heavily upholstered, wood-inlayed room to the view of the city outside, as though to say that someday soon all this would be mine. Around the time we got to the tapioca pudding, he leaned forward and made his point.

"You should be *very careful*," he said, shaking his head somberly. "You need to think about the *motivations* of the people you're working with."

His fear and loathing of the New York crowd was as dark as the thunderheads gathering in the late summer skies outside the tower. He seemed genuinely concerned about my personal safety. When he started to talk about Owen, he became visibly disgusted and had to put down his giant cup of watery coffee.

"I think certain people are looking at this in a transactional way," he shuddered. "They just want to do a deal. They don't want to build anything. Just look at the people you are dealing with. Just *look* at them."

When Roland and Owen invited me back to New York to make polite conversation, I could tell that they had considered the possibility that I, too, might have gone over to the other side. In the office, the paranoia was as thick as the air on a hot summer afternoon. The hallways felt like the setting for one of those science fiction movies in which aliens secretly take over the bodies of earthlings. Chicago posted an armed guard in the

New York lobby and sent a private detective to ruffle through partners' files, which were, after all, still their property. Their lawyers inexplicably sent a hostile letter to my mother, causing her to lose some sleep. At some point I had used her address as a mailing address, so they saw fit to warn her against participating in potentially perfidious acts.

In the course of the next two weeks or so, after some more double- and even a few triple-crossings, 10 of the original 35 members of the Continental Congress had gone the way of Benedict Arnold. Our projected $70 million business shrank to a $50 million business. Among the "traitors" were blond Barry, who had spoken so eloquently against the tyranny of Chicago, and both members of the married couple who had waxed grandiloquent about the virtues of democracy.

I was surprised, even mildly scandalized at the ease with which the double agents switched sides. Yet I should not have been. In all of our discussions about establishing a new firm, there had been a giant whale in the room that had mostly been passed over in silence. Much as I had been charmed by the visions of establishing a postindustrial democracy on some distant planet with my fellow partners, my interest in the venture was ultimately almost entirely financial. I should hardly have been surprised to discover that for the rest of the group, as much as their grand speeches suggested otherwise, it was all about the money too. And for different partners, at different points in their careers, with different competing offers, and with different perceptions of the risks involved, the economic calculus inevitably pointed in different directions. The only surprising thing was the skill with which the double agents had played both sides of the game.

In my case, the math seemed to point unambiguously to New York. Consulting firms are generally organized in the shape of a pyramid, and, whether in ancient Mexico or modern Manhattan, the most fundamental principle of the pyramid is that the money always flows uphill. Thus far in my inglorious consulting career, I had remained firmly in the bottom 80% of the pyramid—the area from which the raw material for sacrifice is drawn. I estimated that the projects I could manage in the foreseeable future would generate about $1 to $2 million in excess cash per year, all of which would rise upward to fund country clubs in the Windy City and beer carts in Gotham.

It is on account of this pyramid principle, of course, that under normal circumstances the opportunity to become a partner in a respectable firm typically arises only after eight or so years of youth-destroying labor—and it is for the same reason, of course, that consulting firms are constantly producing spin-offs like ours. As a group, we liked to pretend that our aim in breaking free from Chicago was the noble one of improving the human condition, but the truth is that we wanted to dethrone the people at the top of the pyramid and occupy those lustrous seats ourselves.

Under ordinary circumstances, I would have had no intention of undertaking the usual slog up the slippery slopes to partnership, and it is fantastically unlikely that I would have survived the process in any case. But now, after less than a year in this group and with a total of a mere four years' consulting experience (plus two years writing a history of philosophy!), I believed I had lucked into a helicopter ride to the upper reaches of the pyramid, at least in New York. By contrast, the offer from Chicago, though it boasted a higher guaranteed base pay, included only an insignificant ownership stake. It offered a leg up in an existing pyramid, not a chance to participate in building a new one.

A further advantage of ownership, I figured—utterly naïvely, in retrospect—was that I would have more flexibility getting out of the business or taking sabbaticals in order to, say, write unpublishable philosophical novels. The Chicago offer, with its fixed periods and corporate language, was clearly not intended for those with philosophical aspirations.

When the dust settled and at last it seemed clear just who was on whose side, Owen and the lawyers drafted and sent around a shareholders' agreement to the remaining rebels for signature. It named Owen the firm's "Managing Director," but otherwise proposed a fairly democratic partnership. I skimmed most of the fine print, which seemed to consist of the usual legalese, and flipped to the end, which specified the amounts and the date for our capital contributions.

In order to launch our new vessel, an investment was required. We would have to pay a buyout fee to the parent firm, we would need working capital, and we had to cover some serious legal bills. My share of the proposed investment came to $225,000—or something under 5% of the total, corresponding roughly to the share of the business my work represented. The amount I was called to contribute, as it turned out, was only a few pennies short of the total amount of money I had saved in the course of the previous year. It would clean me out.

On the date agreed upon, I wired the money into the account of a firm that still did not have a name. I soon learned that I was among the first to do so. Many of my partners apparently waited several days to send in their cash. Some waited weeks. One or two never paid in at all.

The Proper Study of Humankind

I t would be hard to overestimate the impact that Mayo's work had on the subsequent history of the social sciences. To be a social scientist before Hawthorne was to know the bitter taste of frustration and envy. While physicists and chemists were dazzling the world with radar, wonder drugs, and other game-changing inventions, the social scientists could lay claim to only some widely mocked intelligence tests and a clutch of impressionistic essays on the travails of modern life. In Hawthorne, social scientists grasped their chance to play in the game of progress, to do for human society what nuclear physicists had done to the atom. They immediately hailed Mayo's work as the gold standard in research for their discipline.

In 1954, Peter Drucker—who had only recently shed his first career as a professor of political science—declared that "the reports of [Elton Mayo and his associates] on the work at Hawthorne are still the best, the most advanced and the most complete work on the subject [of human relations]."[57] Wallace Donham, Mayo's proud patron and the dean of the Harvard Business School for more than two decades, averred that the Hawthorne research was "the best available 'case' on the question of the value of research to business."[58] The Hawthorne experiments, by consensus, were "management's most influential social science research."[59] Through the reports of Roethlisberger and Dickson, Hawthorne became the scientific rock on which was founded the business

side of the social sciences, which soon adopted the name of "Organizational Behavior" (or just "OB," as the students now fondly call it).

Hawthorne figured so significantly in the origin stories of the social
sciences that its name became attached to a purportedly scientific principle: the "Hawthorne Effect." Coined by social scientists in the 1950s,[60]
the term *Hawthorne Effect* was first defined as the boost in productivity—
allegedly observed by Mayo and friends—that resulted from the mere act
of paying attention to workers in an experimental setting. It soon came
to refer to any unintended (but usually positive) result in social science
experiments emerging from test subjects' awareness of the fact that they
were being tested. From there the idea expanded to include just about
any unintended result in any experiment involving people. In some contexts, the term is now used to mean any unexpected change in behavior
resulting from a change in the environment. The Hawthorne Effect, in
short, has become a "principle" that explains whatever it is about people
that defies explanation.

Among the first and most important of Mayo's successors was Chester
Barnard, a telephone executive who visited Harvard frequently in the
late 1930s and participated in discussions with Mayo and a group of like-
minded social scientists who became known as the "Pareto Circle." An
orphaned farm boy with a gift for numbers, a taste for baroque music,
and a passion for esoteric European sociology, Barnard went to Harvard
in 1906 on a scholarship, left before graduating to take a job with AT&T,
and then rode a 40-year elevator to the top job at New Jersey Bell. He
accumulated positions of responsibility the way that rich people sometimes collect houses, becoming president of, among many other things,
the Rockefeller Foundation, the USO, and the Bach Society of New Jersey.
Known to his subordinates as a "chilly" and "aristocratic" leader, he was
the embodiment of Mayo's "administrative elite."[61]

Barnard shared not only Mayo's interest in Pareto but also his political
inclination to fight the looming threats of unionism and communism. In
his most influential book, *The Functions of the Executive*, Barnard advances
an idea of leadership consonant with Mayo's findings at Hawthorne. In
a workplace where "atmosphere" and "self-realization" matter more
than working conditions and money, Barnard says, formal authority is
mostly a "fiction." He therefore defines real authority in terms of "accep-

tance" by subordinates and makes "communication" a central feature of leadership.[62]

The ideal manager, according to Barnard's way of thinking, is a Moses figure: able to lift his people out of wage slavery and guide them across treacherous waters to the promised land of on-the-job fulfillment. Reading Barnard's work, one develops the conviction that giant corporations did not arise because of technological changes, accumulation of capital, or astute manipulation of the political process in order to secure and maintain monopolistic market positions, but because people just long to labor in the thrall of a great leader. The "mission statements" and tablets engraved with "our core values" that are now an everyday feature of corporate life can be traced back to Barnard and, before him, Mayo.

Perhaps the most accessible representative of the human relations movement after Mayo was Douglas McGregor, the son of a preacher and an able administrator who became president of Antioch College and a professor at the MIT/Sloan School of Management. With his memorable distinction between "Theory X" and "Theory Y"—laid out in an essay of a couple dozen chatty paragraphs and then padded with miscellaneous other writings to fill out a book under the equally memorable title, *The Human Side of the Enterprise*, published in 1960—McGregor expresses with admirable directness some of the basic ideas of the Hawthorne experience. Theory X holds, in essence, that human beings are lazy and irresponsible, and that they need a good beating if they are to do the jobs they are supposed to do. It presumably describes the attitude at Hawthorne before it became an "Effect" and of Taylorists in general. Theory Y says that humans are active seekers of fulfillment and will do a great job if only they are set free to realize themselves.[63] The T Room, at least as Mayo interpreted the experience, was the great example of Theory Y in action.

The most vocal, if not always the most informed, advocates of Mayo's vision in recent times have been the popular management gurus. The buzzwords and catchphrases that most excite today's gurus—"empowerment," "responsible freedom," "the wisdom of teams," "the new organization"—hail from the time of Mayo and his Hawthorne experiments, even if their promoters are not always aware of the fact.[64] "As a nation, we have developed a sense of the value of technology and of a scientific approach to it, but we have meanwhile taken people for granted. What Theory Z calls for is a redirection of attention to human relations in the corporate world," wrote William Ouchi in 1981, a full half century after Mayo put forward his own theory about paying attention to people.[65] In 2007, 80 years after the inauguration of the T Room, Gary Hamel advertised his latest book by making the same "discovery." "Management as it has been practiced over the past 100 years has not been people-friendly," he says in promoting his book. "Today, for the first time since the industrial revolution, you can't build a company that's fit for the future unless it's fit for human beings."[66]

Among Mayo's epigones, pride of place should go to Tom Peters, who earned a PhD in organizational behavior from Stanford, and his coauthor Robert Waterman. In their 1982 book, *In Search of Excellence*, the pair explicitly claim that their work belongs to a "research stream" that was "started in the late 1930s by Elton Mayo and Chester Barnard."[67] They supply a helpful summary of their debt to Mayo:

> Mayo started out four-square in the mainstream of the rationalist school and ended up challenging, de facto, a good bit of it. On the shop floors of Western Electric's Hawthorne plant, he tried to demonstrate that better workplace hygiene would have a direct and positive effect on worker productivity. So he turned up the lights. Productivity went up, as predicted. Then, as he prepared to turn his attention to another factor, he routinely turned the lights back down. Productivity went up again! For us, the very important message of the research that these actions spawned is that it is *attention to employees*, not work conditions per se, that has the dominant impact on productivity. (Many of our best companies, one friend observed, seem to reduce management to merely creating "an endless stream of Hawthorne Effects.")

This passage should serve as a helpful reminder that having a PhD from Stanford is no guarantee that one will not harbor a thoroughly distorted view of the foundations of one's own discipline. Mayo was never a "rationalist," as we know; he wasn't anywhere near Hawthorne when the illumination experiments took place; and these experiments did not in any case produce meaningful results. More important, the passage illustrates how the Mayo legend continues to work its transcendental effects. Central to the functioning of the legend is the notion that Professor Mayo was a disinterested scientist (a "rationalist" even), that Hawthorne was his road to Damascus (the site of an illumination), and that the result of his labors is thus a scientific finding of great significance (an almost magical technique for getting more out of labor without putting very much of anything in). It is the breathlessly imagined tale of discovery, in short, that elevates the climax—the Hawthorne Effect—to a position of such scientific significance.

It is, of course, remarkable enough that Mayo's successors should have looked to the parody of science that he passed off as research as the putatively scientific foundation of anything. It is much more remarkable, however, that a scientific foundation should have been sought for a set of claims that has no need for one. Mayo's legacy was not a finding per se, but the very idea that the kinds of things he talked about should be counted as "findings." And it was this attempt to cloak his ideas in the specious garb of science that had the most detrimental effect on his successors.

Mayo's interpretation of the T Room experience, no less than Ouchi's and Peters and Waterman's garbled paraphrases of it, undoubtedly expresses a seductive insight. Management *is* all about people. Paying attention to employees, encouraging teamwork, and helping each worker achieve some psychic satisfaction are all good things, and undoubtedly form part of an effective manager's job. If you are nice to people, in other words, they will usually be nice back to you. But this insight is a timeless precept, grounded in ethics, barely rising above tautology, and emerging naturally from the experience of being a human being surrounded by other human beings. It is not and never will be a "scientific finding."

Mayo's "finding" had, in fact, been "discovered" countless times before Mayo arrived at Hawthorne. Historians of management thought will know that Mary Parker Follett, an independent scholar who lectured at the Harvard Business School and elsewhere in the 1920s, had said pretty much what Mayo said before he said it. A century earlier, the British industrialist Robert Owen not only had discovered the Hawthorne wisdom, but even had attempted to implement it in his textile mills in Manchester. Owen, too, maintained that a happy worker is a good worker, that workers achieve fulfillment through recognition, and that everybody wants to participate usefully in advancing the good of the whole. He fought against child labor, invested in decent housing and education for workers, and established motivational systems with color-coded rewards to recognize and encourage good performance. "If, then, due care as to the state of your inanimate machines can produce such beneficial results," Owen declared, "what may not be expected if you devote equal attention to your vital machines [i.e., people], which are far more wonderfully constructed?"[68]

Owen, however, was merely borrowing from Jean-Jacques Rousseau, perhaps the most influential exponent in modern times of the idea that humankind is born good, suffers corruption under society, and must seek out a new and more humane social contract. And Rousseau himself was juggling ideas that have been around since ancient times. The ancient Greek historian Thucydides contrasted the productivity of the free citizens of Athens with the inefficiency of the peoples subject to the yoke of eastern CEO potentates; and Aristotle had plenty to say about the self-realization of individuals by social means. Many people would say that their religion teaches them the basic truths that Hawthorne purportedly proved. The Hawthorne wisdom, in short, comes to us either by virtue of being alive or with the aid of an ethical education.

What Mayo's predecessors understood, to put it in abstract terms, is that management involves not just a bundle of *techniques* for organizing human activity, but also a set of *norms* governing the ways in which individuals should relate to one another within an organization and within a society. Ask anyone to talk about a great manager they know, and, after some recognition of the individual's technical skills, the discussion will almost always take place in the language of moral obligation: respect, consideration, fairness. To put it all in Greek, one could say that management relies on both a *techne* (meaning "skill or craft," and the root of our word *technology*) and an *ethos* (meaning "a pattern of behavior, or character," insofar as it discloses bonds with other individuals in a group or society). While *techne* aims in a general way at the goal of efficiency, *ethos* is concerned primarily with building trust. Trust is the infrastructure on which the marvels of technology deliver their gains in productivity. Where trust is lacking, efficiency is rarely possible; conversely, inefficiency erodes trust.

To a certain extent, of course, there is a *techne* associated with *ethos*—that is to say, a craft or body of techniques that can reliably help build character in the individual and trust among groups. The Greeks had a word for this craft: *ethics*, which derives from the conjunction of *ethos* and *techne*. Those who master ethics, the Greeks added, may lay claim to a kind of practical wisdom called *phronesis*—distinct from *sophia*, or theoretical wisdom. One could say that this kind of practical wisdom, or *phronesis*, is the natural end of management. It is the ideal toward which the gurus, in their better moments, urge us to strive.

With his Hawthorne tales, Mayo tapped into a tradition that has long understood that ethics is the foundation of management. The insight at the center of his idealized (and largely fictional) interpretation of the T Room is that mutual trust in the workplace is the bedrock of efficient cooperation. But his contribution to the tradition was the attempt to reduce *ethos* to pure *techne*. He intended to manufacture trust in the same way that one manufactures coat hangers. But trust is not something to be fabricated; it has to be earned. The Hawthorne Effect, to the extent that it does what it purports to do, can serve only to conjure the illusion of trust. It is an attempt to trick our ethical intuitions—that is, to make workers believe that they are being well treated when in fact they are being exploited.

Much of the academic discipline of Organizational Behavior that has grown up around Mayo's humanized idol perpetuates this confusion between the study of human behavior and the study of good behavior. As with Taylor's purported general science of efficiency, most efforts to concoct a general science of organizations fail not because the universal principles they put forward are wrong—they are usually right—but because they don't belong to an applied science. They properly belong to philosophy.[69]

The insistence on driving the stake of science into the muddy ground of philosophy does worse than beget textbooks full of opaque "experiments." It advances the illusory utopian vision that has hobbled management thought since Frederick Winslow Taylor. The humanist version of this utopian illusion is perhaps most clearly visible in McGregor's work. The crucial, unstated assumption behind Theory Y—the view that workers will do a great job if left free to seek their own bliss—is that "rationality" and "cooperation with management" are always mutually consistent. That is, insofar as workers pursue their rational self-interest in self-realization, they will cooperate with management. But the same assumption, paradoxically, informs Theory X. According to Theory X, workers fail to cooperate with management because they are irrational in a general sense; that is, they are not capable of acting in their true self-interest without the application of external force. Excluded from both X and Y is the possibility that a worker might be both rational and uncooperative with management—that an individual's reasonable quest for self-realization might actually conflict with the aims of the organization.

In hopes of achieving the kind of immortality accorded to McGregor, I will argue that Theory X and Theory Y both depend on Theory U—for *utopian*. Theory U is a theory about the nature of human collectivities, and it holds that all conflict in society reduces to misunderstanding, or, to look on the bright side, that if we all made proper use of our reason, we'd have heaven on earth. Perhaps the most forthright statement of Theory U comes from Robert Owen. When he failed to persuade fellow mill owners to adopt his version of T-Room humanism, Owen bought a town in Illinois called New Harmony and attempted to establish a utopian community there. "The happiness of self," he declared, "can only be attained by conduct that must promote the happiness of the community."[70] Within two years, New Harmony dissolved in anarchy and Owen abandoned the project in disgust. Taylor, Mayo, Barnard, Drucker, McGregor, almost all other management theorists, and a very large number of bad novelists are U-men.

Theory T (for *tragic*), by way of contrast, says that some degree of conflict is inherent in all forms of social organization. Sometimes the self is at odds with the community, sometimes the community is at odds with itself, and sometimes, as Thomas Hobbes pointed out, it's a war of all against all. Individuals acting in good faith and with adequate knowledge may still have reason and desire to exploit their fellows, and they will do so unless constrained within a system wherein these tendencies are adequately checked and balanced. Theory T makes for good governments and good literature. Shakespeare, the framers of the US Constitution, and the inhabitants of ancient Greece (with the notable exception of Plato) are T-types—and so, too, are most successful managers in the real world.

The great problem with the U-types, of course, is that their visions of eternal sunshine usually involve a form of tyranny. Like Taylor's class of scientific managers and Plato's guardians, Mayo's "administrative elite" has the ultimate authority over the "science" with which it is to rule the world. Since the "science" amounts to a "noble lie" (in the most optimistic interpretation), the result of Mayo's humanistic philosophizing is really just the legitimation of an unchecked power in the workplace. What Mayo offered was a new tool for manipulating workers for the benefit of management.

The chief novelty in Mayo's form of managerial authoritarianism is that it seeks control over something that Taylor himself probably didn't know existed—the human psyche. In place of Taylor's distinction between thinkers and doers, Mayo offers a division between thinkers and feelers. Whereas Taylor reduces labor to a mass of machinelike muscles, fit only to receive precisely specified instructions from management, Mayo reduces labor even further, to a quivering bundle of emotions, fit only to be manipulated by management. Indeed, Mayo's drive for control makes Taylor look like a placard-waving champion of the workingman. The father of scientific management may have referred to his workers as "drays" and "oxen," but with his incentive-based piece-rate systems he nonetheless took for granted that these beasts of burden had the capacity to make economic decisions for themselves on the basis of their material self-interest. In Mayo's world, however, the workers of the world lack this basic rational capacity to act in their own self-interest.

Management was not slow to take advantage of the opportunities for manipulation identified by Mayo. In the Western Electric Company, Mayo's corporate backers immediately saw in the Hawthorne research the promise of "a new technique of management" that would aid in their efforts to keep the unions at bay and stave off efforts from government, consumers, and capitalists to break up their monopoly.[71] They were quick to scan the bottom line of Mayo's work: paying attention to employees could prove a better investment than paying them more money. The Hawthorne research, in effect, put a scientific gloss on the strategy of welfare capitalism that the Western Electric Company had been pursuing long before Mayo arrived. In subsequent decades, management around the world has absorbed the lesson that a warm smile and "an endless stream of Hawthorne effects," to use the words that Peters and Waterman attribute to an anonymous friend,[72] can be more profitable than a better pension plan or health benefits. For the workers of the world, management humanism always sounds pleasant on first hearing; but insofar as it is a way of substituting beautiful words for substantive negotiation, it is a swindle.

Mayo's humanistic "science" was a creature of the formative years of higher education in business, so it is inevitable that some of its most important effects are to be found in the theory and practice of modern business education. When Mayo's patron, Wallace Donham, took over the reins of the Harvard Business School from Edwin Gay in 1919, he nurtured a bold vision. He oversaw both a dramatic increase in enrollment and a distinct shift in the tone of the business school experience. Sloughing off the "trade school" stigma that had hobbled his predecessor, Donham labored to turn Harvard into the cradle of a new profession— the profession of business management. He introduced the case-study method of teaching—perhaps his most enduring reform—on the basis of an analogy with the other professional schools. Doctors and lawyers learn by studying cases; why not business managers? He fully expected that the members of this new profession would become what Mayo called "the administrative elite." "Effective responsibility has passed rapidly from capital to a new *managing class*, the executive heads of great corporations and firms," Donham said. "This class is not yet equipped for its task, but it must be."[73] His job, as dean of the Harvard Business School, was to select and train the people who would rule the universe.

The professionalization project that began with Donham has two sides: a technical one, and a moral one. The aim on the technical side is to teach the administrative skills required to operate a business—that is, to make his professionals "experts." The aim on the moral side is to promote the use of those skills on behalf of the common good—that is, to create professionals in the ethical sense of the term. The first corresponds to what we sometimes call "management"; the second, loosely to "leadership." To paraphrase Warren Bennis: managers are people who do things right; leaders are people who do the right thing. Donham wanted his MBAs to be both.

Mayo's contribution to Donham's project was to conceive of a discipline according to which moral leadership can be made into the subject of a technical course in the business school curriculum. In 1959, long after Mayo and Donham had retired, the highly influential Gordon and Howell report on business education seconded the notion that studies of the sort initiated by Mayo are essential in the preparation of business leaders: "Of all the subjects which he might undertake to formally study, none is more important for the businessman-to-be than human behavior."[74]

This institutional need for a discipline that fits into the mold that Mayo created explains why, even after catching up with the fraud, social scientists seem unable to extricate themselves from the Mayo legend. Upon acknowledging that the Hawthorne research failed to establish the motivation for the relay assembly workers, for example, a recent Organizational Behavior textbook turns around and says that "whatever the reason, Hawthorne gave the budding human relations movement needed research credibility."[75] Some social scientists offer the very falsity of Mayo's work as evidence for the socially constructed nature of knowledge, and then perversely use this as justification for the meretricious discipline Mayo founded.

Donham's professionalization project, however, rests on a fatal misunderstanding about ethical foundations of a profession. The ethical integrity of a profession rests not on science or any technical subject, but on trust. In any serious profession, just as in any stable society, furthermore, this trust relies on a fair and perspicuous system of punishments and rewards. Medicine is a profession not on account of research in molecular biology but because it has licensing requirements, standards commissions, and policing mechanisms for controlling malpractice. The "profession" of business management as Donham and Mayo conceived it has none of these features. It merely exhorts good behavior on the basis of putatively "scientific" findings. It asserts as a matter of Hawthorne-validated fact that there is no gap between public virtue and private gain. Prospective business managers can be confident that there is nothing outside the often ill-informed reactions of the market and wide latitude offered by the legal system to limit the trade-off between their public duties and their self-interest. Most managers, to be sure, are good people; and it seems unlikely that a couple of years of pseudovocational training will spoil them. But it is foolish to imagine that they will behave well merely because they are told in business schools that they should regard themselves as professionals.[76]

Donham's professionalization project rests on an even deeper misunderstanding about the nature of an ethical education. Insofar as an education can have any effect on the ethical life of the individual, it can do so only by forming intellect and character. For that purpose, the study of obtuse textbooks on organizational behavior will always rate as a very feeble alternative to the study of Aristotle or Shakespeare. In fact, prospective managers are undoubtedly better off finding a good novel or film than laboring over the alleged researches supplied by Mayo and his successors (which, in fact, are the epistemological equivalent of badly written novels). As the best programs in liberal education show, an ethical education is ultimately accomplished not by training but by example. Such a classical approach to education, of course, is not guaranteed to succeed. On the other hand, the approach taken by the business schools is guaranteed to fail. Most students have the ability to sense when a subject they are being taught is mere puffery; what they infer from such an experience about the purpose of an education and the quality of their instructors can hardly be expected to improve their character.

At bottom, of course, as anyone with experience in managerial situations will confirm, Mayo remains correct in the basic insight that management is all about people. But management is all about people in the sense that raising a family is all about people. Advice and research—from academics, old pros, or radio talk show hosts—are always potentially useful. The key to success in such endeavors, however, has never been to study "human relations" in a formal way; it is to become a better person.

The Pyramid and Its Discontents

A few months after the traumatic birth of the firm, at the end of 1994, Mexico suffered an economic meltdown. The peso broke free from its government-controlled rate and plummeted to one-half and then one-third of its former value. A steep recession followed. I like to think that our work in the field of risk management helped our clients survive the crisis, though I can't really be sure. For them, in any case, we were now entirely unaffordable. Our already exorbitant fees, in pesos, were now two or more times what they had been. So, after struggling for a few months into the new year, I closed the shop and retreated to New York, thinking that, as a partner in the new firm, I should find work there.

In New York I made a number of surprising discoveries about the firm of which I was now part owner. For example, I noticed that from time to time a portable therapy bed would turn up in various partners' offices. I soon learned that the "shrink" Roland had earlier mentioned was so important in the lives of the partners that he was, for all practical purposes, on the company payroll. "Dr. Bob," as the therapist was known, was a ghostlike presence hovering over every meeting in the New York office. He treated many of the more influential partners. I have little doubt that they talked about one another with him and through him. Dr. Bob also advised the partners on how to meet the psychic needs of client executives—something I'm sure our clients would have been delighted to hear. Owen called it the "Personal Skills Development" program; others talked about getting "Bobbed."

Dr. Bob was a premium-priced therapist. After all, consultants accustomed to resting their mortal coils on first-class airplane seats and five-star hotel beds would expect nothing less for the treatment of their ego needs. Dr. Bob specialized in "business/industrial psychiatry," according to his promotional material, though he also happened to be a mystery novelist in his spare time. One of his novels involves a group of therapy patients who, rather alarmingly, start getting murdered, one by one. The bills from such a talented individual naturally added up, reaching half a million dollars in at least one 12-month period. As I learned belatedly, one of the bones of contention in the battle between New York and Chicago was that Chicago got fed up with paying such huge sums to alleviate the alleged psychological sufferings of its New York office. The Battle of the Beer Carts, I gathered after the fact, was small potatoes compared with this warfare over the psychologist.

Dr. Bob's clients undoubtedly had much to talk about. Sex, for one thing, could never have been very far from their minds. Among the partners and senior consultants in the New York office, a 1-2-3 rule applied. For every 1 consultant there were roughly 2 marriages and 3 extramarital affairs. A large number of the affairs seemed to occur within the office. Not all of them were consensual. Over the years, and especially in its last days, the firm received a steady stream of sexual-harassment complaints, and eventually settled at least three lawsuits involving partners, to my knowledge—though I have little doubt that these represented a fraction of the violations.

Patrick, our newly appointed CFO, seemed particularly fond of his tipple and developed quite a reputation as the master of the festivities. When the job of human resources coordinator opened up, Trickie had no trouble deciding who to promote to a position involving the oversight of a growing staff of hundreds. He chose a young assistant with a winsome smile and no prior experience in the field. She eventually filed suit against him for sexual misconduct. (The suit was settled.) Another assistant also filed a sexual-harassment complaint against him. In an internal parody memo, a learned wag among the partners identified Patrick as our "CFO *Priapus*." It proved to be something more than a fortunate coincidence that one of Patrick's responsibilities as CFO was to oversee the firm's voluminous dealings with lawyers.

In a fast-paced, team-based business such as consulting, where small groups of bright and ambitious young people come together in faraway towns and work under tight deadlines, it is natural that the members of a firm should develop intense personal bonds and a deep familiarity with one another, so that they become in a sense a "family." Indeed, as real family lives atrophy under the stress of such jobs, the relationships of the workplace begin to take on the intimacy and complexity traditionally reserved for the home. Whether this is a good thing or not in general is an interesting question. How good or not it is in any particular case depends on the circumstances. There are families and there are families.

The New York office was the kind of family that one expects to find on daytime talk shows. Internal meetings with members of Dr. Bob's circle of patients often had the feel of life in a third-world government ruled by distant cousins. People did not occupy jobs, so much as positions on the family tree. When they glared at each other across the table, you could be sure that the issues at stake went well beyond the usual concerns with profits and losses. I realized that the atmospheric paranoia I had sensed on earlier trips hadn't entirely dissipated with the end of the Chicago war.

Sibling rivalry, I came to understand, was one of the dominant motifs in the New York office family. Apart from a distinction between board members and others, there was no formal ranking among the partnership. We were, in the jargon of the management gurus, "flat." And yet, perhaps because of this lack of clarity in the hierarchy, the competition for status was intense—for, as Tocqueville pointed out about democracy in America, it is precisely when individuals are most equal that they work hardest to distinguish themselves. A number of the New York partners also seemed to have an acute grasp of the fact that undercutting a rival could be just as effective as succeeding in one's own work. I sometimes got the impression that they devoted only slightly more energy to performing their own work than to sabotaging one another's.

The only position in the family tree that seemed unambiguously fixed was that of the father. Owen was everyone's daddy. "For Owen, it's not about the money," one of his supporters explained to me. "He has already made enough."

At a dinner event, I sat next to Owen's second wife, our own First Lady, who later came to play a strangely prominent role in the firm's affairs. She told me I reminded her of one of the characters on the sitcom *Friends*. "So what drives Owen?" I asked her sweetly. She shot me a startled and perhaps somewhat disdainful look. "He wants to build something bigger than himself," she replied, equally sweetly, turning away toward the dinner companion on her other side.

"Divide and conquer," Roland told me one day, nodding approvingly. "Owen is a master of balancing people against each other." When I suggested to Roland that, as investors, we should find this approach somewhat concerning, he shrugged, waving in the direction of New York. "It's the way they are," he said, adopting a philosophical tone. "They thrive on the competition. They're street fighters. Frankly, they're lower class, if you know what I mean. They all have chips on their shoulders."

I wasn't so sure. One of the New York partners, a diminutive figure who subsequently came to be known among some members of the firm as "the Prince of Darkness," seemed representative of the most problematic aspects of the culture, I thought; but there was no chip on his shoulder. On the contrary, he was one of dozens of Harvard MBAs in the firm, and the remarkable thing about him was just how highly he thought of himself. He was a decent analyst and a capable organizer; but in his own mind he was a Nobel Prize–caliber intellect and the rightful leader of the free world. The gap between his sense of self-worth and his actual value was enormous and apparently immune to correction from external evidence. He treated the people around him like Kleenex, suitable mainly for receiving his expectorations before being thrown away. One of his drivers—he kept a stable of them at the ready, engines running, even when he was going nowhere—once confided to me that he had pulled up next to a pile of trash hoping that the Prince would step in it.

People with this personality type—commonly referred to as "assholes"[77]—are among the most dangerous in any organization. Most of the time, to be sure, they get "selected out" of important positions. They infuriate too many people. But one or two of them always sneak through. Unalterably convinced of the value of their own opinions, they attract followers and assume leadership roles even as they push relentlessly ahead in their own self-interest. Once in power, they sabotage whatever they can't steal and take credit for whatever they are unable to destroy. They are capable of inflicting terrific brutality, casually ruining other people's careers for the sake of some good that only they can see. The frightening thing is that they will remain serene throughout, secure in the narcissistic conviction that only they know what's best.

On a visit to our London office, where the atmosphere seemed quite sane, relatively speaking, I had a chat with Charles, who I felt certain was not one of Dr. Bob's patients. "What on earth are you doing in New York?" he said, shocked to hear that I'd been spending time there. "Don't you know that they are savages there? It's the broken-arm club."

Charles was onto something important, I thought; something that went beyond the neuroses of our own particular firm and that applies to many similar organizations, though usually to a much lesser degree. Psychologically speaking, the fundamental reality of an organization such as ours is the pyramid. The pyramid is a kind of game wherein labor and ownership—that is, those who produce the surplus and those who appropriate it—all evolve from the same pool of players. Although it is to be found in purest form in private partnerships, the pyramid may also characterize corporate hierarchies to some degree, insofar as corporate managers usurp the role traditionally assigned to shareholders. It is, in a sense, the default model for society at large.

The fundamental fact about life on a pyramid is that it is dangerous. To succeed, players must continue moving up the pyramid. As the funnel narrows, the math inexorably requires those who fail to move up to be tossed out the side. In the end, just about everybody who plays the game is a loser. I once heard that, at an internal presentation on the long-term future of McKinsey, the presenters began by jokingly observing that in the long term of 10 years or so, only about 1% of their audience would still be with the firm.

The pyramid game belongs to the family of games that require players both to cooperate and to compete with one another. Success depends on two apparently incompatible skills: the ability to work with other players and the ability to ruthlessly exploit (and even exterminate) the very same people. Exactly which of these two skills matters more depends on the kind of balance achieved within any particular organization. Since a high degree of cooperation is usually desirable for the organization as a whole, most healthy organizations adopt selection processes that place a strong positive value on an individual's perceived cooperativeness. At the same time, no such process can gainsay the fact that the ability to oppress or annihilate one's competitors also contributes to an individual's success. In more competitive ecosystems, the most desirable trait is the talent for appearing cooperative even while obliterating one's fellows.[78]

The Pyramid Game

	Cooperative Moves	Noncooperative Moves	
Superiors	Accept guidance and do good work. (+10 for you, +10 for them)	Suck up. Flatter their self-delusions in order to distract from your own lack of merit. (+5 for you, –5 for dumb boss) Commit patricide. Betray one to help the other. (+20 for you, +10 for the new boss, –10 for the sucker)	
Peers	Build partnerships to get things done. (+10 for you and them)	Take credit for their work. (+10 for you, –10 for them) Sabotage their work or start a whispering campaign. (–10 for them)	
Inferiors	Serve as mentor, developing their skills. (+5 for you, +10 for them)	Squeeze them like lemons and throw them out. (+10 for you, –10 for them)	

Rules:
1. Players make moves on each other every day for one year.
2. At the end of each year, the player with the lowest number of points in each level is kicked out.
3. Players must spend twice as many years in each level as in the previous level before advancing to the next.
4. New players enter at the bottom.

Charles' point concerned the internal damage inflicted on participants in the pyramid game. My New York partners, almost all ex-McKinsey, had broken their arms by falling down a pyramid. As bright, insecure, and self-loving youngsters determined to win the great race of life, their careers had peaked when they gained admission into The Firm. They had set their sights on scaling the pyramid there, but then, some years later, for the first time in their straight-A lives, they had failed. Not only that, but, by virtue of the competitive-cooperative dynamic in the pyramid, they had very likely experienced some sort of betrayal on their way out. The truth is that it was just a game and the odds were against them from the start. But that is typically little consolation to the kind of people who get into McKinsey.

In top-tier consulting firms, the 24-hour evaluation process can make the pyramid game particularly damaging. Consultants are probably the most "evaluated" people in the working world. After every project, and often in the middle, consultants receive multiple evaluations on their performance. Every six months, these evaluations are compiled into a performance review, and every year, at the least, a consultant can expect to receive a detailed, formal assessment of his or her value to the firm, always expressed in the best euphemisms that the human relations movement in management thought can supply. No individuals are told that they are failing at their jobs; they are patiently informed that they have certain "development needs." After such relentless, paranoia-inducing scrutiny, 99% of consultants are eventually told about the many "development opportunities" that lie outside the firm and are thus, in the most humane terms imaginable, "counseled out."

How gracefully (or not) one loses in life generally matters much more to one's present happiness than does how spectacularly one succeeds. In our firm, there were very many good and healthy people who knew how to make the best of their lives and succeeded on the only metric that counts—one's own. Others, however, had clearly come away with the curdled wisdom of victims. Having pulled the knives out of their own backs, they were convinced that the only way to win was to start sticking them in other people. They had absorbed one of the more unseemly lessons of management humanism: that the best way to exploit people is look them in the eye and smile while you're doing it.

I observed a rough correlation between how twisted they were and how long they had worked at their previous employer. Those who left after two to four years usually emerged with no lasting damage. For them, their first consulting experience was merely a finishing school or a bridge to real work. Those who left after six years had scars. They could not pretend it didn't hurt. Owen, whose career spanned decades, was in a class by himself. When I looked at his watery eyes and lupine smile, I sometimes felt that every bone in his body had been shattered into a mass of splinters. I was far from the first to note with alarm that he seemed consumed with a desire to exact revenge on the monstrous firm that had done him so much damage.

At one point in my anthropological wanderings around the New York office, I sat down with Owen to discuss a business proposal. As a result of the work I had done in Mexico, I had come to think (and continue to believe) that many financial institutions have woefully underinvested in their ability to understand and control risk. So I wanted to share my ideas about building a consulting practice in the area with Owen and get his help in mobilizing resources.

"I'm proposing that we build up this practice area," I said, or words to that effect.

"Did you move around a lot as a child?" he replied.

"Huh?" (I had not yet mastered the art of third-order conversation.)

"Sometimes people who move around a lot as children have trouble feeling 'permanence.' You know, your parents drag you from one military base to the next, and pretty soon you feel that you can never settle down."

My father, as it happens, had been an officer in the US Marine Corps, and we had indeed moved around a lot when I was growing up. But I had never mentioned those facts to Owen. I had, however, recently mentioned them in passing to one of the other partners. I now realized that I had been "Bobbed" in absentia. Owen had conferred with at least one other partner about my psychological situation, and then he or they had very likely discussed my ego needs with Dr. Bob. My business proposal was irrelevant, for my pathology was now laid bare. I had been fucked-up since childhood. All I was really asking for was a hug.

"If you need someone to talk to about all this . . . ," Owen continued.

I could see where the conversation was going. He was inviting me to join the family. Soon, if I followed Owen's humanistic plan for me, I, too, would be confiding my "issues" to Dr. Bob, who would be "processing" them with Owen and his fellow patients. I'd be called "Mattie," and I would spend the rest of my life toiling in a cubicle a few steps down the pyramid from the great pharaoh. I'd have a few incestuous affairs and otherwise do my bit to develop a tight-knit group culture—all in order to help Owen realize his fantasy of building something bigger than himself, something even bigger than becoming a director at McKinsey. It would have felt a lot less sordid, I realized, if we had just agreed up front that it was all about the money.

Roland happened to be arriving at Heathrow at the same time, so we shared a taxi into London. He was in a bubbly mood.

"Business is good?" I asked.

"Business is great! Hey, you know, Charles is looking forward to working with you."

The idea for building a practice in the risk management area had gained more traction in Europe than in the New York office. So I had agreed to come over and help Charles kick off a project in the area. I was thinking mainly about Plan B, however.

"You're gonna find working here a real treat. Charles is a totally classy guy . . ."

"Great! But you know, I've been thinking . . ."

The experience in New York had served to remind me that I had once again exceeded my mission. I went to Mexico in search of a brief adventure and some spending money, and came back with a whole enchilada of commitments to a new business venture. I wanted to return to writing unpublishable philosophical novels. And although there were many good people in the firm, I did not relish the prospect of working alongside Dr. Bob's circle of potentially homicidal patients. My analysis of the financial situation, too, had changed. I owned part of a successful firm, but there was no obvious way to realize the value of my stake. I could see that Owen was hell-bent on expansion, and expansion would entail dilution of my shares as well as extra risk. I could foresee ending up with nothing while he built something bigger than himself. I had discussed this financial analysis with Roland, and I knew he shared my concern.

Plan B was for me to quit after fulfilling the obligation to Charles. I figured I could always come back in on a freelance basis when the money ran low. Since I couldn't see any way to realize the theoretical value of my equity stake in a reasonable period of time, I was simply going to ask for my money back. As we approached the Hammersmith flyover that leads into central London, I resolved to deliver my sayonara speech then and there.

"Roland, I'm really happy that I had this opportunity to participate in getting this firm started . . ."

"It's been great!" Roland said, interrupting me. "Hey, before I forget, I've got to tell you, I've just got Owen to sign off on a plan that is finally going to make it very clear how the founders of the firm, like you and me, are going to realize the value we created by founding the firm."

"Oh?"

"We're going to create a founders fund. Every year, the firm is going to put a percentage of its gross revenues into the fund. In five years, we will start to divvy it up according to the share each of us had in the firm at the beginning. And of course, we'll still have our equity and the usual compensation and bonus."

He went into the details about the percentages involved. By the time we reached the other side of the bridge, I had done the math in my head. Assuming an ambitious but achievable growth rate for the firm, the value of my share in the founders' fund would be as much as $3 million. With robust growth, it could be more. I hastily put Plan B on the shelf.

"I'm looking forward to getting started," I said, as the cab rolled up to the London office.

It was clearly a Faustian moment. I have since drawn from the experience at least two lessons concerning so-called "golden handcuffs." The first is that they are generally a very bad idea. When you offer people far more than they can expect to make elsewhere in order to get them to stay someplace, they will tend to stay there far longer than it is in anyone's interest that they should. The handcuffs only have their intended effect precisely when the effect should no longer be intended. The other lesson is that, before slipping on a pair of golden handcuffs, one should make very sure that they really are golden, and not the shiny plastic kind.

III. Thinking Ahead

How Strategy Became a Business

S trategy derives from the Greek word for "military general," and everyone can agree that strategy is the kind of thing that generals do. In everyday usage, doing "strategy" means understanding the lay of the land, assessing the enemy's capabilities, grasping the possibilities, setting objectives, and making plans. It could be defined as "seeing the big picture and figuring out what to do about it"; or perhaps, "spotting the whale"; or, in very general terms, "thinking ahead." In this general sense, strategy is undoubtedly a vital task for managers. Experience tells us that in every large organization, there are never enough people with the ability and ambition to step back, take it all in, and assume ownership of an enterprise from its foundations. One of the writers in the strategic planning literature concludes his book on the subject with a quote from the seventeenth-century Spanish Jesuit Baltasar Gracián that sums up this general sense of strategy: "Think in anticipation, today for tomorrow, and indeed for many days. The greatest providence is to have forethought for what comes."[1]

In the heavily consulted corporate world, however, the word *strategy* has come to mean something more than it did among ancient Greeks and Spanish Jesuits. It refers to a modern, professional discipline, bound up in lengthy textbooks, purveyed by consultants, and practiced within elite departments of large corporations. It has a language of its own, and even a distinct picture vocabulary, including a variety of widely used matrices and diagrams. Though the person on the street can usually "plan" a thing or two, only a properly schooled individual can know what it means to engage in "strategic planning"—or, for that matter, "strategic positioning" or (to use the new grammar) "strategic visioning."

At my firm, the word *strategy*—in this second, specialized sense—was the sexiest word in business. We identified ourselves to the outside world as a "strategy consulting firm." We looked with disdain upon the much less virile "body shops"—very large firms that did tediously technical projects at risibly low rates. We told our parents that our job was to supply the large corporations of the world with our expertise in strategy. (They scratched their heads.) Fresh recruits basked in the impression that they would soon be hashing out strategy with CEOs late into the night. As we grew from 140 professionals to 700 and from $50 million in revenues to about $250 million in the space of four years, we trumpeted the success of our own strategy. We *were* "strategy."

There is good reason, however, to doubt whether these two senses of strategy have much to do with one another. At my firm, for example, the fact that we were experts (by stipulation, at least) in the arcane discipline of "strategy" by no means implied that we were particularly good at the task of thinking ahead. In fact, at the height of our success, our real strategy was—depending on the moment and angle of viewing—nonexistent, in constant flux, or deeply twisted. We began a formal "strategic planning" process only after the firm ran into serious trouble. And we settled on a definitive strategy only after it became clear that we were falling off a cliff.

From a historical point of view, in any case, the interesting question is this: When did strategy become "strategy"? That is, at what point did strategy become a business that could employ people like me along with thousands of planners, professors, and consultants?

History, in this instance, provides an unusually precise answer. In 1964, Peter Drucker sent to his publisher a draft of a book under the title *Business Strategies*. When he and the publisher test-marketed the title on business executives and consultants, however, they were strongly advised to drop it.[2] "'Strategy,' we were told again and again, 'belongs to military or perhaps to political campaigns, but not to business,'" Drucker recalled more than 20 years later. So Drucker agreed to change the title to *Managing for Results*.

Almost the next day, *strategy* became the hottest word in management circles. In later years, Drucker, who liked to claim credit for having invented the very discipline of management, proffered his 1964 book as evidence that the discipline of strategy, too, was his creation—though he petulantly insisted that *Managing for Results* was a better title, even if it was "less 'sexy.'" But in fact, the treatment of strategy in the book is notable today because, in contrast with what was to follow in the field, it is modest in its ambitions for the topic.

The story of Drucker's unloved title offers a curious reminder that for many years—indeed for the entirety of history before 1965 or so—management got along quite well without "strategy." Taylor, Mayo, and the rest of the early generation of management theorists thought of managers mainly as organizational and administrative types, far removed from the hurly-burly of commercial confrontation. Chester Barnard gave the impression that descending to the marketplace was beneath his dignity in his position as the leader of New Jersey Bell. As the journalist and commentator Walter Lippmann put it in 1914, "managers stand . . . outside the shrewdness and strategy of competition."[3] The business schools offered courses on what was then called "Business Policy," but these were accorded relatively modest importance by teachers and students alike. In the years leading up to the publication of Drucker's retitled book, however, the idea of strategy underwent a mysterious and remarkable transfiguration. Around 1965 or so, it burst onto the scene as the essential discipline of management. It became—and has remained—the defining task of CEOs, the copestone course in business education, and the product supplied by the world's most expensive consultants.

The discipline of strategy was not the invention of a lone genius, as Drucker wishfully insinuates. Rather, it emerged out of a fundamental transformation in the organization of economic life. In his 1962 book *Strategy and Structure*—perhaps the first major business book with strategy on the cover—the historian Alfred Chandler describes the relevant underlying structural change. In order to realize their business goals, Chandler argues, General Motors, Standard Oil, DuPont, and a number of other leading corporations developed a decentralized, multidivisional form of organization, referred to now as the "M-Form" organization. (The *M* is usually understood to refer to *multidivisional*, or sometimes *multifunctional*; but some would say that it derives from the fact that the boxes on organizational charts now cascade down in what looked to some eyes like the shape of an M.) In such an organization, the "top" or headquarters unit limits itself to general functions, such as planning, coordination, and, above all, resource allocation, while each subordinate division assumes operational responsibility for a particular line of business or function. With the help of consultants such as McKinsey, gurus such as Peter Drucker, and the growing numbers of graduates from the nation's business schools, the M-Form became the standard among the world's large corporations.

The M-Form Corporation

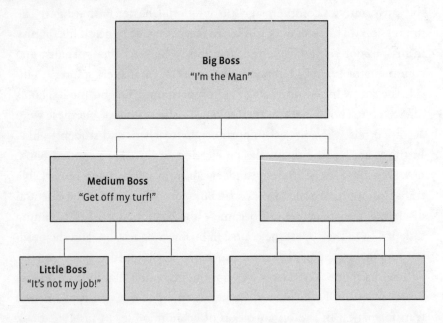

In his well-received book, Chandler's principal thesis is that the M-Form structure followed from the business strategies of these pioneering corporations. As far as the history of business goes, this claim undoubtedly has merit (though some might quibble whether it suggests more conscious agency in the process than was the case). In the history of management thought, however, the reverse is nearer the truth: the discipline of strategy followed structure.

Strategy took hold because it provided an intellectual superstructure that explained and justified the functioning of "top management" in the new M-Form corporations. It grew because it represented the interests of consultants who served this new tier of management. It achieved permanence by furthering the institutional ambitions of the business schools, which expanded rapidly to serve the needs of the new corporations and their vendors. The strengths and limitations of the new discipline of strategy follow mainly from its institutional origins.

Of the many individuals involved in the creation of the new discipline of strategy, three stand out as the most original and at the same time the most representative of the movement. One was a corporate manager assigned a new kind of task, one was a consultant who foresaw a new business opportunity, and the last was an academic who took it upon himself to create a new field of study.

The Planner

One day in the middle of the Cold War at the sunny Burbank headquarters of the Lockheed Corporation, H. Igor Ansoff met with his boss, Robert Gross, to discuss his new job. Ansoff, a PhD in mathematics, was 38 in 1957, and he had worked previously for the Rand Corporation, a defense think tank, where he had analyzed, among other things, the Soviet nuclear threat to the US Strategic Air Command. Robert Gross had been the company CEO, president, and chairman of the board for the previous 23 years. Lockheed was one of the nation's leading defense manufacturers, producing fighter planes, spy planes, bombers, and nuclear missiles.

Despite the corporation's illustrious record, Gross explained to Ansoff, its growth and profits were sagging. Gross had recently created a Corporate Planning Department and charged it with finding a way to restore long-term growth and profits. The rest of the department, Gross explained, was busy developing a long-range plan for the existing businesses. Ansoff's assignment was straightforward enough: his job was to come up with "a plan for diversification" into new businesses.

The assignment was just one in a list of almost random events that would mark a decisive turning point in Ansoff's alarmingly unpredictable life. Born in Vladivostok to an American father who wanted someday to return home and a mother who was "600 percent Russian,"[4] Igor had grown up in Moscow in the years following the Bolshevik Revolution. On account of his father's nationality and his mother's bourgeois origins, he had never felt entirely welcome in communist Moscow. He had compensated by investing his considerable energy in academics and becoming very active in the Pioneers, a breeding ground for future leaders of the Communist Party. In later life, to judge from the photographs, he remained the kind of clean-shaven man who always carries a well-sharpened pencil.

At the age of 18, Igor had sided with his father in the long-running domestic dispute over whether to move to America. His decision, he later admitted, had rested on "shaky grounds": the strategic plan was to go to America in order to see firsthand the depredations of capitalism, to make contact with the oppressed American Indians (James Fenimore Cooper's books were popular in Russia), and then to return to Moscow with a searing report for his fellow communist youth leaders. As it happened, the family escaped Russia only moments before Stalin's purges and the advent of the Second World War would have made such an exit impossible. When he arrived in New York, Igor's English was so poor that he could not understand a word that his teachers and fellow students were saying at the Stuyvesant High School. Five years later, he graduated at the top of his class at the Stevens Institute of Technology in Hoboken, New Jersey.

Ansoff asked Gross what was meant by "diversification." "His frank response," Ansoff later recounted, "was that neither he nor his colleagues had any idea what diversification meant."[5] The neophyte planner returned to his desk and, after some research, discovered that the academics didn't have much that was useful to say on the subject either. So, in the following year, he built from scratch a conceptual framework for analyzing the entire range of manufacturing industries in the United States and assessing the attractiveness of potential acquisitions for Lockheed. He spent the following two years "playing chess with companies" as Lockheed's director of diversification, and he was then moved to a line job as vice president in charge of a division of one of the newly acquired companies.

At the age of 44, after struggling to turn around his loss-making division, Ansoff had a midlife crisis. While literally standing in front of the proverbial shaving mirror, he realized that he lacked a strategic plan for his life. He packed up the family and headed for a two-week vacation on Cape Cod, where he allowed his beard to grow wild and engaged in some "strategic self-introspection" with the help of half a case of scotch. Six empties later, he had formulated a new life strategy. He realized that he did not want to be a line manager for the rest of his life; he needed to diversify. His objective now was to become a professor of management. Upon returning from the beach, he immediately set to work writing down all the things he had learned in the course of developing Lockheed's plan for diversification. Two years later, in 1965, he published *Corporate Strategy*.

Strategy, as Ansoff presents it, centers around an existential question: What do we want to do? "Strategic decisions," one of Ansoff's disciples elaborates, "are primarily concerned with external rather than internal problems of the firm and specifically with the selection of the product mix that the firm will produce and the markets to which it will sell."[6] Thus, the output of a strategic planning exercise, in condensed form, might read something like this: cars in France, toothpaste in gas stations, and insurance to old ladies.

To assist planners in their task of selecting the appropriate mix of products and markets, Ansoff supplies a set of "strategic planning tools." His work sparkles with the kind of things that consultants call eye candy: matrices, charts, and, above all, lists. Perhaps the most celebrated of his matrices is the product mission matrix, in which he represents in graphic form the crucial distinction between "present" and "new" products and "present" and "new" markets. To each of the four boxes Ansoff assigns a "growth vector"—a source of future profit growth. For present products in present markets, for example, the vector is "market penetration." For new products in new markets, it is "diversification."

The charts that populate the work of Ansoff and like-minded strategic planners exhibit a fascinating variety of shapes. Aside from the software-style flowcharts, there are conceptual x-y charts from economics, sometimes extending into three dimensions; Venn diagrams; pies; time lines; boxes within boxes; organizational charts; and Gantt charts. The "environment" is typically represented by an irregular blob, whereas organizational units tend to be boxes, and concepts are circles or ellipses. The many lists that Ansoff and his epigones provide include lists of questions to ask about a business (Who are our customers? What are our products?); lists of metrics to consider in measuring performance (profit margin, sales per employee); lists of the kinds of resources at a company's disposal (raw materials, product inventories); and lists of factors for planners to analyze (competitors, environment).

One later innovation in which Ansoff takes particular pride is his scale for measuring the "turbulence" of a firm's environment. He maintains that, around 1950 or so, the world economy as a whole left a period of relative stability and entered an age of turbulence. To survive in such a chaotic world, he argues, strategic managers must be constantly engaged in the process of selecting new products and new markets to enter. He introduces a scale describing five levels of turbulence, where 1 is "repetitive" and 5 is "surpriseful" [sic]. On the basis of this five-point scale, Ansoff declares himself an authority on the topic of "managing in turbulent environments."

For Ansoff, strategic planning is a kind of applied science. He describes the turbulence scale and its accompanying material, for example, as a "real-time response technology." "The technology of strategic planning has now been around for some 15 years," he writes in 1976, as though referring to the invention of color television.[7] The value of strategic planning, he insists, derives from "the systematic method of science."[8]

Ansoff's book was rapidly accepted as a classic when it came out in 1965. Soon, hundreds of corporations formed strategic planning departments, and began filling out the kinds of matrices and lists that Ansoff supplied. Other writers threw their energies into the genre. One of the more prominent planning experts of the time, George A. Steiner, interestingly, also happened to be a graduate of the Lockheed Corporation's Corporate Planning Department. With the help of proponents such as Secretary of Defense Robert McNamara, the planning bug swept through government. Ansoff hailed the Program Planning and Budgeting System (PPBS) with which McNamara oversaw the Vietnam War as "an advanced version of the strategic planning system."[9]

Within the burgeoning community of strategic planners, Ansoff's supporters were distinguished by their fervor and their orthodoxy. The "research domain developed by Ansoff encompasses *all* variables," gushes one acolyte. "His work is comprehensive and *virtually* exhaustive."[10] In their eyes—and those of many other observers, too—Ansoff had earned his place in the history of management thought as "the father of strategic management."

The Consultant

On a Saturday morning in the fall of the same year that Ansoff published his first book, all 12 members of the Boston Consulting Group gathered to discuss the purpose of their existence. Presiding over the meeting was the firm's founder, Bruce Henderson. A lanky, 40-something southerner and son of a Bible salesman who favored the kind of thick-rimmed glasses that serious people wore in those days, Henderson joined the purchasing department of Westinghouse upon leaving the Harvard Business School. After a rapid climb up the corporate ladder there, he moved over to the consulting firm A. D. Little before venturing to set up his own consulting shop in the bowels of a Boston trust bank.

Henderson's firm was just two years old in 1965. To compete against much larger, established rivals like McKinsey & Company, Henderson told his staff, they could not afford to be generalists. They would have to present themselves to prospective clients as specialists in one area or another. The question was, What exactly were they specialists in? For some time that morning, the young consultants debated in which of various possible fields they should claim to be experts.

According to the later account of Robert Mainer, one of the men present, at a certain point in the discussion Henderson asked a "momentous" question:[11]

"What about business strategy?"

"That's too vague," Mainer objected. "Most executives won't know what we're talking about."

"That's the beauty of it," Henderson replied. "We'll define it."

Henderson later described consulting as "the most improbable business on earth": "Can you think of anything less improbable [*sic*] than taking the world's most successful firms, leaders in their businesses, and hiring people just fresh out of school and telling them how to run their businesses and they are willing to pay millions of dollars for this advice?"[12] Even more improbable, one would have thought, is that a dozen men with no obvious claim to fame should, one fine Saturday morning, declare themselves experts in a subject whose contents they themselves would get to define, and then turn around and expect the world to pay for such expertise. And yet, against all odds, the world proved eager to buy.

In the following year, on assignments for Texas Instruments and Black & Decker, Henderson's consultants observed that manufacturing efficiency improved not just as a function of scale, but as a function of accumulated production. That is, the more widgets a company had produced throughout its past history, the lower the unit cost of those widgets was in the present. Henderson promptly rolled out his first strategy product: the experience curve, which purported to show that for each doubling of total accumulated production, a company could count on a 20% to 30% reduction in unit costs. The strategic implication was that companies should aggressively seek dominant market share in order to outdo their rivals in accumulated production and thus costs. Since companies could now anticipate future cost reductions, furthermore, they could acquire market share by reducing prices to levels that their competition thought insane. The euphoria over the experience curve probably reached its peak when Henderson circulated a pamphlet in 1974 titled "Why Costs Go Down Forever."[13]

Three years after their fateful strategy session, Henderson and his group concocted the product on which much of his firm's fame would rest: the portfolio matrix. At the time, corporate managers were beginning to experience difficulties in managing the diversified empires they had accumulated over the previous decade. Henderson's insight was that, instead of focusing on year-to-year profits from their many divisions, a corporation's general managers should view each division as a business unit in its own right. They should invest or divest in those business units according to the future prospects of each, rather than according to last year's numbers. The prospects of a business unit, Henderson asserted, could be assessed with two variables: the growth of the market in which it operated, and the unit's share of the market.

The famous portfolio matrix thus comes with four boxes. Business units with a high share of a low-growth market Henderson calls "cash cows." These should be milked, he suggests, but should not receive large new investments. Those with high share and high growth are "stars" and should be lavished with as much love and milk as they can take from the cows below. Those with low share and low growth are "pets" (this was later changed to the more biting "dogs"). Pets, says Henderson, "are not necessary"; they should be put to sleep. As for high growth–low share businesses, Henderson seems to have run out of imaginative labels, so he calls them "question marks," by which he means that they maybe deserve to get milk and they definitely need to be subject to some additional consulting work.

Whatever doubts one may have about its substance, there can be no denying that the four-square pattern with its memorable icons is a very pretty package. The matrix made BCG. Soon CEOs around the world were to be found milking those alliterative cash cows, sending their dogs to the pound, and thanking their lucky stars. The matrix became as ubiquitous in boardrooms as the Bible in hotel rooms. It soon made the leap into classrooms, where it served business school professors as a prop for teaching the new discipline of strategy. Most important for Henderson, the matrix appeared to validate his concept of consulting. Consultants do not need to have any special knowledge of the businesses whose executives they advise, he let the world know; they bring to bear general principles of strategy that are common to all businesses.

McKinsey, which had hitherto dominated the top end of the consulting market, paid BCG the ultimate compliment by trying to imitate it. The Firm cast aside the elaborate organizational diagrams for which it had become famous and reinvented itself as a "strategy consulting firm." Perhaps hoping to one-up its upstart rival, it unveiled a three-by-three matrix for categorizing business units according to composite measures of industry attractiveness and business strength.

By that time, though, Henderson and his group had already established themselves as the smartest people in the room. The staff of 12 apostles who had met on that fall day in 1965 multiplied faster than any of the tribes of Israel, doubling in number on average every five years to reach 3,900 by 2007.

The Professor

In 1969, the year after Henderson first sketched his immortal matrix, Michael Porter, a young Princeton graduate in aerospace engineering, matriculated to the Harvard Business School. A gifted athlete and the son of an army officer, Porter excelled in his academic pursuits. Upon receiving his MBA, he moved across the Charles River to study for a PhD in the Department of Economics.

Porter describes the move across the river as a "surreal experience."[14] On both sides of the Charles, the professors were talking about industry structure and firm behavior; but neither group seemed to have much to say to the other. The Business School leaders still eschewed the formal study of strategy. The authors of the Harvard textbook *Business Policy: Texts and Cases*, in the edition that dates from before Porter's matriculation, defend the case-study approach on grounds that it is impossible to "make useful generalizations" about business strategy because too many variables are at work.[15] The economists, on the other hand, lived for generalizations. From their point of view, the business school approach to strategy must have seemed like the moral equivalent of reading the business tabloids. (Which in fact is pretty much what it was.) Porter aimed for a third way. With respect to the business school approach, he says in a recent interview, "I set out to add more rigor." As for the economics approach—the best way to put it is that he turned it upside down.

Porter's timing was impeccable. In 1959, Gordon and Howell had shaken up the university world with their report *Higher Education for Business*, sponsored by the Ford Foundation. The state of business education, the authors said, was out of joint. Business school faculties were woefully underqualified; students were mediocre; and, above all, the subjects of instruction lacked a proper foundation in research. The report exuded more than a whiff of the skepticism about the whole business school project that was then widely shared in the rest of the university and in the business community—and that the business schools had never, since their inception, managed to shake. Determined to quash the doubts for good, Gordon and Howell proposed a solution that, perhaps unwittingly, followed precisely the lines that Harvard's Edwin Gay had first pursued when he made the pilgrimage to Boxly. They urged the business schools to bring a higher degree of rigor to their research, and thus to put their discipline on a scientific foundation.

A decade is a very short time in the life of a university, of course, so when Porter arrived at Harvard in 1969, the business schools had only earnest reports and good intentions but few results in the effort to make business management into an academically respectable subject. The subdiscipline of strategy, in particular, which held the allure of a potential copestone course, had progressed somewhat in the accumulation of "data," but it lacked what the German academics of the nineteenth century would have called "system."

The economics department, naturally, had, if anything, a surfeit of "system," and therein lay the key to Porter's achievement. Porter's specialty in economics was the subdiscipline known as Industrial Organization. IO, as it is often called, concerns itself with the behavior of firms. One would have thought that all economists study the behavior of firms, but in fact, most of the rest of the discipline tends to assume that firms do not exist, since, on the assumption that firms are rational economic actors working within perfect markets, their individual behavior typically does not affect the outcomes of economic models. IO is for that reason sometimes described as the subdiscipline that deals with "imperfect markets."

A Harvard-trained economist named Joe S. Bain helped launch the field in the 1950s with a startling observation—startling, that is, to classical economists. According to the elegant equilibrium models of classical economic theory, in a perfect market all industry sectors should, over the long run, gravitate toward a single rate of return on capital, adjusted for the risk of capital loss. When business is good in any one sector, says the theory, new investors will pile in, driving the rate of return back down to normal levels. When things are bad, capital will flee, allowing the returns on the remaining capital to move upward. And yet, Bain and colleagues noticed, rates of profitability do vary across industry sectors over long periods of time. Above-average or "excess" profits are real and persistent. How can this be?

In his 1956 book *Barriers to New Competition*, Bain argues that persistent excess profits can be explained by market imperfections that he calls "barriers." That is, the structure of an industry can make it difficult for potential competitors to enter the markets, thus allowing existing firms to enjoy artificially high profits. A central insight of Bain's analysis is that the threat of competition from new entrants or substitute products can matter more than actual competition from existing firms. Bain discusses at length three major types of such barriers: economies of large scale, product differentiation, and absolute cost advantages of existing firms.

The agenda behind Bain's analysis is straightforward: "Since higher barriers to entry tend in general to be associated with higher degrees of monopolistic output restriction and larger excess profits . . . a good beginning for policy should be to reduce high barriers to entry wherever this is feasible."[16] The point of IO work is thus to identify and help eliminate "soft monopoly" situations that create artificially high profits—that is, situations where, even in the absence of an actual monopoly or oligopoly and without violation of basic antitrust laws, firms engage in anticompetitive behavior, with the attendant disadvantages for society at large.

So the bespectacled, tweed-wearing academics on the north side of the Charles thought excess profits were a bad thing. But, as Porter could not have helped but notice, the flashy go-getters on the other side of the river thought excess profits were just fine. In fact, the point of their courses on business policy was to figure out how to make them all the more excessive. So Porter asked, why not stand the discipline of IO on its head and call it "strategy"? Instead of using the IO research to pursue the economists' goal of reducing the market imperfections that cause excess profits, why not use this same research to pursue the goal of exploiting market imperfections in order to create and sustain excess profits? In 1979, 10 years after matriculating to the graduate school, Porter published an influential article on this novel approach to the problem of strategy,[17] and in the following year he released his landmark book on the subject: *Competitive Strategy*.

On the basis of this inversion of IO theory, Porter announced that all strategy aims for a single, measurable goal: excess profits. And since, according to IO economists, excess profits derive from the structure of industry sectors, Porter declared that strategic analysis begins with the analysis of industry sectors. "The strength of competitive forces in an industry," he writes, echoing the theoretical core of IO economics, "determines . . . the ability of firms to sustain above-average returns."[18]

The purpose of strategic analysis, in this view, is to discover sectors (and positions within sectors) where competitive forces are kept at bay. "The economists' 'perfectly competitive' industry offers the worst prospect for long-run profitability," Porter explains. The "weaker the forces" of competition, on the other hand, "the greater the opportunity for superior performance."[19]

Porter then lays out a framework of five forces that allows one to determine the competitiveness of an industry sector. The five forces are (1) the bargaining power of suppliers, (2) the bargaining power of buyers, (3) the rivalry among existing firms, (4) the threat of new entrants, and (5) the threat of substitute products. The stronger any or all of these forces are, the more competitive the industry will be, and thus the lower the prospects for excess profits. The framework captures one of Bain's central insights: that the threat of new competition can be more important than the existing competition in a sector. Barriers to entry are thus a crucial feature of Porter's analysis. His aim is essentially to expand and develop Bain's list of barriers so that they cover the universe of strategic options faced by a business manager. In Porter's new vocabulary, a company that occupies a position within a sector that is well protected by market imperfections such as barriers to entry is said to have a "sustainable competitive advantage."

Porter's book is very, very long, but for many readers the practical upshot is the idea that there are three "generic" strategies that bring success for most businesses most of the time. The three generic strategies loosely follow Bain's discussion of barriers to entry. The first is to aim for "overall cost leadership" in a sector—that is, to be able to produce goods at a lower cost than the competitors do. The second is to "differentiate" one's offerings so as to make them unique within a sector. The third is to "focus" on a particular market niche. The strategies are, for practical purposes, exclusive, in Porter's view (albeit with some exceptions). That is, if you try to be both low-cost and high-quality, chances are you will end up "stuck in the middle," which is bad.

Porter's tome landed in business school libraries just in time to plug a gaping pedagogical hole. Teachers and students were excited to learn more about the hot topic of strategy, but the discipline lacked focus and a solid foundation in theory. The work of consultants like BCG may have been insightful, but it did not appear to be systematic. Ansoff and his crowd of strategic planners, as Porter himself notes, were plenty systematic, but they had really only laid out the questions of strategy.[20] What students wanted to learn and teachers wanted to teach were the answers. They wanted a theory that would tell them which strategies generate profits and which ones don't. Porter offered just such a theory, and as a result he became to the new discipline of strategy what Aristotle was to metaphysics. At business school campuses across the world to this day, thanks to Porter, one can hear students challenge each other with the cry "So, what's your competitive advantage?"

Other theorists stampeded through the gate Porter had opened. A number of influential theorists saw that, in his inversion of IO, Porter had left some pieces of insight still standing right side up. Back in the 1950s and '60s, for example, the IO economists had realized that the new field of game theory could be used to understand the behavior of firms, in particular in oligopolistic markets. As economists first noted in the nineteenth century, perfectly competitive markets at one end and pure monopolies at the other are easy to analyze. In both cases, buyers and sellers are assumed to behave according to their own interests, and economists can rest safe in the assumption that the moves individual players make won't upset the parameters of their tidy models. In oligopolies, however, moves made by one player can change the playing field, and so bring about different responses by other players, resulting in very different global outcomes. In analyzing such markets, game theory can be quite useful.

Both Ansoff[21] and Porter[22] understood that game theory would also, by process of inversion, be of use in helping firms conceive of business strategies—especially in oligopolistic markets. But their actual discussions of game theory are somewhat general and do not live up to the promise of the subject. In recent times, Adam Brandenburger and Barry Nalebuff, among others, have taken up the challenge of applying game theory within a Porterite project of academic theorizing about strategy in their influential book, Co-opetition.

Brandenburger and Nalebuff begin with the insight that competition in business is not always a zero-sum game. Competitors can often help increase the total market or "the size of the pie," and to that extent their relationships are win-win. It is only when it comes to dividing up the pie that the game becomes win-lose. The same is true of relationships between buyers and sellers: insofar as they can collaborate to increase the benefits on both sides of a transaction, the game is win-win; when it comes to deciding who gets what, the game switches to win-lose. The authors capture this mix of cooperation and competition with their neologism *co-opetition*. They also introduce the term *complementors* to describe pairs of entities that can enhance one another's returns—such as, for example, hot-dog makers and mustard makers. Complementors can be thought of as a "sixth force" in Porter's five-forces framework for industry sector analysis.

Yet another untapped vein in the IO mine opened by Porter had to do with studies that looked within the firm itself to understand growth and profit differentials. In her 1959 book *The Theory of the Growth of the Firm*, economist Edith Penrose argues that a firm should be viewed as "a collection of production resources at the disposal" of management, and that it is the differences among firms in resources and in their application that create opportunities for growth.[23] In his 1957 book *Leadership in Administration*, Philip Selznick expresses the central insight perhaps more succinctly with his concept of "distinctive competence."[24] By carving out of its own resources a distinctive competence that other firms would have difficulty matching, he says, a company can achieve the kind of sustainable excess profits that Porter would later seek. Igor Ansoff, too, has a fair amount to say about analyzing the capabilities of an organization. In his 1984 article "A Resource Based View of the Firm," MIT/Sloan Professor Birger Wernerfelt[25] revives these ideas and formalizes them into what is now referred to simply as the "Resource-Based View," or RBV.

Although the RBV movement clearly adds something to Porter's theory of competitive advantage and is sometimes presented as being at odds with it (not least by Porter himself[26]), in a deeper sense it represents a continuation. Following the logic of Porter's theory of competitive advantage, it posits excess profits as the singular goal of strategy; and it attributes excess profits to the kind of market imperfections studied in IO economics. The principal novelty of the RBV approach is that it looks inside the firm, at its own resources, for the barriers to entry that Porter tends to see on the outside, in the firm's positioning with respect to its competitors. RBV can be thought of as an "inside-out" approach to strategy, in contrast with the "outside-in" approach of Porter.

Wernerfelt's work met with radio silence (in a 10-year anniversary edition of his 1984 article he notes ruefully that in its first three years it received three citations, two of which were from his own graduate students). Then Gary Hamel and C. K. Prahalad popularized the idea in their 1990 article in the *Harvard Business Review* titled "The Core Competence of the Corporation." In other articles and in their subsequent book, the best-selling *Competing for the Future*, the authors also introduce to a wider world the notions of "strategic intent" and "stretch." "Strategic intent," they tell us, is "an ambitious and compelling dream . . . that provides the emotional and intellectual energy for the journey to the future." *Stretch* means, roughly, that the dream is going to involve a lot of work. The theoretical nexus for Hamel and Prahalad, however, remains that of the RBV theorists. Aside from the rather obvious points that it should contribute to product value and offer potential for new applications, "a core competence should be difficult for competitors to imitate," Hamel and Prahalad say, making clear the link with Porter's theory of competitive advantage.[27]

Strategy, or Strategic Management, is now a thriving discipline, populated with a teeming multitude of theories, studies, and controversies. In its fundamental structure and content, the discipline Porter launched embodies the vision set forth by Gordon and Howell in 1959. Strategy, it is thought, will succeed where Taylor and Mayo have failed. It will become the discipline that synthesizes all of the other functional subdisciplines of management into a meaningful whole. It defines the purpose of management and of management education. Such, at any rate, is the hope that Porter and his successors have set out to fulfill.

A Case Study in Strategy

" t's amazing how people will consistently undersell themselves," Owen said mostly to himself, shaking his head with a wry smile as he got off the phone. "But that's our opportunity."

He looked like a poker player reluctantly collecting winnings from people who just shouldn't have been at the table. I knew he was talking about yet another senior recruit. We were hiring them by the dozen at the time. As it happened, I had come back to New York to discuss hiring some partners for a new office I wanted to help open in Spain. Owen's words stayed with me long after the details of the negotiations faded. As only gradually became clear to me, they expressed the essence of one version of our firm's business strategy—the twisted version. There was, in fact, no shortage of other strategic frameworks to explain what we were doing. One of them must have worked for a while, at least, because the firm did very well in its first years.

The first theory of the firm, which we discussed on "Independence Day" and which provided the initial rationale for the venture, loosely followed the style of Michael Porter's theory of competitive strategy. Our overall goal was to become a "Type 1" or "prestige" consulting firm. That is, we were going to pursue what Porter would call a "quality" or "differentiation" strategy. We said "Type 1" or "prestige" in deference to an awkward fact about our industry. The dirty little secret of the strategy consulting business is that most of the work involves strategy only in the sense that cleaning the kitchen can involve strategy—at least, when the boss tells you to do it. The term *strategy* in "strategy consulting" actually means "high-ranking." A strategy consulting firm is one that works for people higher up in a bureaucratic hierarchy. Not coincidentally, *strategy* in this context is also a synonym for "extremely expensive." The most reliable way to distinguish a strategy consulting firm from a body shop is that the former will charge up to three times as much in fees per consultant.

The more specific, Porterite argument for our existence had to do with the subsector of the extremely expensive high-ranking consulting market from which our group had historically derived most of its work—the sector serving large financial institutions. In this highly profitable submarket, it was observed, there was one dominant player—McKinsey—which accounted for more than half the market, and a number of much smaller players (such as my previous employer) who for one reason or another could not or would not compete at scale. The theory was that we could turn McKinsey's quasi monopoly into a duopoly. Clients would welcome having a choice between similar firms (most of our consultants were ex-McKinseyites, after all), and we might even be able to claim an edge by being specialists in the sector. At the same time, we presumed, whatever barriers were keeping other potential entrants out would remain in place, allowing us to share the spoils of a sheltered market with our hated/admired parent/nemesis. The practical implication of the theory was that we would locate our offices in major financial centers of the world and concentrate on serving this one industry. Thus, our "ambitious and compelling dream," to use the language of the gurus, was to become a Type 1 firm in the financial services submarket.

Within six months of the start-up, the theory was no more. It was a nice idea; but it had no predictive value. It turned out to be much easier to sell work when we weren't competing directly against McKinsey than when we were. When it further proved possible to generate business outside the financial services industry, we did so. Why try to predict the potential sources of profit with a theory of competitive strategy, we reasoned, when actual experience will simply tell you where they are? Soon, we had launched practices serving clients in media, telecommunications, and other sectors. We then began to open offices wherever we happened to find reliable client work or wherever partners wanted to live. Many of our 15 or so offices ended up far from the world's major financial centers. Every few months, usually as the result of some random event, such as the acquisition of a new client or of a new partner, we added yet another market segment to the mix.

For the benefit of recruits, clients, and a number of disgruntled partners, the firm continued to pay lip service to its "strategic intent." But the business we actually pursued did little to further our ambition of becoming a Type 1 firm. Throughout the expansion, about two-thirds of the firm's revenue came from a single kind of consulting project. We called it "the miracle of sourcing." Sourcing is a bundle of techniques for reducing the amount of money a large corporation spends on purchased goods and services. It involves turning company supply offices into miniature versions of Wal-Mart. Some of the cost reductions come from simply rationalizing demand—that is, coordinating purchases across organizational units to achieve bulk discounts. Some require working with suppliers to reduce costs. Most result from brutal and competitive negotiations. Some of these negotiations involve using market power in rather questionable ways—to squeeze suppliers, form de facto buying cartels, shake down workers, or exploit tax loopholes. In the early 1990s, many large corporations had inefficient purchasing operations. Among the items they had not figured out was how to source the sourcing service itself. As a result, we were able to charge extraordinarily high fees.

Many good and bad things could be said about sourcing; one thing that is certain is that it had almost nothing to do with "strategy." It wasn't the kind of service that makes for a "Type 1" firm. Fresh recruits who had been expecting to hash out global expansion strategies with CEOs were chagrined to discover that, in fact, their jobs involved negotiating discounts for photocopying and waste disposal services. Sourcing was a "Type 2" or "body shop" product not just on account of the relatively low intellectual demands it made on staff, but because of the "leverage"—that is, partner-to-staff ratio—it permitted. In Type 1 firms, as a consequence of the relatively artisanal nature of the service, the number of associates per partner ranges from 5 to 8. In sourcing projects, on the other hand, one partner could easily oversee a team of 20 or 30, broken up into sub-groups burrowing into one microscopic category of purchased goods or another.

The other curious thing about sourcing, incidentally, was that it was not our invention. In fact, we snatched it on the way out the door as we left our "host vessel" in Chicago, which had developed the idea in its work on behalf of large manufacturing companies. From the perspective of the theory of competitive strategy, our position would have been very hard to justify: we were selling a stolen good with consultants who had been pushed out of other firms. According to Porter's logic, such a structural disadvantage should have doomed us. But in fact, the sourcing business did very well, and our many later troubles were caused not by the business proposition itself, but by the firm's response to it.

Our massive reliance on a single "me too," Type 2 product occasioned some heated strategic discussions among the partnership. The debate roughly followed the contours of the BCG growth share matrix. We had a "cash cow," the theory went, so the time had come to start investing in question marks and stars. Every few months, someone would cobble together a presentation listing the new markets we would penetrate and the new products we would develop in order to realize our destiny as a Type 1 firm. The only certainty about our product matrix discussions was that within six months they would be entirely forgotten. And then, of course, we'd see that two-thirds of our revenue was still coming from our trusty cash cow, so someone would present a new vision of the future with the same touching fervor.

The matrix did little for us because it merely restated a simple problem but did nothing to change the underlying dynamics that had created the problem. Indeed, by stating the problem in such a clever way, it served the purpose of many so-called therapies: it allowed us to pretend we were doing something about it when we weren't. Sourcing dominated our portfolio because it was the easiest way to make money. It maintained its dominance because certain partners with a particular interest in the product very clearly saw it as a way to gain power for themselves within the partnership. We ultimately did nothing about our wish for a better portfolio because the more senior leaders, and especially Owen, did not take the issue of product concentration very seriously.

Owen seemed to view our fitful strategy discussions mainly as therapeutic opportunities for partners. "At McK, we were always worried that we were too dependent on one product," he said many times. "Then, a few years later, a new product would come along, and then, a few years after that, people would start worrying all over again. Worry is healthy." I formed the impression that, at this exalted point in his career, Owen no longer did much work for clients. He seemed to have only a dim idea of what the rest of us did for them. His focus, as always, remained relentlessly inward.

Owen did from time to time make an effort to enliven the matrix discussions by offering his thoughts on future product development. At one point, he became enthusiastic about the prospect of selling services connected with the "Y2K" bug that was supposed to bring the world to an end at the turn of the millennium. He manifestly saw the Y2K mania as a device for scarifying clients. But the average member of our firm was a "technology consultant" in the sense that an MBA who buys a surfboard becomes a "surfing consultant." We didn't know what we were talking about.

Sometime toward the end of year 3, Owen began to hold what he called "4×5 meetings." I can no longer remember what the 4 and the 5 referred to, but even at the time they didn't matter. The meetings were all about numbers that had no meaning. They were a gesture in the direction of strategic planning. On Owen's orders, Patrick (our concupiscent CFO) and his cronies from the New York office created a set of planning spreadsheets and then asked partners from offices around the world to fill them out every month or two and present them to the so-called 4×5 committee. The spreadsheets included projections for future revenue, staffing levels, recruitment plans, market analysis, and so on.

"This is such bullshit!" Roland groused. And it was. The plans purportedly peered into the future, but in fact they were simply a distorted way of looking at the past. They merely mixed up data from our recent activities with our most ardent present desires. Often out of date even by the time they were presented, they served mainly as scoreboards for political infighting: the partners with the most political influence landed the biggest "projections," so they got the biggest budgets. The most amazing thing about the plans was that they were almost instantly forgotten. As soon as it became clear that the future wasn't turning out like the past, the planners simply cooked up new spreadsheets.

Despite the absence of any consistent, formal strategy, the firm was, in all outward respects, very successful during the first three and a half years of its existence. The basis of this success—our real "strategy," as it were—was at bottom something much simpler than anything that the fancy theories and matrices of the strategy discipline would suggest.

In life and in business, the most reliable strategies follow a threefold path. The first and most important step, by far, on the path to glory is to be in the right place at the right time. There is no substitute for being born well. As Woody Allen said—perhaps intuiting a version of the Great Whale Principle—80% of success in life is just showing up. Machiavelli figured that about half of anyone's claim to fame comes from what he called *Fortuna*—and the other half comes from skill in responding to whatever *Fortuna* throws at you. The second step in any successful strategy, assuming you are so lucky as to find yourself in the right place at the right time, is to bet big. In fact, bet massively (especially if other people's money is involved). The final step, having landed in the right place and put everything on the table, is to work very, very hard to make sure that you aren't proved to be an idiot. Jack Welch sums it all up in a memorable way: "In real life, strategy is actually very straightforward. You pick a general direction and implement like hell."[28]

Our strategy followed the threefold path to success precisely. First and foremost, we were born into the right business at the right time. To be in the business of management in the last decade of the twentieth century was good; to be a management consultant was heaven. In that golden age, the corporate skies opened and the cash rained down on the management consulting industry. The expensive end of the sector was growing at 15% to 20% per year, year after year. Our strategy, to a first order of approximation, was to put out lots of buckets. We bet big. We didn't let ourselves be slowed down by fussing over the color of the buckets—whether they had fancy words like *strategy* on the side or not, or whether they were all in exactly the right places. We just worked very, very hard to get them out there as fast as we could. The result was that we grew at a rate of about 40% per year.

The buckets in this case were consultants. The overarching theory of the business was that we weren't selling a product or a service; we were simply finding and packaging bright people. Hire the smartest people in the room, the theory goes, and they'll figure out on their own how to extract money from the other people unlucky enough to be caught in the same room. Our focus, as Roland had hinted early on, was on the "supply side"—or, more appropriately, the "sourcing"—of consultants. To paraphrase the guru Jim Collins, ours was a "who" strategy, not a "what" strategy.[29]

We trafficked in two kinds of consultants. The first were the "shiny people"—the fresh graduates of universities and business schools. Jim took charge of rounding them up. He spent his days traveling from one school to the next, dragging along his tattered briefcase and his increasingly grating shtick about the mother ship, the host vessel, the noble history of the profession of consulting, and all that. He'd come back with a planeload of young people who glimpsed in his very incomprehensibility a sure sign that we must be the coolest, the most uncorporate, the most purely professional, and the most "strategic" firm in the world.

Because it would have taken years to grow senior consultants through internal processes, we opted to snatch them out of other consulting firms. Owen seemed to devote almost all of his time to this effort (when he wasn't running otiose "planning" meetings, that is). He lured in quite a few new partners with the promise of becoming a leader in a blazing-hot Type 1 firm. One might have thought that, with the industry growing so rapidly, preowned consultants would be in short supply. On the contrary, however, owing to the pyramid structure of most consulting firms, there was always an oversupply. In most firms the funnel at the top to partnership was still narrow enough that many ambitious consultants found themselves facing premature ejaculation. Owen, no doubt on the basis of his own experience, believed firmly that these abused consultants still had a lot of value left in them. With the market for consulting services growing so rapidly, it turned out that he was mostly right. So, in some sense, we were simply filling a hole in the market created by the existing firms' reluctance to grow as fast as they could.

At the same time, with his deep and personal understanding of the psychology of abuse, Owen also seemed to think that these consultants were willing—in the words I heard him use that day I saw him in New York—to "consistently undersell themselves." He thought we could buy them on the cheap. Our strategy, to a second level of approximation, involved a kind of arbitrage. We were exploiting a pricing anomaly in the consulting compensation market, a gap between the market value of consultants and their self-esteem.

It certainly worked for a time. But even from a cursory review of our case, questions about our foresight are impossible to overlook. Such a rapid expansion—essentially a doubling of the firm every two years—in any business is always inherently risky. Expansion at such a rate really makes sense only in the context of a clear business focus and a strong culture capable of building mutual trust among people who are essentially strangers, not to mention a lot of cash and a solid administrative structure. Yet our business focus, such as it was, reflected some deep and very obvious contradictions that could hardly have been expected to augur well for our cultural integrity. A key to our expansion was our ability to sell ourselves to junior and senior recruits as a Type 1 firm. Yet our expansion was, in fact, based on the rapid migration toward a Type 2 business. What would happen when all of our Type 1 people realized what was happening to them and to their firm? This question brings up an even more troubling one concerning Owen's theory about the consulting compensation market. Consultants are paid to place a value on things; and they have never in recorded history been known to place a low value on their own opinions. Is it really plausible that they would undersell themselves? Or were they being oversold? Were they, in fact, being promised more than they were going to get? In which case, what would happen when they found out?

Planning While Rome Burns

gor Ansoff loved to make to-do lists. The granddaddy of all his to-do lists goes like this:

> The procedure within each step of the cascade is similar.
> 1. A set of objectives is established.
> 2. The difference (the "gap") between the current position of the firm and the objectives is estimated.
> 3. One or more courses of action (strategy) is proposed.
> 4. These are tested for their "gap-reducing properties."
>
> A course is accepted if it substantially closes the gaps; if it does not, new alternatives are tried.[30]

For example,

1. You want to eat.
2. You don't have any food.
3. You propose (a) going out for Chinese; (b) making a run to the grocery store.
4. Your strategic planning department forms a committee tasked with evaluating the gap-reducing properties of chicken chow mein versus the local Safeway.

While waiting for the report to come back, you order pizzas all around.

George Steiner expanded Ansoff's list from 4 to 13 steps. According to Steiner, the first step is "plan the plan." Step number 11 is "carry out the plan."[31]

Ansoff was determined that no conceivable eventuality should escape his comprehensive and exhaustive plan of plans. When warned that, in his focus on "externals" (e.g., products and markets), he had overlooked key "internals" (e.g., organization and culture), he meticulously added the study of those internal factors to his to-do lists. When it was pointed out that his frameworks favored the analysis of "hard" variables over "soft" ones such as "political" and "sociological" conditions, he added some extra blanks to his charts to make room for the soft variables. When, long after his ideas had entrenched themselves in the corporate landscape, critics pointed out that many efforts in strategic planning had failed, Ansoff replied that there was nothing wrong with the theory—how could there be? The problem, he wrote, taking a page straight from Taylor's playbook, was that only a "handful" of companies had implemented "genuine" strategic planning. So he added "implementation" to the list of things to do. It seems that there was nothing that Ansoff could not accomplish with his well-sharpened pencil and paper.

There is a kind of madness in strategic planning. In Ansoff's case, it is hard to resist the speculation that his manic list making was a mechanism for coping with anxieties that arose in the face of the chaotic forces that sporadically ruptured the fabric of his own life. Just as Mayo's desperate celebration of harmony in the workplace belied a hysterical fear and loathing of industrial conflict, so Ansoff's frenetic planning seems to have had its roots in an instinctive hypersensitivity to the uncertainties of life in the free market. His response to the maddening multiplicity of experience was of the kind pioneered by the philosopher Hegel: he planned to trap it all within a wrought-iron conceptual system. He was determined to suppress the knowledge that some things in life will never go according to plan.

Ansoff's neurosis may have been extreme, but his approach fills a certain psychological hole in the management soul. In the context of complex decisions with uncertain outcomes and no obvious right answer, the managerial mind inevitably longs for some handrails to grasp amid the smoke and flames. Strategic planning offers that consolation—or illusion—of a sure path to the future.

Ansoff's purported "technology" of strategic planning is, in fact, a permutation of Taylor's universal science of efficiency. It aims to bring science to bear in determining the relation between any given means and any given end. But there is no such science. Ansoff's work, no less than Taylor's, involves a serious epistemological confusion—a confusion that afflicts almost the entire discipline of strategy. "As a first step, we need to establish some concepts and definitions," Ansoff writes in a typical preamble to one of his pieces.[32] But, in fact, *everything* that follows consists of concepts and definitions, most of which are merely analytic. The distinction between existing and new products, for example, is no different in principle from a distinction between, say, purple products and not-purple products. Ansoff's science, like Taylor's, rests on a bed of nonfalsifiable tautologies, generic reminders, and pompous maxims. It is an obtuse way of saying, "Think very carefully about what you want to do; then do it."

To be sure, conceptual frameworks of the sort promoted by Ansoff, stripped of their pseudoscientific pretensions, can be useful and require a degree of artistry to produce. Who among us could live without Ansoff's concepts of "synergy" and "success factors"? At their best, such frameworks offer a handy vocabulary for communicating the common features of experience. Insofar as their purpose is normative as well as descriptive, they can help suggest reasonable courses of action.

The value of Ansoff's vocabulary list, however, only barely exceeds the effort that goes into acquiring it. His definitions and concepts are worth about one weekend of study. As Richard Rumelt, professor of strategy at UCLA, has famously quipped, "If you know how to design a great motorcycle engine, I can teach you all you need to know about strategy in a few days. If you have a Ph.D. in strategy, years of labor are unlikely to give you the ability to design great new motorcycle engines."[33]

Sometimes even a weekend is too much. The problem with conceptual frameworks like Ansoff's is that they readily become temples into which the light of experience does not enter. They extend the umbrella of nonfalsifiable certainty over claims that can and should be subject to empirical scrutiny, and thus they provide a refuge for dogma and hidden agendas. They often have to be unlearned—at great cost.

Among the many crypto-empirical claims that Ansoff attempts to pass off as certainties of reason is his cherished "turbulence scale." What on earth could have moved Ansoff to pick 1950 as the dawn of the age of turbulence? Had he forgotten about the Bolshevik Revolution, the collapse of the Weimar Republic, the crash of 1929, the Great Depression, and those two world wars? Why are there 5 levels of turbulence and not 4 or 10? What exactly counts as the "environment"? What are the chances that any two analysts will agree on whether a particular environment is "changing" (level 3) or "discontinuous" (4)? Are there *any* CEOs out there who would *not* categorize their environment as "surpriseful" (5)?

The most troubling dogmas in Ansoff's conceptual framework are those that bias planners toward a particular strategy and those that implicitly favor a particular form of corporate organization. The idea of strategic planning, far from providing a rational basis for choosing a strategy, is to some degree a rationalization for a strategy already chosen—as well as a rationalization for the power of those who favored that strategy in the first place.

When Igor Ansoff first walked into Robert Gross's office on that day in 1957, the essence of Lockheed's strategy had already been decided. The corporation was going to diversify. Ansoff's job was not to formulate the strategy, but to implement it. Lockheed's thrust to diversify was typical of many of the large, M-Form corporations of its time. "Concern with strategic management," Ansoff explains, "arose in the 1950s in American business firms which increasingly confronted flagging sales growth and unsatisfactory profitability."[34] The concern with falling numbers was not one that troubled the economy as a whole, which was in fact expanding vigorously for most of the period. Nor did the concern arise necessarily from shareholders, who in principle would have been content to retrieve excess capital from unprofitable corporations and take it elsewhere. It *was* a problem for top management teams of large corporations in mature and declining industries, who did not want to see their empires get smaller. For managers working within M-Form corporations, diversification was the obvious solution to this problem of slow growth: there is in principle no limit to the number of subsidiaries that can be managed in a cascade of "M's."

Here and elsewhere, it is important to note, the idea of strategy, like the owl of Minerva, typically arises just as the sun is setting on an organization. An old saw has it that strategy is when you're running out of ammo but you keep firing on all guns so that the enemy won't know. As a rule, corporations turn to strategy when they can't justify their existence in any other way, and they start planning when they don't really know where they are going. Shareholders who hear the word *strategy* would be well advised to reach for their wallets and hold on to them very tightly.

The pro-diversification bias of strategic management is evident in the fact that it is essentially a helicopter-based activity. The strategic manager rides high above any specific business, and his job is to select target markets and products in which to invest. Thus, merely to exist as a strategic manager is to be engaged in a diversification strategy. Ansoff's "turbulence scale" helps convert this logical necessity for diversification into a physical necessity. Because the world as a whole is now at the upper reaches of the turbulence scale, warns Ansoff, old products and old markets are constantly disappearing. Managers who fail to diversify will therefore soon be unemployed. Although Ansoff does hedge his bets, insisting that diversification strategies should be united by some common thread, he continued throughout his career to define strategic management in terms of entering new markets with new products and heaped scorn on claims that corporations should "stick to the strategic knitting."

Embedded in strategic planning's pro-diversification bias is the strategy discipline's central contribution to the development of management thought since Taylor—namely, the idea that the science of management extends even to the mastery of markets themselves. Implicit in Ansoff's thinking is the notion that managers, not markets, are the ultimate authorities when it comes to the allocation of productive resources. Indeed, in Ansoff's world it is difficult to explain why capital markets exist at all. Shouldn't we all just hand over our capital to a planner who can buy and manage every company worth having? The ideal world, for Ansoff, is the managed world. The stability of the plan is the bedrock reality against which the capital markets are found wanting. "Turbulence," in his conception, is an unpleasant environmental force that must be tamed and ultimately liquidated. In the real world, of course, the reverse is nearer the truth. The one constant in a market environment is turbulence; and the thing that changes most is people's plans.

Ansoff's ideal of a planned world, in fact, looks very much like the communism in which he was raised and that has lurked in the shadows of management theory since Taylorism first landed in the Soviet Union. It is more than a coincidence that strategic planning was cradled in the quasi-socialist command economy of the military-industrial complex, and it should hardly come as a surprise that the biggest customers for strategic planning outside the trophy corporations of the capitalist world have been the governments of the communist world. Just like Taylorism, strategic planning is at bottom a managerial assault on capitalism.

The dogma most deeply embedded in the strategic planning framework involves not the specific strategy of diversification but the form of the organization that gave rise to it. From the perspective of the history of management thought, perhaps the most important consequence of the rise of the M-Form corporation is the division of the world of management into two classes: "top management" and "middle management." Top management takes responsibility for deciding on the mix of businesses a corporation ought to pursue and for judging the performance of business unit managers. Middle management is said to be responsible for the execution of activities within specific lines of business.

This division within management has created a new and problematic social reality. In earlier times, there was one management and there was one labor, and telling the two apart was a fairly simple matter of looking at the clothes they wore. The rise of middle management has resulted in the emergence of a large group of individuals who technically count as managers and sartorially look the part but nonetheless live very far down the elevator shaft from the people who actually have power. In essence, middle management forms the backbone of a new kind of working class, made up of so-called white-collar workers or, in optimistic trend-spotting books, "knowledge workers." The emergence of the M-Form marks a crucial first step toward a world in which almost everybody is a "manager" of one sort or another, even if the distribution of real managerial power remains as concentrated as it ever has been.

The concept of strategy as it emerges from the work of the pioneers in the field, such as Ansoff, is essential in defining the function of top management and distinguishing it from that of its social inferiors. "There are two types of management," asserts George Steiner, Ansoff's colleague at

Lockheed. "That which is done at the top of an organizational structure is strategic management. Everything else is operational management."[35] Michael Porter, Bruce Henderson, and almost all the other contributors to the strategy genre insist on this distinction between strategic management and lower-order operational management. Strategic, or top, management, they tell us, is a complex, reflective, and cerebral activity that involves interpreting multidimensional matrices with pictures of farm animals and other icons. Operational management, by contrast, requires merely the mechanical replication of market practices in order to match market returns. It is a form of mindless action, suitable for capable but perhaps less intelligent types.

Steiner draws a chart showing that the farther one moves up the corporate ladder, the more time one spends peering into the distant future. According to his handy analysis, a CEO should "ideally" expend a mere 18% of his or her valuable time on items that come due in the next six months, and 67% on the things that take at least two years to plan. A lowly "group supervisor," on the other hand, should devote 98% of his or her time to planning tasks six months ahead or less, and no time at all to anything one year or more in the making.[36]

Thus, on the one side are the high-brow, mentally endowed, far-seeing rulers of men; on the other are the low-brow, eyes-to-the-ground, brawny types whose duty ends with obedience. The distinction between strategic and operational managers, it is easy to see, marks a return to Taylor's division between thinkers and doers. Igor Ansoff may be the father of strategic management, but its grandfather is undoubtedly Frederick Winslow Taylor. The twist is that whereas Taylor's doers are manual laborers, the strategists' doers are middle management. In the same way that Taylor supplies the metrics required for managers to gain power over pig-iron loaders and the like, Ansoff and his planners give top managers the metrics they need to control middle managers. Strategic planning is a species of rhetoric—a kind of "expert talk"—that justifies the power of top management over the middle.

For all the strategy pioneers, strategy achieves its most perfect embodiment in the person at the top of top management: the CEO. Embedded in strategic planning are the assumptions, first, that strategy is a decision-making sport involving the selection of markets and products; second, that the decisions are responsible for all of the value creation of a firm (or at least the "excess profits," in Porter's model); and, third, that the decider is the CEO.[37] Strategy, says Porter, speaking for all the strategists, is thus "the ultimate act of choice." "The chief strategist of an organization has to be the leader—the CEO."[38]

This picture of CEO-superdeciders does much to justify their huge compensation awards and the congratulatory press coverage, and yet it has little foundation in fact or logic. As a matter of fact, CEOs do not decide on all or even necessarily the most important matters of strategy. In a McKinsey survey from 2007, only 8% of 2,000 managers said that the CEO is primarily responsible for strategy in their businesses. In a study of actual executive behavior in the office, Henry Mintzberg proved to the academics what anyone who has done time in the cubicles already knows very well: that Steiner's idea that CEOs spend their daylight hours pondering the distant future is just baloney.

As a matter of logic, the case for the CEO as warrior-god is even less compelling. Insofar as strategy consists of things like making to-do lists, seeking out market imperfections, and applying the concepts of game theory, it hardly describes an activity that can or should be confined to executive suites. The lowliest car salesman does all of those things too. Inasmuch as some subset of strategic activities pertains to the whole of an enterprise, it does not follow that such an overall strategy is necessarily or ought to be the result of some unique act of decision making on the part of a single person. A firm's overall strategy may well be embedded in its very existence. It may be part of the firm's charter. It may evolve over time and emerge out of the work of many people and a confluence of events of which CEO decisions form only one part. If the strategy has an initial launch point and logical resting place, then that would be not the CEO but the board as representatives of the investors—at least, it would have been in the days before the board became an extension of the CEO.

The notion of the "strategic CEO" typically involves an anthropomorphic fallacy. It represents what the philosopher Francis Bacon called an "idol of the tribe"—an error characteristic of the limitations of the human mind. Human beings think a lot about other human beings, and indeed they often still think about human beings when they think that they are thinking about rain clouds and steamships. So perhaps it is no surprise that they do the same with their own collective organizations. We often speak of corporations as though they were idealized human beings with a single conscious mind and a unitary set of intentions and desires—even though, if we keep our senses, we know that the underlying reality is far more complex. Once human beings start thinking about a multifarious organization as just another human being, however, they tend to make the further inference that there is a unique individual who embodies the collectivity. That would be the king, the pope, or, as the case may be, the almighty CEO, on whom the people tend to heap praise or scorn for what are, in the end, their own virtues and vices. According to this view, the individual *is* the organization and the rest of the people associated with it are mere appendages. Strategy theorists, who necessarily concern themselves with the actions and intentions of a corporation viewed as an individual actor, are especially prone to this fallacy. Indeed, inasmuch as they take their directions from CEOs, they are paid to make this kind of false inference.

The rationalist framework of the strategic planners provides a way to overlook the fact that CEOs—and indeed all other sociopolitical structures of authority—exist as much on account of human irrationality as on the basis of rational decision making. In the world according to the strategists, the absolute authority of the CEO purportedly arises from the dictates of pure reason. But in fact the corporate hierarchy that exists today is a work of customs, cultures, laws, and politics. It is the product of a historical process, not a logical one. Ultimately, it exists for many of the same reasons that warrior aristocracies existed in the ancient world.

Strategic planning, along with the rest of the discipline of strategy, is to modern CEOs what ancient religions were to ancient tribal chieftains. Its rain dances (i.e., budgets) and oracles (i.e., forecasts) ultimately explain the divine right of the rulers to rule. It is actually a covert form of political theory. As the tribal imagery of modern strategists makes plain, however, it is a political theory that has advanced little from its origins in the prehistoric era.

Ansoff's conceptual distinctions may have been nonfalsifiable, but the hypothesis that one should hire a department of people versed in these distinctions and trust them to improve the fortunes of their employer is one that can be tested against experience. As a matter of fact, this hypothesis has now been falsified at least to some extent. Although it obviously makes sense for corporations to engage in some kind of planning activity, various studies and an overwhelming amount of anecdotal evidence now suggest that corporations that engage in formal planning exercises perform no better than those that don't.

Henry Mintzberg, who chronicles the fate of Ansoff's baby in *The Rise and Fall of Strategic Planning*, concludes, "Ultimately, the term 'strategic planning' has proved to be an oxymoron."[39] Michael Porter says, "Strategic planning in most companies has not contributed to strategic thinking."[40] Brian Quinn of Dartmouth adds, "A good deal of corporate planning . . . is like a ritual rain dance. It has no effect on the weather that follows, but those who engage in it think that it does."[41] Richard Rumelt, in an interview with *McKinsey Quarterly*, notes that strategic plans have generally amounted to long-range budget projections garnished with fanciful market forecasts. He proposes ditching the label "strategic" in favor of "long-range."[42] There is a sad kind of irony in this: Ansoff and Steiner began their movement by insisting on the distinction between the existing "long-range" planning efforts and their own brand of "strategic" planning.

The strategy of diversification that strategic planning tended to justify has also generated less than encouraging results—for shareholders, that is. By the early 1970s, academic studies were suggesting that heavily diversified corporations underperformed their peers.[43] In 1987, Michael Porter studied the diversification records of 33 large companies—many of which had reputations for good management and were leaders in their principal fields of business. "The track record of corporate strategies has been dismal," he concluded. "The corporate strategies of most companies have dissipated instead of created shareholder value."[44] The same is almost certainly not true, however, of their effect on senior management compensation.

The Lockheed Corporation—that original spawning ground of strategic planning—fared worse than most. Ansoff's performance in implementing Lockheed's diversification strategy, it turns out, fell short of the corporation's preestablished goals. It seems that he got tangled up in his own flowcharts and to-do lists and did not buy enough new companies to keep the top brass happy. "I viewed Lockheed's diversification as a problem in cognitive logical analysis," Ansoff later confessed. "In retrospect, I see that this narrow problem focus on analysis was responsible for the limited success of Lockheed's diversification program."[45] Naturally, in preparing for future assignments, he added noncognitive logical analysis to his to-do lists. In the meantime, he was "promoted" to a line job, while Lockheed, under a new director of diversification, carried on with its diversification strategy.

It soon became clear that Lockheed's diversification strategy succeeded mainly in providing the corporation with a dog's breakfast of underperforming subsidiaries. Its planners devoted the 1970s to unloading the purchases they had made in the previous decades. Still intent on colonizing markets, Lockheed's senior managers took to bribing foreign officials in order to secure contracts for its airplanes and weapons systems. In the ensuing scandal, the corporation came close to bankruptcy. It has since merged into a larger defense conglomerate.

Ansoff had the misfortune of living to see his plans for planning thwarted. In 1991, at the age of 73, he responded to the detailed criticisms of the strategic planning movement offered by Henry Mintzberg: "According to Mintzberg . . . all of the prescriptive schools for strategy formulation should be committed to the garbage heap of history," he fumes.[46] It seems somehow appropriate that he chooses here to express this dread of a disorderly end with the help of a metaphorical refuse receptacle that he perhaps unconsciously borrows from the writings of Karl Marx. For Ansoff, this is personal. "If I am to accept Henry's verdict," he continues, switching to first names, "I have spent 40 years contributing solutions which are not useful to the practice of strategic management."[47] For one last time, Ansoff sharpens his pencil and, adding a few minor items to his to-do lists, proves yet again that nothing can conceivably escape the exhaustive logic of his conceptual framework.

How to Profit from Planning

I spent the most interesting part of year 2 helping a client bank "undo" its strategy. Some years earlier, under previous management, the bank had decided that its strategic intent was to become a global financial institution. It wished to diversify away from its home market. The strategy naturally came wrapped up with many plans and maps of potential conquests. Because the bank had no distinguishing assets other than a strong position in its home market and it was not particularly long on capital, however, this strategy in practice amounted to a shopping spree on which it traveled to other countries and blew out all its credit cards acquiring a string of third-tier banks that nobody else wanted to buy.

By the time we arrived, it was obvious to most sentient beings connected with the matter that this "strategy" had resulted in serious destruction of value and would have to be undone by selling off the worst of the acquisitions and shaking up the rest. Although we were ostensibly hired to assess the situation, in fact our main job was to read the writing on the wall out loud so that everyone who needed to hear could hear. Our principal client contact, who had recently assumed responsibility for the portfolio, was smart enough not to tell us ahead of time what the wall was saying.

It was an illuminating and entertaining case, involving lots of strong personalities and trips to some of my favorite European cities. It also served to vivify the truism that sometimes the worst thing a corporation can do is develop a strategy. In retrospect, I should have paid more attention to it as a classic example of the perils that befall shareholders when management indulges in uninhibited expansionist ambitions.

As the end of year 3 of our own firm's miniature experiment in expansion approached, money became a very serious problem. The firm's hyperactive expansion naturally called for massive investment to cover sign-on bonuses, new office space, recruiting, and client development expenses. Although the business was generally running at or close to capacity, the cash flow wasn't enough to fund the expansion, and, until very late in the process, banks were understandably leery of lending us anything. The money therefore had to come from the partners.

Partners in the firm expected to receive half or more of their compensation in the form of a bonus that, in ordinary circumstances, would have been paid at the end of the year. Upon Owen's suggestion, and after rancorous debate, the partners agreed to reinvest a large part of the first year's bonus in equity in the firm, and then to delay receipt of bonuses for subsequent years by one year, and then even more. At the dawn of year 4, the net cumulative cash payout to some partners was actually below that of some of the senior associates who worked for them.

I soon began to sense that money was even tighter than it should have been. One day Roland approached me in an unhappy state, waving in front of me a letter from a partner who had joined and then decided to leave. Our former partner was protesting that his capital investment in the firm had not yet been refunded to him as promised.

"How do you feel about belonging to a firm that doesn't honor its obligations to former partners?" he asked me sarcastically. I agreed that it looked very bad. "I'm gonna get on Patrick's case about this," he muttered, and stormed off.

Patrick was the chief representative of the other nagging problem with our emerging strategy. As the firm expanded, its tendency to mimic the least desirable features of third-world governance grew. It became a nexus of secret deals, backdoor compromises, and silent understandings, with Owen at the center of an expanding group of people who did not know and had little reason to trust one another. The absence of an authentic, homegrown culture resulted in still further concentration of power and information at headquarters, mainly in Owen's hands. As a result of all the backroom dealing to acquire new partners, the finances of the firm—and, above all, the compensation of partners—became shrouded in bureaucratic secrecy. Our shareholders' agreement had established a board to oversee the management of the firm, but the board had become increasingly irrelevant. Clustered around Owen in the New York office, there emerged an apparatus of partners like Patrick who assumed control of the administrative machinery of the firm and hoarded all of its secrets. Like Patrick, these individuals owed their careers to Owen—they were family (in some cases, literally).

Many partners were getting restless. Keeping consultants away from their bonuses, it turns out, is something like hanging a fresh carcass just out of reach of a pack of hyenas. The incidence of sexual harassment and other forms of deviant behavior rose appreciably. Some partners had already left in frustration, and others were now engaged with one another in vicious territorial conflicts. A number, including Roland and me, began to voice concerns about the competence of the firm's management.

Owen responded to the pressure by turning up the volume on his 4×5 planning process. The result was more internal meetings and more numerological forecasts. Many partners were now taking a significant portion of their time away from serving clients in order to fill out their quota of planning forms. The entire process represented everything against which we had earlier rebelled in the battle with our erstwhile parent firm in Chicago. Like many successful revolutionaries, we had somehow reestablished an apparatus even more fearful than the one we took down.

"It's all about control," Roland whispered to me one day. He had a point. Strategic planning for us was a good illustration of Michel Foucault's idea that the discourse creates the subject and thus establishes the relations of power. Our discourse of strategic planning didn't do much for the business but, by establishing a pattern of routine and surveillance, it constructed the roles of the "CEO" and his underlings. It was a ritualized, spreadsheet-based form of obeisance that constructed the office of our dear leader. The process also co-opted the partners who got involved in it, granting those who made the reports a certain preeminence over those who did not.

The ultimate meaning of our firm's strategic rituals was finally revealed in year 4 when the results of the compensation committee's clandestine labors were leaked. An associate working with one of the members of the committee had found the partners' compensation list on a desk and made a photocopy. It soon made the rounds.

The list showed that, even as the firm was struggling to find money for expansion, Owen had decided to pay himself $2.8 million for the previous year. "And that doesn't count the renovations on Owen's house that we're paying for," Richard, our in-house military historian, fumed. On another list, I saw that Owen's total take was $3.2 million. The man who had by now become known as the Prince of Darkness and another one of Owen's closest friends, who were also on the committee, had settled for about $2.5 million apiece. A handful of the other partners made over $1 million each, and the rest of us, the new proletariat, were deep down in six-digit territory. One of Owen's minions eventually produced a graph that mapped the partners' compensation numbers against a Pareto curve. The graph actually revealed that the distribution of our compensation was even more skewed than Pareto's formula would have allowed. It was a whale on steroids. Owen had sighted his Moby Dick.

At around the same time, Roland discovered that even while Owen was finding the money to compensate himself for the arduous task of running pointless planning meetings and hiring unneeded partners, the founders' fund was not being funded.

To say that the partnership was not happy at this point would be something of an understatement. "It's like there's a mugging taking place in the middle of the street, and everybody is just watching," one partner said to me. "And we're the ones getting mugged!"

It is, of course, hard to summon very much sympathy for people making on average about half a million dollars a year, but he did have a point. The revelations showed that we so-called partners weren't partners in any real sense at all. We had become employees. Our nominal status as "shareholders" was of no consequence. The firm, it was now clear, had been conceived and was being run as a machine for enriching Owen and his closest friends. The firm's success rested to some degree on cultivating the Ponzi-style illusion among prospective partners that their investment in the firm would entitle them to participate in the control of the firm and receive compensation commensurate with their contributions. The partners had not undersold themselves; they had in fact been grossly oversold.

In a curious way, Owen had achieved for himself what we often advised our clients to attempt. Our firm was, in microcosm, the kind of managerial state that characterizes the global macrocosm. From democratic origins, we had witnessed the rise of a management class that soon devoted itself to building empires, setting its own compensation levels, and reducing shareholders as well as workers to mere instruments of its good fortune. All of our fatuous discussions about "strategy" had served only to legitimate the position of the "chief strategist" or "CEO" who ruled over us.

In his flustered attempts to justify the firm's grotesque compensation policy, Owen sounded all the beautiful notes in the chorus of academics, journalists, and consultants who sing eternally in favor of lavish executive compensation policies. His salary, he said, was comparable to that of his "peers"—the directors of other "prestige" consulting firms. It was based on "an objective evaluation process," he claimed. No one doubted him when he pointed out that he could have roped in a "compensation consultant" to bless the arrangements. As the firm's CEO, he further maintained, he had decided upon and executed its successful strategy. The firm's value was his value. We were supposed to have been grateful for his existence, and even eager to pay him more.

In fact, the firm's compensation policies, like those of the bloated management sector in the rest of the economy, served only to illustrate the universal principle that when people take charge of their own compensation, they tend to pay themselves ridiculous amounts of money. Owen's ex-post rationalizations simply instantiate the corollary that people can justify just about anything to themselves as long as their salary depends on it.

Trust is always the most important foundation of management.

Indeed, management at its most elemental level is the vesting of trust by those who own resources in those who will control them. But trust is an eggshell, and Humpty Dumpty cannot be put back together again. At this point in the short and colorful history of our firm, trust among the partnership had been shattered beyond repair. The mood began to turn very ugly. Lawyers began showing up at meetings in the office.

With the legal clouds gathering on the horizon, Owen appointed a "counsel" for the firm. As with many of his previous appointments, this one, too, occurred behind closed doors and was announced after the fact. It turned out that our legal counsel was a close relative of Owen by marriage. "Pretty bloody convenient," Charles said with scorn.

Roland, Charles, Jim, and four other aggrieved members of the emasculated board huddled together in a secret meeting at a hotel near Gatwick airport and plotted a response. With the encouragement of partners like me, the "Gatwick 7," as they became known, decided to express our frustrations in a letter to Owen. After reaffirming our faith in the beautiful founding principles of the firm, the letter takes on a stern tone:

> A large and growing number of partners have grown fundamentally to distrust the motives, actions, and competence of the firm's leadership . . . We are on dangerous ground . . . We must IMMEDIATELY ensure that there is an open environment for debate, including prohibitions against any efforts to inappropriately consolidate leadership by a few through deals or retaliation against partners who are staking their claim for change.

The letter was intended—and no doubt received—as a declaration of war. Its not-very-well-hidden agenda was to get rid of Owen or at least kick him upstairs—and to fire the appalling Patrick. The language was indeed hot and bothered. But the actual demand, in retrospect, was absurdly tepid. The letter called only for the formation of a "strategy review" that would allow partners to discuss the firm's compensation policies, governance, and business strategy. It was a typical product of the consulting profession. Instead of doing what we had to do, we were going to consult ourselves about what to do. Our strategy was to talk "strategy." Appropriately enough, this proved to be a fatal mistake.

What Consultants Talk about
When They Talk about Strategy

> **The Consultant's Guide to Profitability**
> The most reliable way to make money from strategy is to sell it
> to other people.

The most striking thing about the BCG portfolio matrix is its sheer preposterousness as an analytic tool. The matrix proposes to decide the fate of a corporation's multimillion-dollar business units on the basis of a binary evaluation of two variables: market share and market growth. Most people use more variables to decide which movies to go see than BCG sees fit to analyze in situations where thousands of jobs are at stake. The failure to provide any coherent specification of just what constitutes a market, and of how to estimate growth and share and where to draw the line between "low" and "high," renders even the crude analysis of these two variables moot. Lacking any real substance, the matrix becomes a hortatory noise—another nonfalsifiable grunt intended to encourage companies to invest in good businesses and divest from bad ones. If Ansoff's vocabulary is worth a weekend of study, and Porter's requires a more painful two weekends, then BCG can be out the door in 30 minutes.

Perhaps the best evidence for the vacuity of the matrix and its brand of farm-icon portfolio analysis is the near randomness of the results it supplies. In any attempt to apply the matrix analysis to a real corporation, it is an almost trivial exercise to shift units from one box to another. A small change in arbitrary assumptions can easily turn a dog into a star. In a study where four slightly different portfolio management techniques were applied to the same 15 business units of a single corporation, only one unit got the same grade according to all four, and only five got the same grade in three of the techniques used. Nearly similar results could have been achieved by having four monkeys throw darts at a few matrices.[48]

Like the other strategic frameworks, the otherwise vacuous matrix comes with a surreptitious set of strategic commitments. By making market share one of only two variables in assessing a business, the matrix is inherently biased toward an expansionist strategy. Since profitability per se is not a variable in the matrix, one could argue that the matrix implicitly favors acquiring market share without regard to profits. In this respect the matrix follows on the theme of BCG's experience curve, which also argues for acquiring market share at almost any cost. Unfortunately, it seems that a number of BCG's early clients took this kind of reasoning seriously. Texas Instruments never quite recovered from the price wars that ensued from its attempts to gain market share with unsustainable price cuts. In 1989, Henderson penned a bizarre piece for the *Harvard Business Review* in which he drew a strained analogy between Darwin's theory of natural selection and life in the free market and belatedly let his clients in on the secret that "market share is malarkey."[49]

The matrix, in keeping with the fundamental thrust of the strategic planning tradition, presumes that managers can do a better job of allocating resources among businesses than the market can. The matrix presumes, for example, that it is better to invest the milk from cash cows in the limited portfolio of stars and question marks available to a corporation than to send it back to shareholders. It further presumes that the funding of stars and question marks should be constrained by the capacity of whatever cows the corporation has on hand, rather than through the infusion of new capital. The matrix thus describes a self-contained pseudomarket within the corporation—a planned economy controlled entirely by managers. The entire global economy could be represented in a BCG matrix, if the managerialist fantasy of turning the world into a giant M-Form corporation were ever to come true.

Strategy, in the matrix and in general, is simply a word used to cover the transfer of authority that had traditionally rested with owners over to management. Although Henderson claimed that the practice of "strategy consulting" represented a new kind of consulting, in a certain sense his firm was doing only what McKinsey had been doing all along with its "organizational consulting." Both were legitimating the new order of management power in the M-Form corporation—one with explicit organizational diagrams, the other with the implicit dogma of its conceptual matrices. "The beauty of it," as Henderson might have put it, is that managers used shareholder money to pay for the consultants who would legitimate this imperial grab for shareholder resources.

Apart from its role in buttressing managerial power, there is little evidence that BCG's famous matrix had any useful effect on corporate strategies. As is the custom among consulting firms, BCG has provided no reliable data on which to judge the performance of its invention. In 1994, years after the matrix fad had passed into history, a pair of professors conducted an experiment in which they showed that business school students exposed to BCG's matrix overwhelmingly preferred *un*profitable investment opportunities over profitable ones if the matrix sent them in that direction. The professors also discovered that corporations that used the matrix actually had a slightly lower average return on capital than those that did not.[50] These results should hardly be surprising. In corporations run by the matrix, after all, general managers care less about their business units than they do about the films they go to see, and they analyze their portfolios by having monkeys throw darts at a wall.

Whatever its effects on corporate clients, there can be little doubt that the matrix was a boon to those who produced and marketed it. And this points to the source of some of its most serious limitations. Consultants will not push an approach to strategy that does not involve significant sales of consulting work. It should hardly come as a surprise, then, that the discipline of strategy has been shaped in ways to suit the needs of this industry. In a memoir titled *Whatever Happened to the British Motorcycle Industry*, an executive named Bert Hopwood recorded the following exchange: "The chief executive of a world-famous group of management consultants tried hard to convince me that top-level management executives should have as little knowledge as possible relative to the product. This great man really believed that this qualification enabled them to deal effectively with all business matters in a detached and uninhibited way."[51] The important thing is that the consultant in question—could it have been Bruce Henderson himself, whose firm, BCG, was at the time consulting for the British motorcycle industry?—was advancing a view of the nature of top management that, however improbable, is deliciously convenient for the consulting industry. If top managers need know little about the particular businesses in which their firms are engaged, then consultants need know nothing at all.

The matrix has another feature that makes it especially attractive from a consultant's point of view. It is aimed squarely at the one person who knows little about the businesses but nonetheless wishes to gain maximum control over them—namely, the CEO. In principle, it covers all of a corporation's activities. There is really nothing of interest in a corporation that exceeds its synthetic grasp. Thus, one good matrix can beget dozens of follow-on projects. Consultants can whip up a decent matrix in a matter of weeks or months; but they can spend years turning around dogs, burnishing stars, optimizing cash cows, and, above all, dealing with those pesky question marks.

The most general and far-reaching consequence of turning the discipline of strategy into a consulting product has been the creation of an artificial need for newness in the business—for fashions in strategy. In the 1980s, as it became clear that the matrix was losing its luster, BCG announced that "today time is at the cutting edge." The firm promptly began to tout time-based competition—the idea that, roughly speaking, the last one to market is a rotten egg—as the basis for all strategy worthy of the name.[52] By the early 1990s, however, time had evidently run out on the time-based movement. Facing spirited new competition from the "core competences" crowd, BCG's strategy gurus rolled out a "me too" product: "capabilities-based competition." Later in the same decade, as the dot-com bubble loomed, the very same gurus declared that "every business is an information business." As Roseanne Rosannadanna used to say, "If it's not one thing, it's another."

The strategy fads, like most management fads, run a predictable course, as many researchers have noted.[53] They begin with the euphoric conviction that the solution to the corporate world's troubles is on the horizon. A handful of leading corporations decide to test the new pastures. Initial reports are very promising, so the rest of the herd pushes through the gates. As the fad works its way through organizations, the enthusiasm becomes difficult to sustain. It becomes clear that not all problems will be solved by the four-box method, or whatever it is. The consultants notice that the opportunities for follow-on and implementation projects are diminishing. Once a critical number of large corporations have passed this tipping point, the market for the product begins to sour. The conventional wisdom then cries out that the world's corporations are at a strategic impasse and demands a new approach to strategy. It points to deficiencies in the earlier approach as the source of the malaise. Consultants are ready and waiting to come to the rescue all over again. Planned obsolescence turns out to be a desirable feature not just of cars, but of the products of the strategy industry as well.

Consultant, Consult Thyself

Machiavelli pointed out that if you are going to strike at a king, you had better strike to kill; you don't usually get a second chance. The rebellious partners at our firm would have been wiser to consult Machiavelli on this point than all the experts in the modern discipline of strategy.

Owen's response to the letter from the Gatwick 7 was masterful. Indeed, it reflected the same genius at manipulating organizational and legal processes that had propelled his ascent to the top of our cheery little corner of the consulting world. Rather than reject the petitioners' proposal for a "strategy review," he agreed wholeheartedly to the plan. He said we should establish three "task forces"—on "business strategy," "compensation," and "governance." But—big but—he declared that he, as the firm's managing director, had the prerogative to name the leaders of the task forces.

The rebels balked. In their act of rebellion, they had made the grave mistake of substituting a process for a decision; now they were asked to surrender control of that process to the very people the decision had been intended to eliminate in the first place. But, at a special board meeting, Owen produced a well-groomed corporate lawyer to confirm that, in his capacity as managing director, he did indeed have the authority to appoint the leaders of the task forces.

It came as something of a surprise to many of the shareholders that we had no direct control over such an elementary process in the firm that we notionally owned. Many people continue to believe that America is a capitalist country, but in fact the laws of the land are written for the benefit of managers, not owners. Our firm's own constitution, the shareholders' agreement, as it happens, was written for the benefit of one person in particular. As one partner later explained to the press, "The shareholders' agreement was a document written by lawyers to be read by businessmen, who wouldn't understand what actually was being said—in other words, a lot of the things in there that were added to offer comfort to the partners were meaningless legally." The one partner who knew the meaning of all the words to which we had agreed, of course, was Owen. He had made good use of that law degree he had picked up from Harvard. The law was almost always on his side.

Owen named the Prince of Darkness and two other of his closest friends to head each of the three task forces. He also hired an external consultant, a professor from Columbia University, to "assist in the process." The result of the rebellion was that we, the consultants, were going to experience a taste of the medicine that we all had long been dishing out to client organizations.

In retrospect it is astonishing, given how many times we as consultants had served CEOs in similar situations, where we were hired to pacify a collection of rebellious underlings, that so many of the partners agreed to go along with the new plan. The partners signed up not because they trusted Owen, however, but because they did not really trust one another. They were not quite ready to take blood oaths for the sake of a new revolution. Each submitted to the process in the belief that he or she might be able to master it and turn it to his own advantage.

Although he probably had no formal schooling in the subject, Owen had a firm, intuitive grasp of game theory. In co-opting the strategy review, he had skillfully set the stage for a version of the "prisoner's dilemma" among the partners. If all of the partners cooperated with one another, they could easily overthrow Owen and secure a mutual benefit. But if some of the partners betrayed the others and cut a deal with Owen, they potentially stood to profit greatly, while those who remained faithful to the revolution would lose everything. The highest card in Owen's hand was the same absence of mutual trust within the partnership that he had helped foster.

For over three months, the firm's business activities slowed dramatically as the partners met with their task forces, formed subcommittees, sat through long video conferences, and drafted hundreds of pages of charts and analyses. Owen's consultant went around interviewing all the partners and asking them questions that he had suggested. As the end of year 4 approached, the final reports were ready and, with the benefit of all that internal reviewing and external consulting, the firm at long last had a "strategy."

Strategy in the Classroom

The final resting place of the strategy business today is not the corporate planning departments or the consulting firms but the academy. Although the efforts of planners like Ansoff and consultants like Henderson are of heroic dimensions, strategy today is mostly what the professors tell us it is. Under ordinary circumstances, this fact would ensure that the discipline in question is a harmless affair, unlikely to do more than disturb the sleep of a few students for a semester or two. But in this particular case, the reality is disconcertingly different. The academics have achieved the remarkable feat of creating a discipline that is both bad for business and bad for society.

Michael Porter and His Pointed Framework

A conceptual framework is a way of breaking up the landscape of experience into meaningful pieces. It is intended to help individuals engaged in a particular practice to describe and analyze the context of their actions. It is often expected to provide normative guidance on what to do.

Some chefs will undoubtedly find the "five forces of cooking" framework supplied here useful in these ways. Student chefs in particular will be keen to master whatever secrets they imagine to be lurking in the framework. Academics, as is their wont, will inevitably dispute aspects of the framework and propose amendments or alternatives—such as, perhaps, a talent-based view of cooking. Most chefs, however, will immediately sense that the whole endeavor is an atrocious waste of time. A framework, they will point out, has never fried an egg.

The Five Forces of Cooking

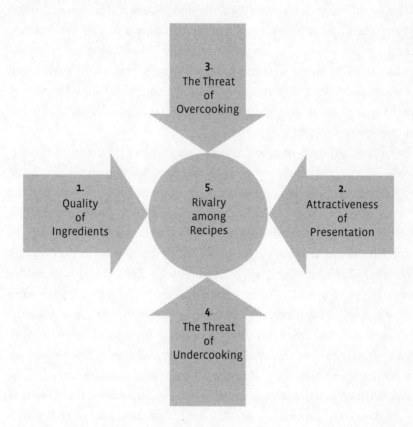

The most obvious way to read Porter's work on competitive strategy is as a conceptual framework. In the introduction to *Competitive Strategy*, he promises to deliver "a comprehensive framework of analytical techniques."[54] In an interview, he adds that his aim is to supply "frameworks rather than models."[55] A model makes predictions about outcomes of certain kinds of processes under specified conditions, and its value is measured against observed experience. A framework, on the other hand, justifies itself in terms of its utility. If it helps practitioners change the world in positive ways, then that is good enough.

That some management practitioners perceive Porter's framework to be useful is beyond doubt. Many academics, too, have found it useful—if only to make a living by disagreeing with it. Many more practitioners pay lip service to the framework—they pepper their conversations with "competitive advantages" and "barriers to entry"—but they don't actually use it (or, in many cases, even properly understand it). Most practitioners haven't the slightest interest in it; but then they are under no obligation to use it. On the whole, if one is concerned only to know that it is perceived to be useful by those who use it, then Porter's framework must count as a success. In fact, it is certainly the most successful such framework in the discipline of strategy, and arguably the most successful in all of management thought.

Perceived utility is, of course, a rather weak test of the merits of a framework. Astrological charts and voodoo dolls, too, have a high perceived utility for many people. Qualms about such frameworks arise from the fact that they do more than simply slice up experience into convenient chunks. They also involve propositions about the world that can be tested against experience—and that should be tested, if the framework is not to work potentially harmful effects, even on those who claim that it is useful for them. Porter's framework is a case in point. Embedded within it are a number of empirically and logically testable hypotheses that should be tested.

The claim that there are three generically successful business strategies, the claim that the analysis of industry sectors is the foundation for strategic analysis, the claim that all successful strategies involve the exploitation of structural barriers or market imperfections, the claim that strategy-making processes should aim at the singular goal of excess profits, the claim that strategy is embodied in a set of decisions made prior to action—all of these are not self-evident truths or reasonable stipulations in an anodyne framework, but hypotheses that should be tested against experience. It turns out, in fact, that these hypotheses are mostly false or unsubstantiated. In some contexts, to be sure, they are close enough to the truth to be useful; in other contexts, they give rise to systematic distortions of experience and harmful normative guidance. The problems with Porter's framework afflict the bulk of the strategy discipline that Porter launched and can be traced to the institutional setting within which the discipline emerged and achieved prominence.

The obvious way to test the theory about the three generic strategies for success would be to line up a series of companies that have adopted these three strategies and a number of companies that have not, and then track their relative performance in a future period. Probably no conclusive evidence on the matter exists, but there is no shortage of real-world cases that would seem to refute the theory by counterexample. In the very same years that Porter was insisting that a company had to be either the low-cost producer or the high-quality producer but not both, for example, a number of Japanese manufacturers proved to the dismay of their American counterparts that one could indeed be both.

The theory that the structure of an industry sector is what determines the possibility for excess profits can and has been studied by comparison of profitability rates among companies within sectors. The results, while not conclusive, are not promising for the theory. Although no one doubts that industry sectors have an important place in strategic thinking, a number of studies of company profitability have found that company-specific effects often matter much more than sector-specific effects.[56]

The more alarming problem here, however, is not that the theories are possibly untrue, but that Porter does not, as a rule, submit them to test. On the contrary, they function within his work as nonfalsifiable propositions. Porter deduces the theory about the three generic strategies, for example, not from a study of firm behavior but from an analysis of the framework he puts forth for categorizing the competitive forces in an industry. Thus, we are asked to believe in the theory because it follows in a purportedly logical way from his assumptions about the generic structure of markets. (It does not help his case, incidentally, that the deductions he offers are weak. He asserts with little cogent argument that the low-cost strategy will create a barrier to entry, for example, and then turns around and acknowledges that such barriers can rapidly succumb to "industry evolution.") Porter likewise defends his industry-sector approach largely by conceptual fiat: it is simply part of his framework.

This tendency to defend a questionable theory on the basis of a non-falsifiable framework reaches its unfortunate climax in Porter's presentation of his most important idea: that the structural barriers that protect a position of "sustainable competitive advantage" are the sole basis for excess profits and thus the logical object of all strategic thought. This general theory of competitive advantage could, in principle, be framed as a testable theory. One could, for example, identify a collection of firms that possess an attribute called "sustainable competitive advantage," as well as a control group whose members do not, and then measure their relative performance over time. But Porter instead presents his theory as a deduction from the fundamental axiom of his conceptual framework.

The axiom on which all of Porter's discipline of strategy rests is that excess profits always derive from market imperfections. Mere "operational efficiency," he cautions, by way of contrast, provides no sustainable basis for excess profits. On the contrary, it may lead to the "self-inflicted wound" of "hyper-competition," in which companies whittle one another's margins to the bone as they drive a market toward perfection.[57] It is only insofar as a company can shelter its activities from competition that it can claim excess profits. In cruder terms: according to Porter, the only real money is monopoly money.

As axioms go, Porter's fits into a category that one might call "definitional." That is to say, in his world excess profits and the class of market imperfections that give rise to excess profits ultimately become analytically identical. To make excess profits (over the long run, discounting for temporary irregularities due to business cycles, company-specific operational idiosyncrasies, and so on) is, by definition, to occupy a position in such an imperfect market, and to occupy a position in such an imperfect market is to make excess profits (or substandard profits, if one is caught on the wrong side of the imperfection). To say that a company has "sustainable competitive advantage" is thus merely to restate the fact that it makes excess profits.

The problem for Porter is that, though such a definitional axiom may belong to a conceptual framework and may *explain* excess profits, it does nothing to *predict* them. It does not give us a set of attributes independent of the concept of excess profits that will allow us to predict their occurrence. It boils down to the equivalent of saying, "If you take the ingredients you need and mix them according to the best recipe you can find, then you will have a great meal." When Porter cites real-world cases that appear to confirm his "theory" of competitive advantage, in fact he is merely celebrating coincidences between empirical data points and the contours of his preconceived framework. He is saying: "Look at Chef Pierre! He is using great recipes and great ingredients and his meals are great. My theory is true!"

This confusion between explanation and prediction afflicts almost the entire discipline of strategy and sheds light on one of its more paradoxical features. As anyone with more than a few pages' worth of familiarity with the genre will know, the strategists' theories are 100% accurate in hindsight. Case study after case study shows that XYZ Corporation, for example, succeeded because it had established a sustainable competitive advantage (or did whatever it is that the strategist insists is the right thing to do). Porter's writings are replete with interesting examples of companies that succeeded in generating long-term excess profits by ensconcing themselves securely behind protective barriers. Yet, when casting their theories into the future, the strategists as a group perform abysmally. Although Porter himself wisely avoids forecasting, those who wish to avail themselves of his framework do not have the luxury of doing so, for it is the very purpose of the framework to predict the future outcome of strategic decisions. And it is safe to say that the number of failed companies that were once credited by one strategist or another with having a sustainable competitive advantage substantially exceeds the number of successes. The point is not that the strategists lack clairvoyance; it's that their theories aren't really theories—they are "just-so" stories whose only real contribution is to make sense of the past, not to predict the future.

By reducing his principal thesis—that strategy is all about the search for structural barriers—to an axiomatic part of his system, Porter appears to immunize it from critique. And yet it should be critiqued, for there is good reason to think that it is not just wrong but dangerous. In the theoretical landscape Porter describes, all strategy worthy of the name involves avoiding competition and seeking out monopoly profits. Strategy is therefore all about figuring out how to secure profits *without* having to make a better product, work harder, or be smarter. It is a form of cheating—a way of doing better than the merits alone would allow. In the real world, however, plenty of companies and plenty of people skip the search for monopoly money and succeed instead by adopting the "strategies" of making a better product, working harder, or being smarter. Porter's framework for the discipline of strategy isn't just an epistemological black hole; it's antisocial and bad for business. It accomplishes the unlikely feat of goading business leaders to do wrong both to their shareholders and to their fellow human beings.

To be clear, the concern here is with a conceptual tendency inherent in Porter's framework. Michael Porter the person, as it happens, has shown keen concern with antitrust issues and anticompetitive practices. He has argued that the "competitive advantage" of nations depends on the effectiveness of their antitrust regulation, and he has further encouraged antitrust regulators to look well beyond the usual measures in gauging the competitive health of a sector and of proposed mergers and acquisitions. It is curious, however, that in hopes of providing assistance to regulators, he offers them, too, his five-forces framework for assessing the strength of competition in industry sectors. This, of course, is precisely what his predecessors in IO economics proposed to do—before Porter turned the discipline upside down to help companies seek out and create uncompetitive markets.

In his attempt to conflate an axiomatic framework with a predictive theory, Porter overplays his hand in a way that obscures one of the insights embedded in his premises. The most immediate and important implication of Porter's axiomatic framework is not that companies should seek out competitive advantage but that they should avoid competitive disadvantage. The two are not the same thing: showing up for a job interview naked will incur a competitive disadvantage (in most cases), for example; but showing up properly attired doesn't usually amount to an advantage. From a theoretical standpoint, avoiding competitive disadvantages is easy and follows in an analytic way from Porter's basic premises. If all the firms in a sector benefit from scale economies, for example, then it is a matter of simple deduction to show that a new entrant operating a subscale facility will find itself at a competitive disadvantage.

Finding a sustainable competitive advantage, from a theoretical standpoint, is much harder—indeed, despite Porter's best efforts, it may well be impossible from a purely deductive point of view. For, inasmuch as the underlying framework includes the assumption that markets always tend toward perfection (or what Porter calls "hyper-competition"), then all barriers are in some sense temporary or artificial and do not follow analytically from the original premises of the framework. Attempts to claim a sustainable competitive advantage require a surreptitious synthetic judgment—that is, one that relies in part on a claim that cannot be justified within the framework. In a very abstract sense, this is the same logical trouble that bedevils Ansoff's manic conceptualizing of strategy. Strategy makes sense as a project only in the context of uncertainty, or, more generally, in a context where pure reason will not deliver a definitive answer to the question "what is to be done?" But a purely rational framework, such as those offered by Ansoff and Porter, leaves no space for such "irrationality." So the framework solves strategic problems only in a context where there is no possibility that such problems will arise.

According to Porter, who implicitly judges the importance of a task according to its theoretical complexity, avoiding competitive disadvantages is a nontheoretical, nonstrategic, and merely operational task, distinct from the higher-order (and theoretically problematic) quest for sustainable competitive advantage. From a practical standpoint, however, there is nothing trivial about avoiding competitive disadvantage. In fact, one could argue that this is the principle task of management. Avoiding mistakes, getting things right, and making sure everyone gets dressed in the morning may not make for a sexy business of strategy, but in some ways it is what management is about.

Porter's theory that strategists must aim for the singular goal of excess profits is a version of Taylor's dogma of the singular metric. It follows in a deductive way from the premises of his framework, but it has no foundation in experience. In practice, individuals and organizations pursue multiple goals, and just about no one succeeds by measuring all potential decisions against a single, scalar metric. People and organizations behave this way not because they are irrational (necessarily) but because they lack the information and the certainty required to organize all of their activities according to a single metric. The ultimate measure of success in business may well be profits or some other such singular metric, but the strategies and actions that get firms to their destination can almost never be deduced from the metric.

The fallacy of the singular metric, incidentally, reveals itself in a curious way in a paradox that emerges from contemplation of Porter's framework. Since Porter's framework looks the same no matter who is looking at it, everyone looking at it should come to the same conclusions about the relative strength of competitive forces and hence the prospects for excess profits for all possible positions in all industry sectors. So everyone should choose to invest in the same positions in the same sectors. But if everyone invests in the same things, the excess profits will disappear. The paradox arises only because we assume that everyone has access to equal information and then, by virtue of the deductive analytic framework, comes to the same conclusion. But in actual experience people do not have the same information, nor, given the uncertainties, will they reliably apply any framework to arrive at the same conclusions. So they will inevitably pursue a multiplicity of strategies to arrive at the same goal of excess profits. Indeed, strategy is really only possible in such a context of uncertainty and lack of information. But, in precisely such a context, Porter's analytic framework lacks its crucial inputs and therefore no longer works.

Porter's undisclosed theories govern not just the nature of successful strategies, but also the nature of successful strategy-making processes. Implicit in Porter's approach is the idea that strategy making is a decision-making process that takes place prior to and largely independent of any action. As with Ansoff, the output of such a process is principally a set of commitments to do business in a specified set of markets and products in a specified way (low cost, differentiated product and so on). Although some strategy making may occur in this way, it seems likely that much—perhaps most—does not. Most successful strategies emerge through action; they become perspicuous only in hindsight. And this play-it-by-ear kind of strategy making does not result necessarily from a lack of foresight; it often stems from a healthy recognition that the world is generally too complex for our simple plans.

Also implicit in Porter's approach is the idea that successful strategies involve developing a comprehensive theory of the world, or at least of an industry sector. As Porter presents it, strategy making seems like a problem in calculus. You research all of the parameters about an industry sector, put them into the equation, and out pops your strategy. In classroom settings, it is easy enough to fill out a diagram of the five forces in action for any tidy and prepared "case." In practice, strategy formulation *never* follows the logic of a universal method. To most people with practical business experience, in fact, Porter's framework doesn't seem wrong so much as idealistic. A framework such as Porter's may include useful reminders (watch out for product substitutes!) and important insights (the threat of new entrants may keep prices down even when actual competitors don't), and it can certainly help structure research and discussion. But in the real world, no single framework can be counted on to deliver reasonable results in all contexts. Some strategies may call for an analysis of 83 forces; others—more likely to be successful—boil down to one simple idea. The choice of framework, and not what any particular framework says, *is* the analysis.

The Resource-Based View, or How to Be Good at Being Good

The "Resource-Based View," or "core competences" theory, that claims to supplant Porter's theory of competitive advantage offers no escape from the epistemological quagmire of the academic discipline of strategy. Like Porter's theory, the RBV rests on the axiom that excess profits arise from market imperfections—the difference being that it locates such imperfections inside the firm, in its distinctive and inimitable competences. By analogy with Porter, however, the RBV creates an analytic identity between a company's competences and its ability to generate excess profits. When a company does well, according to the exuberant RBV theorists, we know that this success must be on account of its unique culture, the one-of-a-kind interaction of its many parts, or, in sum, its ineffable it-ness. The "theory" here boils down to the tautological assertion that a company's ability to make money rests on its unique ability to make money. Like Porter's "theory" of competitive advantage, this explains everything and predicts nothing. When the RBV theorists cite company after company that has succeeded by building its resources or competences, they aren't supplying evidence for a theory; they are merely expressing joy at seeing their preconceived interpretive framework reflected back to them in the world.

Hamel and Prahalad, proponents of the "core competence" version of RBV, should really serve as cautionary examples of the kind of overconfidence that irrefutable conceptual frameworks tend to imbue in their adherents. In the 1990 article that launched their movement, they reserve their highest praise for Japanese electronics manufacturer NEC. In the subsequent decade and a half, NEC has turned in an underwhelming performance.[58] In their 1994 book, *Competing for the Future*, Hamel and Prahalad spill the ink for, among others, General Magic, a venture that aspired to unite the world with intelligent personal communication devices. General Magic vanished like pixie dust with the emergence of the Internet and cell phones. "[Hamel and Prahalad] are probably as good as there is in their field," Bill Gates commented in 1998. But "every example they gave, with the exception of Hewlett-Packard, was a total joke."[59] By the time Gates made this comment, however, Hamel had moved on, now touting Enron as America's "most innovative company."

The Rules of the Game Theorists

The work of the game theorists who followed in Porter's footsteps offers perhaps the best illustration of the nefarious consequences wrought by the academic conquest of the discipline of strategy. In *Co-opetition*, Brandenburger and Nalebuff choose an interesting set of heroes. They lavish much attention on Nintendo, for example, the Japanese game maker that, for a time in the 1990s, achieved a market capitalization comparable to that of Toyota. Nintendo, the authors crow, showed itself a master of game theory in the marketplace as much as on the video screen. By imposing harsh conditions on its software suppliers, engineering shortages of its own products, manipulating retail prices, and willfully holding back on the development of better gaming technology, Nintendo established just the kind of sustainable competitive advantage that academic theorists have always championed. The company's enormous profits, the authors gleefully explain, derived from "the added value of a monopoly."[60]

After joyfully detailing how Nintendo screwed its suppliers and overcharged customers for inferior products, the game theorists note indignantly that "some people called Nintendo's practices into question."[61] "Some people" turns out to be—the horror!—"a Democratic congressman." The authors fight back by quoting a writer for *Barron's* insisting that Nintendo was "a real business success story." (In an endnote they acknowledge that Nintendo eventually paid a settlement to the FTC over its pricing policies.)

Other heroes of the game theorists include De Beers, the secretive worldwide cartel that has kept diamond prices artificially high for decades, and Microsoft. On the other hand, IBM, which allowed Microsoft to corner the market in operating systems and then compounded the error by opting for open architecture for its PCs, counts as a sucker, in their estimation. (The fact that consumers enjoy computer hardware that to this day is cheaper and more advanced than the software that runs on it does not appear to enter into the authors' analyses of the outcomes of the games in question.)

For those companies not in a position to secure a de facto (but perfectly legal!) monopoly along the lines of Nintendo or De Beers, the game theorists offer a number of proposals that they promise are almost as good. "Complex pricing schemes," they point out, "create a fog that obscures the true price."[62] Their favorite scheme is the loyalty program. The American Airlines frequent flier program that got it all started they describe as "a stroke of genius."[63]

Why? Most analysts had thought that American's frequent flier program became moot as soon as Delta and the other airlines copied it. But in fact, the authors argue, the effect of such programs is that customers are less likely to switch from their preferred airline to another in response to a price cut. Thus, thanks to American's AAdvantage program, Delta has less incentive to lower its fares; thanks to Delta's SkyMiles, American is less likely to lower its fares. And, still more joy, both airlines can even start to raise fares, knowing that customers are less likely to leave in the event of a price increase. In essence, by atomizing individual consumers, loyalty programs create soft, micromonopolies on the market to individuals. The result for the airlines is "greater price stability," the authors say, by which they mean higher fares. They happily chalk it up as a "win-win" for American and Delta—never mind the fact that, according to their own analysis, consumers collectively end up paying more in exchange for having expressed their individual loyalties.

Of course, as every business traveler knows, the airline programs work in no small measure because businesses pay the fares while travelers collect the miles.[64] "So are bosses the losers?" the game theorists ask. "Not necessarily. Frequent-flyer miles are a tax-free way for companies to compensate employees who undertake a lot of business travel."[65] Thus, according to the experts, in the profoundly unlikely event that an extra tens of thousands of dollars in business class fares is your company's way of gifting you a once-a-year trip to Hawaii, then it is the taxpayer who foots the bill! So it's a win-win all around—except for those who pay taxes.

The authors' enthusiasm for this kind of "strategy" reaches fever pitch in their discussion of General Motors' credit card. The car company's program of offering discounts to customers who use its credit card they qualify as "a runaway success."[66] Ford's copycat move counts as "healthy imitation."[67] As in the case of the airline loyalty programs, the cause for celebration is that the competing card programs allowed GM to collude with Ford in raising the prices of their cars. It was a case of price fixing without any of the untidy legal complications.

So, are car buyers losers? "Not necessarily," the authors cheerfully assert. "Competition sinks sunk costs . . . If manufacturers can't earn prof-its today, they don't invest, and consumers don't get better and cheaper cars tomorrow. So, perhaps over the longer run, higher prices may lead to a win-win outcome for both the automakers and their customers."[68] According to this kind of reasoning, consumers should be clamoring for higher car prices. In fact, they should be demanding that Congress find ways to funnel extra profits to car companies and shelter them from competition, since car companies are evidently so good at investing the extra money in consumer-friendly ways.

As the game theorists praise one company after another for corner-ing markets and duping customers, one can't help but wonder, whatever happened to the long arm of the law? To their credit—or perhaps on their lawyers' advice—the authors decide to confront the legal cloud sur-rounding their work directly. "To our knowledge," they say, "none of the contracts we've discussed raises anti-trust concerns."[69] To be on the safe side, however, they recommend you check with your lawyers too.

This is a good thing, because in fact by their own admission, many of the contracts they discuss do indeed raise antitrust concerns. After championing buying coalitions as the preferred game theory method of ganging up on suppliers, they sheepishly add, "American antitrust law does put some constraints on buying coalitions."[70] After lauding a kind of contract known as a "most favored customer," or MFC, as a way for companies to gain control of their markets "almost through the back door," they let slip that "MFCs are a practice that has come under quite intense anti-trust scrutiny."[71] After putting forth their bizarre position that anticompetitive behavior is good for consumers because it allows companies to make ungodly profits that they will then surely invest in socially constructive ways, they add, "We're not convinced that current U.S. antitrust law appreciates this perspective."[72] In sum, their position is that everything they propose is perfectly legal, and the law deserves to be broken anyway.

As is the custom in the management theory literature, Brandenburger and Nalebuff organize their ideas about strategy under an easily remembered acronym: PARTS (which stands for *p*layers, *a*dded value, *r*ules, *t*actics, *s*cope). At the conclusion of their book they ask, "Is PART the whole of strategy?" Answer: "In principle, it is."[73] Thus, the lesson seems to be that befuddling your customers with complex pricing schemes and concocting tricky loyalty programs is what making cars, for example, is all about. The game theory approach to strategy is, in this sense, simply a more pronounced version of the theory of competitive advantage and its kin. Strategy, in this understanding, is about how to arrange a cartel without having to enter a smoke-filled backroom, how to organize a monopoly without going to the trouble of bribing government officials, and, in general, how to make extraordinary profits without having to make extraordinary products.

The game theorists inadvertently supply good evidence that such an approach to strategy is as bad for business as it would seem to be for society at large. While GM and Ford occupied themselves with their game theory–approved credit card "strategies," Toyota was busy building better cars. In the decade after Brandenburger and Nalebuff lauded its "runaway success" in the credit card business, GM lost more than half of its market value. Ford, which elected to discontinue its credit card about one year after the game theorists had praised the idea as "healthy imitation," performed somewhat better, losing less than half of its market value. Meanwhile, Toyota, which does not offer credit cards, has doubled its share price and has overtaken both of the American firms to become the largest automaker in the world.

Idols of the Marketplace: Why Academics Manufacture Bad Ideas

How could it be that clean-cut professors like Porter, Brandenburger, and Nalebuff—leaders in those citadels of capitalism, the Harvard Business School and the Yale School of Management—should have become scofflaws and the scourge of free markets? It is a safe bet that these three professors are nice guys. The feckless character of the discipline that they and their colleagues created cannot be the result of any personality disorders. Rather, it must emerge from the institutional setting within which their work takes place.

As Porter understood from his time in the Department of Economics, the foundation for sustainable academic advantage is always a body of general theory. Unfortunately, a general theory that can reliably predict the success of strategies for companies engaged in free and fair competition to make superior returns is very hard to come by. Companies are always trying new ways to make money, after all, and there is much reason to doubt that all of their efforts can be usefully marshaled under one theory. Anyone who did discover such a theory, furthermore, would undoubtedly become instantly rich. But a general theory that can explain how and why a company operating in monopoly or quasi-monopoly conditions can make superior returns is quite feasible. In other words: a theory about how to win in life is hard; a theory about how to cheat is, analytically speaking, a cinch. People in search of tenure, then, are well advised to stick to cheating.

In the case of the game theorists, the antisocial dimension of their work follows from the same analytic bias combined with a more pedestrian case of technophilia. They've chanced upon a neat little analytic tool that has a certain, limited utility in business contexts. They aren't rooting for greedy companies to inflict higher prices and inferior products on consumers; they're just thrilled to have the opportunity to watch their shiny gizmo in action.

The analytic bias of the strategy discipline results in part from the fact that the audience the professors seek most to impress is themselves. In disciplines, such as strategy, where facts are sometimes hard to see through the forest of theories, this inward focus can have alarming consequences. A sure sign that strategy has gone off the rails of reasonable inquiry is the emergence of heroic authority, or "guru," figures within the field. In an encomium for Michael Porter, for example, one prominent proponent of the Resource-Based View recalls with amazement how his colleagues reacted when Porter attacked his theory at a conference: "They congratulated me! While I was focusing on Porter's criticisms of the theory, they saw the bigger picture—that by critiquing the Resource-Based View, Porter was actually beginning to legitimate it as a theoretical perspective. But only Michael Porter could have wielded such an influence."[74] As a general rule, when the truth of a theory (or the "legitimacy" of a "theoretical perspective") is judged not with reference to the facts but according to the state of mind of some unique figure of authority, then what you have is not a discipline but a cult. This kind of authority-based theorizing is what typically turns academic fields into swamps of self-referential babble that have no meaning for those on the outside.

The academicians' drive for monopoly profits, however, stems from more than just the usual foibles of scholastics. It also reflects the fact that business school academics naturally fall captive to a managerial viewpoint. When Porter laments the horror of "hyper-competition," he expresses a distinctly managerial frustration in the face of turbulent markets. Capitalists, as a rule, don't crave "sustainable competitive advantage"; they just want a good return on their money over a reasonable period of time. Only managers want to build something that can withstand forever the forces of the market. The game theorists, too, seem to side unconsciously with their friends in management. As they hail one "win-win" situation after another, it becomes clear that the winners in question are always the management teams of the companies under discussion, and never consumers, the public, or even shareholders. The characteristically managerial apprehension about unruly markets that impels the work of today's academic strategists reflects the same anxiety that led Taylor's disciple Henry Gantt to propose a cartelization of the economy, that drove Mayo into the arms of the Rockefellers, and that induced Ansoff to attempt the implementation of Soviet communism within the American military-industrial complex.

The bond between academic strategists and the managers they serve is more than merely emotional. The most successful strategy professors make most of their money working as consultants to many of the same large corporations whose stories they celebrate in the pages of their books. Porter founded a consulting company that has generated hundreds of millions of dollars in fees from corporate clients (as well as from clients in the nonprofit sector). Brandenburger and Nalebuff advertise their book with a list of a dozen brand-name firms that they have served as consultants. One can hardly fault these professors for playing well the game that the entire business school system is designed to play. The business schools and their various disciplines would not exist as we know them today if large corporations did not contribute to school endowments, fund their research projects, and consume the graduates of their programs. So perhaps it is not surprising that when the academics apply their theories to real cases, they tend to choose the cases where corporations and their managers are the heroes.

The drive for monopoly profits and the conflation of capitalism and managerialism drives the academic discipline of strategy toward the end point for which the entire business of strategy has been striving since its inception in the corner office of the Lockheed Corporation: the triumph of management over markets. Frederick Winslow Taylor set the agenda by declaring management the master of physical labor. Elton Mayo added the human element, or the leadership of society and culture, to management's domain. In defining management as the function of maximizing excess profits (or shareholder value), the strategists have sought to bring the allocation of all resources in society—the ultimate control over the very ability to make useful things—under the sway of management expertise.

The business of strategy achieves its clearest expression in the shareholder-value-maximization model of management that dominates the business schools. According to this model, management alone knows how to make money; so the logical thing for shareholders to do is hand all their cash over to management, along with an incentive plan that encourages management to give some of it back. This dogma is now so ingrained in modern business school practice that it should perhaps be recited as a catechism for all entering students. Its chief consequence is to reinforce students' belief that the only obligation they or their companies have to the rest of the universe is to pursue their own self-interest in the narrowest financial terms conceivable. It confirms them in the conviction that whatever is legal is ethical. (And if it isn't legal, check with your lawyer.)

The attempt to turn strategy into a rigorous academic discipline has done considerable violence to the core value in almost all strategic thinking—the fundamental idea that one should always keep an eye on the big picture. Seeing the big picture means seeing not just what is, but what can be. It is, by its nature, a synthetic activity, not an analytic one. It is essentially creative, not reductive. It happens in an imperfectly knowable world, and it is risky. It is what we mean by *entrepreneurial*, in the best sense of the word. The academic discipline of strategy, like the business school system from which it emerges and the managerial perspective it represents, is fundamentally analytic, reductive, and risk-averse. By the default settings of all such institutions, it is bound to prepare people to become bureaucrats rather than entrepreneurs. We can nonetheless take some comfort in the knowledge that the core value of strategy will surely survive the academic onslaught. After all, there is nothing that a blackboard can do to halt the arrival of spring.

The Market Value of Strategy

As one would expect from consultants, the "strategy" of our "strategy review" was delivered into the world in a screaming bundle of paper. The task forces produced hundreds of dazzling charts and graphs, veritable works of art, like mathematical sculptures, conjured out of numerical backwash of the firm's business activities. The presentations were full of sinuous curves and fulsome pronouncements, but they really signified only one thing. The essence of the firm's new strategy was that Owen's autocratic powers as managing director would be virulently enforced and the world beneath him would be divided into two viceroyalties, headed up by the Prince and Owen's other closest friend. If you wanted to buy a pencil, you needed approval from a member of the new triumvirate. The people who formerly thought of themselves as partners in the firm were now quite clearly to be regarded and treated as employees. In his memos, Owen talked about a "transition to a new management structure" as though we were merely rearranging the furniture in the office. But the situation was more like that of ancient Rome, circa 44 BCE. The Republic was dead, and the Empire was in the throes of a violent birth.

In a parody of a memo from Owen, dating from a few months after the strategy review, when I was no longer a member of the firm, an anonymous partner described the firm's new strategy as the "P3R Program:" "Purge the Firm of troublesome partners, Pacify those that remain, and Perpetuate and Reinforce the historical management structure." To which one should add an *S*, for "Sell the company," since, unbeknownst to the memo writer, the prospect of a sale played an important part in the execution of the other four letters.

The purge began very soon after the counterrevolution. Using their new imperial powers, Owen and his friends picked off the rebel partners one by one. Within six months, all of the Gatwick 7 and a large number of other partners, including me, had been forced out of the firm. In the cases I knew of, the purged partners left in the belief that they were being cheated of money they were owed, in the form of past-due bonuses, equity investments, and interests in the founders' fund.

Charles, who had played a central role in building the firm's European practice, went down without a fight. My impression was that he was too disgusted with the firm and its management to continue in a struggle whose outcome would be bleak in any case.

Roland, on the other hand, was hardly the kind to give up without a fight. Over the previous four years, he had hauled in tens of millions of dollars in revenues on behalf of the firm. So he cleaned off his old whale-hunting harpoon, as it were, stood to face his enemies, and demanded that they come at him in a manly way. After a bruising duel with the Prince of Darkness, he believed he had fought his way to an honorable exit. He was taken entirely by surprise when the knife hit him in the back. "I just don't understand it," he sputtered on the phone. "I had a deal with him. I looked him in the eye. We shook hands." He was soon engaged in litigation with the firm.

The most poignant case was that of Jim. In the last year of its existence, the firm made it into a *Fortune* magazine list of the 50 most desirable places to work, as ranked by graduating MBAs. The unexpected triumph, which put our humble establishment shoulder to shoulder with such giants of career aspiration as McKinsey, Proctor & Gamble, and General Electric, marked the pinnacle of Jim's achievement as the firm's chief recruiter. It was the visible record of his siren songs on campus. Two months before the list was published, however, in an emotionally wrenching scene for many members of the firm, Jim had been fired. The MBAs, as is their wont, were tracking yesterday's star. (One analyst shows that a good way to predict stock market movements is to track the percentage of Harvard Business School graduates who accept jobs in finance: if the number is below 10%, good times are ahead; if it exceeds 30%, a crash is looming.)[75]

The firm soon became the center of a storm of lawsuits, as the purged partners sought to recover their investments in the firm. Under Patrick's oversight, and with the eager assistance of Owen's legal counsel/family member, the firm preferred to invest the money in high-priced lawyers, who were evidently under instruction to make sure that the departing partners received as little as possible. Owen and Patrick were not about to forget the fact that the expelled partners had made attempts on their jobs.

The P3R "strategy," not surprisingly, turned out be a terrific exercise in self-destruction. As partners who had been important to the business were fired, clients naturally stopped doing business with the firm. Other partners, seeing where things were going, spontaneously purged themselves, taking their clients with them. Associates, sensing the turmoil in the senior ranks, mass-mailed their résumés and called around to their buddies in other firms in search of "development opportunities." As invariably happens in such cases, the best performers found their way out first. The firm had entered a death spiral.

In a panic, Owen ordered a decimation of the associates in the Roman fashion. One in every 10 had to go. As anyone who has spent any time in a managerial role knows, laying people off is one of the most difficult and important aspects of the job. No matter how much positive spin one puts on a layoff, it usually involves sacrificing the interest of the individual concerned for the good of the enterprise. The honesty, fairness, and competence one demonstrates in the task can have a huge impact on the morale of remaining staff and on relations with outside groups, such as labor groups and schools, not to mention former employees. When Owen orchestrated his layoffs, according to the memo writer, "Several of the most senior partners distanced themselves from this distasteful event by not being in the office, and may even have been on vacation. In remarkable displays of courage, many partners had their administrative assistants make the calls to set up termination interviews."

At the same time that he was ditching new associates, Owen also rescinded offers previously made to students who had not yet started work. This action forever ruined the firm's reputation with the schools, which in turn signaled to remaining staff that the partners saw no future in the company.

With the firm rapidly taking on water, the remaining partners decided that the logical thing to do was sell it to someone else. Owen hired another one of his friends from his former consulting life, a man named Al, to serve as the firm's new "communications director." Al's job was to communicate to potential buyers the firm's desire to be rescued from itself. The firm shortly contracted an investment bank, which went in search of kindhearted buyers—chiefly, it was presumed, other consulting firms.

The plan for a sale appeared to me to be a ruse. It proved useful in keeping at least some of the remaining partners and staff on board. It soon became apparent that no respectable buyer could be found. The rumors about the firm had already spread around the consulting world. Why would another firm buy into such a mess, when it could simply hire away any individual consultants it deemed worth having?

The parody memo distributed by an anonymous partner, written in the "royal 'we'" voice favored by Owen, describes the trajectory that had brought the firm to this point in its illustrious career:

Much speculation and rumor circulates in the Firm regarding the exact cause of our difficulties. Some suggest our obsession with destroying the opposition irrespective of the consequences has been our downfall (Schoolyard bully theory). Others observe that our automatic recourse to litigation irrespective of the merits of the situation, the likelihood of our success, and the magnitude of our legal expenses has been ill-advised (Win at any cost theory). Some believe that our desire for "vengeance" against perceived wrongs at McKinsey has blinded us to reality (Get even theory). Still others note that our "friends and family" program may have gotten out of hand (Pay for loyalty theory). Others look carefully at our frequent 4×5 meetings and shake their heads at our fixation with quantitative measures (Analysis paralysis theory). Finally, many point to the proliferation of offices and the hiring of non-productive or self-serving partners and directors (many of whom are former or failed

senior consultants from our previous firms or bored and arrogant
former executives from our previous clients) as being at least part of
the problem. ("I need to be a BSD [Big Swinging Dick]" theory).

I gathered from the memo that the pacification, perpetuation, and
reinforcement components of the P3R program were progressing in a
predictably bloody way:

> We will shortly be subdividing the four office units into subdivi-
> sions, planned communities, and—eventually—strategic hamlets
> (as described by Neil Sheehan in his book *A Bright Shining Lie*). We
> will then pacify each hamlet by means of special deals, threats, and
> use of appropriate *force majeur* in order to assure the maintenance
> of the current political environment and the continuation of the
> current management team. Members of unpacifiable hamlets will
> be grouped into retirement communities.

Although I was no longer with the firm at this point, I can see that
behind the memo is quite a sense of sadness about the firm's devolution.
Eventually, the grim reality proves too much for the parodist, and the
memo breaks from its sarcasm:

> The majority of the partners with whom we have talked see the
> situation for exactly what it is—the inevitable consequence of the
> actions of a management team which is attempting to function
> beyond its capabilities and which has lost the respect and trust of
> the partners and the staff at all levels . . .
>
> [The firm] grew out of a belief that fundamentally different individ-
> uals could learn to support each other and respect each other precisely
> because of their differences. But when management lost perspective
> on its own contribution to our success, through its attitude and then
> through its own compensation awards, it was inevitable that mutual
> respect would disappear. The truly unusual partners who created the
> *spirit* of the Firm have all been terminated or have departed.

Not long after this memo was written, I read in the *Wall Street Journal*
that, against all odds, the firm had found a purchaser. The lucky buyer

was a relatively new Internet consulting company that had recently acquired a string of software and web consulting firms. The offer was worth an astounding $300 million in the form of the richly valued shares of the acquiring company. The offer took me by surprise, not just because of the ludicrous amount of money involved, but because I knew very well that the members of the firm collectively had about as much expertise on Internet-related subjects as the average high school graduating class. When I read the rationale for the purchase in the public documents, surprise turned to a good belly laugh.

The purchaser avowed that it was buying a "strategy consulting" firm in order to complement its web consulting with some expertise in "strategy." Three hundred million dollars turned out to be the market value for a big fat word, *strategy*, sitting on top of a pile of old presentations and broken promises whose actual value was exactly zero. This remarkable transaction should serve as a useful data point to measure just how much people will pay for something that does not exist.

Sometime later, after things had come to their inevitable conclusion, communications director Al told the press, "Here was [the acquirer] buying strategy with an inflated stock price, and, at that level, the word 'strategy' meant nothing. So I think you look back and say we were using language at a level of abstraction."

It got even better. I learned that the former CEO and "chief strategist" of the company that believed so fervently in "strategy," a 28-year-old man named Joe, had recently resigned under pressure. In a twist that surely must be emblematic of this very peculiar moment in the history of the modern capital markets, it turns out that Joe also believed that many terrestrial technologies, including semiconductors, fiber optics, and lasers, had been brought to earth by aliens.[76] He would know: he had an intimate conversation with an alien—"a remarkable being, clothed in brilliant white light"—or so he reported on his website at the time. When the company found out about his extraterrestrial activities, Joe voluntarily stepped down as CEO and took the title of "chief strategist." After the press broke the news, however, he resigned altogether and dedicated himself to promoting awareness of humankind's debt to its alien benefactors.

IV. Striving for Excellence

Tom Peters Talks to God

I t was 6:00 a.m. and Tom Peters was mad as hell. His pen hovered angrily over a blank pad of paper. He had just days to condense 700 slides and thousands of miles' worth of first-class travel into a presentation on Organizational Effectiveness short enough not to irritate the notoriously short-tempered CEO of PepsiCo. From the McKinsey office on the forty-eighth floor of the Bank of America building, he looked out over the San Francisco Bay for inspiration. "I was genuinely, deeply, sincerely, and passionately pissed off!" he says in an interview almost 20 years after that morning in 1979.[1] It was good to be mad. "Tom's not happy unless he's madder than hell about something," says his coauthor Robert Waterman.[2]

He was mad at more than just another dyspeptic CEO. He was mad at his erstwhile client, the Xerox Corporation, a bureaucratic monster where brainy MBAs played number games with each other while their company churned out inferior products. He was mad at Peter Drucker, the man he (strangely) blamed for the invention of that senseless implement of torture known as the modern American corporation. "In my mind, Peter Drucker was the enemy." He was mad at his bosses, a band of flaming narcissists from McKinsey's New York office who sneered at the San Francisco office as a "weak sister" that never made any money. "We were the closest thing McKinsey had to hippies." (Being a hippie at McKinsey meant that you didn't have to wear a hat; but Peters and his fellow countercultural types still sported the regulation black suits and thin red ties.) The New Yorkers had just assigned themselves the big internal project on Business Strategy ("please note the capital letters"), leaving for Peters and his fellow freaks "this other little dipshit project" on Organizational Effectiveness.

Peters was in his late thirties at the time and had recently completed an MBA and PhD in organizational behavior at Stanford (he was mad at his professors for the usual reasons). As a Navy Seabee before that, he had been deployed twice in Vietnam and "survived a tour in the Pentagon." (He was supremely pissed off at Robert McNamara—"the Peter Drucker of the Pentagon.") The guiding theme of his fitful career thus far was the overwhelming fear of staying in one place. He later confessed that he dreaded the thought that he might end up like his father, a faithful employee of the gas company in Baltimore, walking through the same door to the same office for 41 solid years.

As he sat there on that morning in the Bank of America tower, in his black suit and thin red tie, chained to his desk, stewing in resentments and frustrations—the very picture of corporate humankind—it is safe to say that the young Peters had no idea what the future held in store for him. How could this choleric company man have guessed that one day soon he would be able to command up to $100,000 a day in speaking fees, appear in boxer shorts on the cover of one of his own books, and raise alpacas on a farm in Vermont?

Peters took his gaze off the San Francisco Bay and closed his eyes. He leaned forward over his desk. "Then . . . I wrote down eight things on a pad of paper. Those eight things haven't changed since that moment." Two and a half years later, they were published as the eight fundamental principles of *In Search of Excellence: Lessons from America's Best Run Companies*, a book that Peters coauthored with Waterman. Peters still speaks of that moment with a reverent awe. It was an epiphany—a conversation with the god of organizational effectiveness.

The Eight Attributes of Successful Companies

1. A bias for action
2. Staying close to the customer
3. Autonomy and entrepreneurship
4. Productivity through people

5. Hands-on, value-driven

6. Stick to the knitting

7. Simple form, lean staff

8. Simultaneous loose-tight properties[3]

All eight of the lessons of excellence revolve around a single insight: "Treating people—not money, machines, or minds—as the natural resources may be the key to it all."[4] *Excellence* marks a wholehearted return to the humanistic tradition of management thought. It is dedicated to the idea that "people are a really important part of business and . . . you can't motivate them by controlling and tyrannizing them." It champions freedom over authority; collaboration over coercion; intuition over rationality; spontaneity over the plan; culture and values over lines and boxes; the individual human being over the bureaucracy; and, in general, everything soft over everything hard. It often reads, as the authors acknowledge, as the kind of book Elton Mayo would have liked to write, if only he could have mustered the energy. "I was scratching the Douglas McGregor itch," Peters admits in his later interview.

It does not necessarily diminish Peters' achievement to note that Mayo, McGregor, and even Drucker—notwithstanding Peters' intemperate aspersions—had pretty much said it all before. What was new and radically different about *Excellence* wasn't the message, but the effect. In the earlier world of management thought, a book that sold a few thousand copies counted as a blockbuster. The publishers of *Excellence*, swept up with passion for their product (and backed up by assurances that the authors would find suitable ways to dispose of many copies), scheduled a wildly optimistic initial print run of 15,000. The people at McKinsey chortled as they ceded to Peters and Waterman the royalties for any potential sales over 50,000 copies. But *Excellence* went on to sell *6 million* copies—and counting. Since its publication, Peters has given, by his own estimate, more than 2,500 speeches before 2 to 3 million people in 63 countries. According to the blurb on the back of one of his more recent efforts, he is "the guru of gurus of management." "We live in a Tom Peters world," *Fortune* magazine exclaims.[5]

It has often been noted that *Excellence* benefited from a timely birth. The book appeared in the midst of a recession, following a spate of articles and television shows on the Japanese conquest of the world economy, at a time when Americans hankered for a celebration of homegrown excellence. But this circumstantial analysis misses the essence of the book's achievement. *Excellence* did not satisfy a demand as much as create one. It inaugurated the management guru industry as we know it today. Before *Excellence*, management theory was a "business-to-business" sector connecting a few hundred scribblers with an elite involved in the management of large corporations. Tom Peters brought management theory out of the boardroom and into the living room. He made it into a *consumer* business. "All business is show business," Peters explains in his second book, evidently generalizing from personal experience.[6] Many others have since entered this new, multibillion-dollar management-entertainment industry, but all are imitations of the master to some degree or other.

It should have been Peter Drucker, say some commentators—not least, Peter Drucker himself. If there is a convention in the annals of commentary on the management guru business, it is that Drucker is "the top dog" of the industry—the "good" guru who makes up for all the charlatans in the sector.[7] Drucker certainly says all the right things, and he is proficient enough (if perhaps not quite as stylish) in the bold reversals and epigrammatic pronouncements required of a guru. Perhaps on account of his origins in a more stratified Europe or his early work at the headquarters of General Motors, however, Drucker never quite breaks free from the top-down perspective of traditional management thought. Peters is the more able psychologist. He understands his audience; he feels their pain. He always looks at management from the bottom up, from the perspective of the underdog at the fringe office fed up with the casual brutality of the headquarters types. He knows where to find the heartstrings of corporate humankind, and he yanks on them for all he is worth.

Drucker did not always welcome being upstaged. Peters made it look too easy, he complained:[8] "All you had to do was put that book under your pillow and it will get done," he sniffed to reporters.[9] "Half of the 2 or 3 million books they sold were graduation presents for high school graduates," he added. "When Aunt Mary has to give that nephew of hers a high school graduation present and she gives him *In Search of Excellence,* you know that management has become part of the general culture."[10] But that, of course, is the lesson from all those graduation presents: It was *Excellence*, more than any of Drucker's works, that led the charge into the retail sector. Drucker established himself as an authority on management well before Peters, but he became a guru (and indeed regularly granted interviews) only after Peters.

On the heels of *Excellence*, a stampede of gurus has rushed to satisfy the public demand for management advice. Some, such as Jim Collins, the author of the *Good to Great* series, have remained true to the theme of seeking out excellence in company life in general. Others identify themselves with one particular cause or fad—such as Michael Hammer and James Champy with the "business process reengineering" craze of the early 1990s. Some gurus, such as Gary Hamel, focus on business advice and strategy; others, such as Charles Handy and Stephen Covey, devote more energy to individual and organizational issues. Among the best-selling gurus are the "I did it may way" pack—successful managers, led by Jack Welch, who promise to share some of the magic for the price of a hardcover. The gurus offer a wide menu of advice, but all are feeding from the pastures that opened on the success of Peters and Waterman's book.

From Peters' remarkable achievement, however, have followed some remarkable paradoxes. Like popular music, management theory in its popular form has become a lively, entrepreneurial response to demand: incoherent and emotive; rebellious in expression, if often not at all so in effect. But is that which pleases the most people necessarily true? Or is it just another thing that you play in the car on the way to work? The gurus promise to reveal the secrets of power, but the secrets they offer sound suspiciously like the kind of secret Mother shared as she was handing you the lunch box on the way to the bus stop. They gurus make no shortage of forecasts and predictions, the large majority of which have been thankfully forgotten. So why do people keep demanding that they look into their crystal balls? It is perhaps not so surprising that the gurus contradict one another; but what is one supposed to think when they contradict themselves? The gurus are often accorded respect as great authorities. But what exactly are their qualifications for the job? What are they authorities in? And why is it that millions of people are eager to pay for instruction on what they should do in the fantastically improbable event that they become CEO of a major corporation? How did management theory become so personal, so spiritual, so impractical?

Three decades after it all began on that morning in the Bank of America tower, for about $1,000—or for free if your company foots the bill—you can still see Tom Peters do his show. For $29.99, you can catch some of the magic on one of his DVDs. You will see him pace furiously back and forth across the stage, his arms pumping, his voice ranging from dramatic whisper to fire-drill loud, his face turning rosy and registering various emotional contortions. He will exhort you to have "fun" on the job and insist that "life at work can be cool," that it's all about passion, persistence, and imagination. At the same time, he will furrow his brow, peer over his granny glasses, and wag his finger as he warns you that the world is changing at hyperspeed and that you'd better learn to color outside the lines before you become roadkill on the highway to global competitiveness. You might think that he is a performance artist, or maybe some kind of postmodern ironist. You might also find yourself wondering if he needs to be taking some hypertension medication.

The Tom Peters experience strikes most listeners as something fun and novel. It is about as hip as management gets. Yet it should also suggest something very old, almost classical. After all, if you stay tuned and wait around for the next show, you're not unlikely to find someone else with a more familiar style warning of the dire perils of modern life and promising that you will be able to perform miracles if you only put your hand on your heart and say, "I believe."

Free at Last

Not long after the firm's farsighted "strategy review" established the new imperial order, I checked my bank account and noticed that I had not received my regular base salary for the previous two months. At the time, I was working mainly in Barcelona, where I was leading a team of about 10 consultants on a large project for a new client. I also noticed that I had not been reimbursed for my travel and other expenses for two months, nor had I received a partial installment on the bonus for the previous year that had recently been paid out to other partners.

I called the firm's accountant in New York. He said he thought it was a clerical error and promised to look into the matter. I faxed letters and left phone messages expressing concern about the missed payments to the accountant, to Owen, and to Patrick.

In the third month, I saw once again that I had received no pay. And once again I made calls and faxed letters. Owen's and Patrick's assistants at first claimed that their masters were not in, but after a few more attempts, they quietly whispered that they had been instructed to screen my calls.

The accountant eventually called me back and sheepishly admitted that there was no clerical error. "You're not on the firm's payroll," he announced. I now knew for sure that I had been purged. Only, the firm's newly self-empowered management had evidently forgotten to tell me about it.

In its particulars, the event caught me by surprise. And yet, strange as it may sound, I came to regard it as one of the luckiest twists in my topsy-turvy career.

For quite some time before my precipitous departure, life at work had not been "cool." To all outward appearances, of course, our firm was "excellent." According to the buzz on campus, we were "hands-on/value-driven," "loose-tight," "antihierarchical," and all the other things that the gurus say you have to be. But the truth was very different.

I had resolved to return to my vocation as an unpublishable philosopher, but I could not bring myself to slip out of the golden handcuffs that tied me to the firm. In theory, through my unrealized equity stake and founders' fund interests, as well as uncollected bonuses, I was one of the chief beneficiaries of the firm's rapid expansion. In reality, my supposed net worth rested on a few pieces of paper that were then in the hands of the imperial elite that had taken over the firm.

Early in year 3, I made an attempt to extricate myself from this unpleasant situation. My idea then was to become a part-time partner, working only two or three months out of the year, and taking the rest of the time off to pursue my other interests. I was, of course, willing to take a commensurate reduction in pay, but I also wanted to preserve my equity interests in the firm, and in particular at least part of my interest in the founders' fund. With Roland's backing, I wrote up a detailed plan and presented it to Owen and Patrick. But Owen only smiled his lupine smile and waved my proposal aside. True to his method, he took the conversation to the third level. He didn't try to read what I wrote; he tried to read my mind—and it wasn't my conscious thoughts he was after, but the unconscious thoughts that he imagined were driving my behavior. Once again, he seemed to think that a session with Dr. Bob would clear things up right away. Patrick took notes like a cop at a crime scene, but said nothing.

While these Kafkaesque negotiations were taking place, I was in the process of setting up a consulting practice for the firm in Spain. I helped recruit three local partners, led by an amiable man named Santiago from a well-connected family whose Rolodex served us well. We managed to attract some business—he, mainly in Madrid; I, in Barcelona, where I had the advantage in speaking the local language, Catalan.

When the news of Owen's extraordinary compensation policy broke, I realized that Owen and Patrick had little interest in negotiating even a partial exit for me, because they didn't think they would have to give me much or anything at all if I left. In their obtuse refusals to consider my proposals, they were effectively saying that I was welcome to stay and continue generating profits for them, but if I left, they would count my years of work and my equity investment as a selfless contribution to their infinitely expanding bonuses.

In the several months preceding the firm's "strategy review," I had come to accept as a matter of abstract truth that I was screwed. If I left the firm, I'd get nothing. If I stayed, I'd get next to nothing. I also under-stood, in a merely logical way, that I was largely responsible for screwing myself. I had invested four years and all my money with a group whose leadership I had come to view as deranged, and I somehow expected that these same people would be both competent enough to collaborate with me in building a viable firm and trustworthy enough to honor their commitments to me. On both counts, I had made a serious misjudgment, attributable to the fault that habitually inflicts pain on investors: greed-induced blindness. So my brain told my legs to walk. But my legs, suffer-ing from a debilitating combination of inertia and outrage, weren't quite ready to get up and go. It particularly galled me to think that, with my misjudgment, I had helped enrich some people who in my opinion did not deserve to be rich.

At this point, I was locked in a zero-sum game with the partners who were in the process of commandeering the firm, and there is a part of me that really, really hates to lose in zero-sum games. At my favorite café in Barcelona, I flipped through the shareholders' agreement with my legally unsophisticated eye, in search of a winning strategy. The agreement did allow that in the event of an "involuntary dismissal *without* cause," a shareholder would be entitled to full participation in the founders' fund, as well as preservation of all other equity interests in the firm. The agree-ment further seemed to specify exactly what an involuntary dismissal *with* cause would look like. It said that the firm was required to give the errant shareholder 12 months' notice, specify the cause in writing, provide an opportunity to cure, and put the matter to a vote of the board. In the best of all possible worlds, I figured, I would be dismissed against my will and without cause. Then at least I'd have a claim of some sort for getting my money back. But how could I get fired without giving cause? And how could it be involuntary if, in fact, I desperately wanted to leave?

With the benefit of a double espresso, I contemplated the possibilities. Could I perhaps allow the New York partners to develop the impression that I should be fired? Could I further allow them to imagine that they would be better off firing me without cause? Could I, in short, turn some of the very same psychologistic tools that Owen and his fellow therapy patients had used to such effect over the previous four years *against* them, by exploiting their psychological weaknesses, which included but were not limited to paranoia, conceit, fecklessness, and delusions of power? It seemed like a twisted and devious idea, worthy of a cold-blooded Machiavellian type. It also seemed ridiculously improbable, so I set it aside. Yet, as much by inaction as conscious effort, this strange idea ended up playing a not insignificant part in the way events ultimately unfolded.

Every month or two, I sent Owen and Patrick another variant on my proposal for becoming a part-time partner. In principle and on paper, these were legitimate proposals. In an honest and psychologically balanced firm they would have been taken as such, and I would have been very happy had they been so received. But in the back of my mind I knew that they would not be so received. Owing to their delusions of omnipotence, my opponents would not imagine that it was in their interest to negotiate in an honest way with me. Owing to their belief in their own mastery of human psychology, I knew, they would interpret my communications as third-order signals of a self-destructive tendency on my part. And yet, given the actual weakness of my position, I sensed it was a good idea to encourage in them the belief that I thought my position even weaker than it was. In the manner of jujitsu, I was manipulating them by pretending to put myself in a position to be manipulated by them.

Information is almost always an advantage in any game, and so, more as a precaution than as part of a concerted plan, I resolved to minimize the amount of information my opponents had about me. I allowed my activities in Spain, from the New York perspective, to be enveloped in a fog. This required almost no effort on my part. I merely avoided all of the opportunities for pointless preening and self-congratulation in which partners in consulting firms obsessively indulge in order to glorify themselves before their peers. When business took me to New York, I worked mainly from my apartment there. I showed up in the office late and in casual clothes, falling naturally into the part of the hippie and the "weak sister" from the "fringe office." The New Yorkers could at any point have penetrated the fog surrounding my work by simply asking me or others what I was doing. But I guessed that they would not do so. I knew that their paranoia and their fundamental belief in the shallow neediness of their fellow consultants would lead them to draw the worst inferences from the absence of ritualistic boasting on my part, and I also knew that their delusions of omniscience would prevent them from pursuing the facts of the matter.

It was, admittedly, a bizarre way to behave. I had become as warped as the firm and the "profession" from which I was desperate to extricate myself. I also did not believe that anything would come of my efforts. I had no cards to play; my only hope was that my adversaries would misplay their own hand. I did not know what kind of mistake they could make, or whether it would come to pass before the whole house of cards collapsed in bankruptcy.

When I first learned that my salary had been cut off, I was astonished and alarmed. I doubted that the moment was opportune for the inevitable showdown. I felt obligated to serve out the contract with my Barcelona client in particular. I told Santiago about the circumstances, and he became extremely agitated when he grasped the potential implications for the business in Spain. He implored the New Yorkers to resume my salary. After the third month, however, when it became clear that I would never get paid again, it was obvious that there was nothing more I could do.

I soon grasped that the firm's self-appointed leaders had delivered to me my holy grail: an "involuntary dismissal without cause." They had fired me without following any of the procedures listed in the shareholders' agreement for establishing cause—indeed, without even telling me that I was fired. So it was with great relish that I notified Owen and Patrick that I was accepting my involuntary dismissal without cause. I requested that they arrange to transfer to me the moneys and the rights I was owed: my unpaid salary and expenses for the previous three months, the unpaid bonuses for the previous two years, my equity interests in the firm at book value, the founders' fund interests accrued thus far and my rights over the full period of the fund, and my "retained interests"—that is, rights to an equity interest in the event of sale, as specified in the shareholders' agreement.

My main concern about the decision at the time was that it meant letting down the main client and the fellow consultants with whom I had been working. When I explained the situation, however, they all agreed that I couldn't very well be expected to work for the firm if I wasn't on its payroll. In the end, the new turn of events worked to the benefit of both the client and my associates. The other key individuals on the project eventually agreed to leave the firm and go to work directly for the client, which was more economical for the client and offered better career opportunities for the individuals.

In response to my declaration that I had been fired, the firm immediately took the position that it owed me no money and no rights—not even the missing three months' salary and expenses. This was, of course, disappointing but not at all surprising.

In my earlier life, I had never imagined that I would one day become one of those people who huffily says, "You'll be hearing from my lawyers." But, with so much money on the line and the prospect of another thrilling zero-sum game ahead, I found myself quite pleased to inform my former partners that they really would be hearing from my lawyers (even though I did not yet have lawyers).

For the second time in four years, I gathered up all of my savings and placed a big bet. Through my brother's contacts in Washington DC, I found exactly the right lawyers for the job: prestigious, driven, snarling, hungry, and outrageously expensive. The partner on the case was the kind of wizened, wise-cracking old beagle who lives for the "gotcha" moments in cross-examination. The real work fell to two very bright young associates who seemed eager to take up the cause. My case was, by their standard, small beer, but I believe that the partner was happy to take it on for its entertainment value. "We're kinda glad to have you," Neil, the lead associate confided. "Most of our clients are, uh, you know, well, they've done something *bad*." Then he rushed off to meet with a client who had just taken up residence in one of those penitentiaries reserved for white-collar types.

My instructions to the lawyers were simple: maximum speed. The firm, I knew, would not be able to stay above water much longer. Maximum speed in the legal world, as I soon discovered, turns out to mean somewhat faster than a tree grows but a lot slower than ketchup coming out of a bottle.

The Science of Excellence

I t seems unsportsmanlike to consider *Excellence* as a piece of research; and yet it is unavoidable, since that is what Peters and Waterman claim their book is. The book cites previous "researchers" (such as Elton Mayo) and offers "findings," many of which are said to be "surprising," and all of which are purportedly based on "rigorous" research. The same predicament holds true of the management guru literature in general. To measure it against the normal standards of rational inquiry feels inappropriate and yet is necessary, since that is how it presents itself. On the assumption that we have not yet adopted a faith in the gurus' preternatural capabilities, in any case we owe it to ourselves to consider whether the evidence they supply justifies the many claims they make.

Viewed as a piece of research, *Excellence* follows a seemingly straightforward premise. The authors begin by selecting a set of "excellent" companies according to a set of highly specific, mostly quantitative criteria. Then, on the basis of interviews and other analysis, they attempt to establish what it is that these companies have in common. They conclude by offering a set of principles—the famous eight lessons—that they maintain will produce excellence in other companies.

The same method remains the preferred one among management gurus to the present. Jim Collins, for example, uses it in his *Built to Last* (coauthored by Jerry Porras) and the *Good to Great* series, with some modifications that turn out to be superficial on inspection. (Peters is mad at Collins, incidentally; but then he also manages to suggest that he taught Collins everything he knows.[11]) It is not at all a coincidence that this is also the standard approach of self-help writers, from Napoleon Hill (*Think and Grow Rich*) to Stephen Covey (*The Seven Habits of* just about anything you might want to know about), who in general aim to tell us what it is that rich people have in common other than the fact that they have a lot of money.

The first obvious flaw in the method of *Excellence* is that it provides for no credible control group. Might there be companies that have applied the lessons of excellence and yet failed? Might there be companies that have applied none of the lessons and still succeeded? We'll never know—which, of course, means that we cannot be at all sure that the eight lessons predict success at all.

The second and equally obvious flaw in the conception of *Excellence* is an elementary confusion between correlation and causation. In framing their approach, the authors assume that whatever attributes their excellent companies have in common are the same ones that can predict success in other companies. They fail to consider the logical possibilities that the attributes may have no causal relationship with excellence or that they may be a consequence rather than a cause of excellence.

It would indeed be quite plausible to conclude that the happy, people-centered cultures the authors observed in their favorite companies were a consequence of their business success rather than a cause. During the bubble years, for example, every dot-com worth its vastly inflated share price had a superlatively humane culture. Ping-Pong tables, free massages, and lengthy bull sessions with top management were all part of the people-first package. Employees at one Internet consulting company received complimentary copies of Jim Collins' *Built to Last*, along with the hearty message that "we are all in this together." Such kindnesses undoubtedly made the 100-hour workweeks seem like a fair trade. After the crash, the Ping-Pong tables and other freebies vanished, but the workweeks often remained the same. The built-to-last company fired huge numbers of its staff and then organized company-wide conference calls to warn the survivors that any more "underperformers" and "slackers" would be weeded out. "We know who you are," the firm's leaders intoned menacingly over the phone.

If the methodological framework of *Excellence* is problematic, the execution is arguably worse. Although Peters and Waterman purport to base their eight lessons on a close study of the chosen 43 companies, they provide the reader with little reason to be confident that the eight bear any relation to the 43. In the book, 15 of the excellent companies are instantly forgotten upon making the list; a further 20 or so receive only cursory references; and only 7 are discussed in depth. Although the authors intimate that they have exclusive access and contact with these 7, closer inspection suggests that their acquaintance with the companies rarely goes beyond that which is available to the diligent magazine reader. Similarly, Jim Collins, making the same noises about scientific research, proudly bases *Good to Great* on "384 million bytes of computer data."[12] And yet, upon closer inspection, it appears that Collins' data trove—which would fit comfortably on a single CD—consists chiefly of press clippings.

From their 7 superexcellent companies, in any case, Peters and Waterman elicit a number of beautiful stories to illustrate their principles; but they provide little reason to believe that anyone intent on illustrating exactly contrary principles couldn't pull out a few stories in the same way from another 7 companies—or perhaps even from the same 7. As is the case throughout the history of management thought, the evidence is all anecdotal—and the anecdotes, for all we know, could be fables. In the final analysis, the eight lessons read very much like what an inspired individual might have cooked up early one morning while looking out over the San Francisco Bay. In the months before *Excellence* became a phenomenon, a reviewer in the *Harvard Business Review* pointed out that the book's main conclusions are "unsupported generalizations."[13]

"Of course we know all this is to some extent phony baloney," Peters confesses in an interview 20 years after *Excellence*.[14] (Actually, in the published interview, his words are "we faked the data"; but in his blog, Peters denies he ever said this and offers the "baloney" comment instead.) *Baloney* refers both to Jim Collins' and to Peters' own practice of selecting excellent companies. "If you try enough variations of plausible, tough long-term financial hurdles," Peters explains, "you can significantly influence the outcome."[15] The selection in *Excellence*, he hints, had less to do with the quantitative and putatively objective screening criteria than with his intuitions and those of his fellow McKinseyites about which companies deserved to be called excellent. Such a tilted selection process, of course, undercuts whatever remaining research credibility *Excellence* has. Instead of looking for independent variables to explain how some companies achieved a state called excellence, the book becomes an excuse for explaining what it is that Peters and his McKinsey colleagues like about the companies they happen to like.

Sadly, it has since become evident that Peters and friends' intuitions concerning the excellence of companies are about as bankable as the average fortune cookie. Two years after the publication of *Excellence*, *Business Week* published an article under the title "Oops!" in which it noted that about half of the excellent 43 were in serious trouble. At the five-year mark, Michelle Clayman, a financial analyst, concluded that the famous 43 "began to decline virtually across the board starting right from the date on which they were selected as 'excellent.'"[16] Over the five-year period, two-thirds underperformed the market. Alarmed, Clayman decided to go "in search of disaster." She retrospectively picked out a portfolio of "unexcellent" companies, reversing the financial criteria that Peters and Waterman had used in their study. Two-thirds of the stinkers outperformed the market, and over the five-year period the disaster portfolio beat the excellent one by over 60%. Peters, who is curiously thin-skinned compared with other members of the guru class, responded by opening his 1987 book, *Thriving on Chaos*, with the oddly defensive line "There are no excellent companies."[17]

Peters and Waterman are hardly the only gurus to wake up to unpleasant realities the morning after. Reading through the gurus' favorite companies from the past two and a half decades is like watching a parade of homecoming queens from years past. The sad procession serves mainly to prove that time destroys every conceit.

The more important lesson to draw from the gurus' underwhelming record is not that they fail to see into the future, but that they are in a certain sense *behind* the times. If there is one idea that unites the gurus, paradoxically, it is that the conventional wisdom is dead wrong. If you want to succeed, they howl in unison, you must break with the pack. But the guru literature itself *is* the pack. True to their calling as mass entertainers, they are followers rather than leaders. Their choices pander to rather than create the mood, aspirations, and conventional wisdom of the moment. Since the perceptions of the public are already factored into stock prices, it is not surprising that the gurus fail to outperform the market. All of this leads to the following conclusion: if you really want to profit from the gurus, listen carefully to what they say and then run fast in the opposite direction.

The other important lesson is that the gurus are easy prey for the all-too-human failing of hubris. We all take more credit than we deserve for our successes and we all blame bad luck too often when we fail. What makes the gurus different is that they are willing to extend the same holiday from reason to their pet companies. When a company succeeds, they attribute this success to an amazing managerial team or an even better management theory. Their winners, riding high on a wave of good fortune, often have no place to go but down. Peters' admission that "there are no excellent companies" is in part a belated acknowledgment that excellence in business is by its nature ephemeral. It is about what works in a particular time and place, and not necessarily next year or in the next town over.

The gurus may be particularly bad stock pickers because they allow their moralizing to cloud their judgment. In guru land, the stories about successful companies always embody a moral. When Peters says that companies succeed because they are "excellent," he means that they succeed because they are virtuous in some sense. The specific moral of most guru stories is that organizations succeed by breaking all the rules, flouting convention, defying authority, and, in general, advancing the cause of human freedom. The title of Marcus Buckingham's contribution (coauthored by Curt Coffman) to the genre says it all: *First, Break All the Rules.* But rating companies according to one's perceptions about how well they embody a certain preconceived moral value is a tricky business, as guru Gary Hamel has learned. In the late 1990s, he (along with many other gurus and a good portion of McKinsey & Company) was touting Enron as a company that achieved spiritual freedom of a sort and hailing CEO Ken Lay as a "revolutionary" and—with unintended prescience—a "rule-breaker."[18]

Although their record in predicting the future is lamentable, the gurus' record in predicting the past is always stellar. This infuriating asymmetry points to a deeper source of trouble in the kind of research represented in *Excellence* and its progeny. The theories that the gurus offer can explain everything and predict nothing because they aren't theories at all. Like the more elaborate conceptual frameworks of the strategy discipline, they are in fact bundles of nonfalsifiable truisms. They are always right—as long as you apply them in the right way.

In *Excellence*, the age-old taste of management thought for nonfalsifiable truisms becomes an uncontrollable addiction. The authors defend their first lesson, "a bias for action," for example, on the grounds that action is better than "sending a question through cycles and cycles of analyses and committee reports." Well of course it is. The authors aren't quite hotheaded enough to dismiss all "analysis": "what we are against is wrong-headed analysis."[19] But then, who would be in favor of "wrong-headed analysis"? "Stay close to the customer" is good enough advice— but then what else should one do? Get as far away from the customer as possible? Since Peters, it has become clear that the market for inanities masquerading as profound insights knows no limits. Aspiring gurus seem to understand that the road to riches is paved with garbled clichés and transparently unsubstantiated pseudotheories. No sentiment is too obvious or banal to count as management wisdom, provided it makes use of one or two bits of jargon and is followed by an exclamation point!

To be fair, platitudes do have their uses. Managers in large corporations do tend to forget that their organizations exist to serve customers, so it is not always redundant to remind them of their purpose. Simple, mnemonic frameworks, such as the "Seven Ss" (don't ask) that Peters and Waterman discuss in *Excellence*, may prove useful to stimulate actions in a world that doesn't fit easily into any model. The aim of management thought, say the gurus' supporters, is not to produce scientifically rigorous theories but to supply practical tools and concepts for the managers of the world. But this kind of pragmatism is ultimately just an insult to the rational faculties of the people who would purportedly make use of it.

Many of Peters' seminar participants remarked that the experience left them feeling like they'd just chugged a triple espresso. They came away juiced, but when they arrived back at their cubicles they didn't quite know what to do with all that energy. So they told Peters to "get prescriptive"—to tell them exactly what to do. Peters naturally listened to his customers. He came up with a "'So you want a fucking list' list" of things to do, which served as the basis for his third book, *Thriving on Chaos*. Presented as a "handbook," *Chaos* offers 45 "prescriptions," shoe-horned into five letter-coded headings.

Chaos in fact serves as a good illustration of the truism that it is better sometimes *not* to heed one's customers. The 45 prescriptions, to begin with, are really about 15 pretending to be a bigger number. Practically minded readers are unlikely to spot the difference between "become obsessed with listening" (C-7), "listen/celebrate/recognize" (P-3), and "Pay attention! (More listening)" (L-5). Many of the prescriptions—"Involve everyone in everything" (P-1)—make painfully clear that their author has never managed anything other than small teams of bright, highly motivated fellow consultants. Some prescriptions—"master paradox" (L-1)—hint at a strangely postmodern sensibility. But most simply suffer from that maddening impracticality of all platitudinous exhortations. Of course one should "simplify/reduce structure"—but where exactly does one start with such a project?

As Peters gamely wades into the battlefield of seemingly practical suggestions and "72-hour action plans," it becomes clear that his idea of strategy is to fire all of your guns at once and explode into space. In *Chaos*, he recommends that you "consider doubling or tripling your training and retraining budget."[20] He also wants you to "consider doubling" your sales force[21] and investing in innovation, manufacturing, and international expansion. While you're at it, you should "provide bold financial incentives for everyone."[22] He probably wants you to have Christmas every day too. After telling you to double up on everything, however, he turns around and demands that you obliterate half of the organization and nuke the hierarchy. In his 1994 book *The Pursuit of WOW!*, Peters lists six of the prominent fads of the moment as top priorities for management, some of which favored the "empowerment" mantra, others of which leaned toward the side of cost reduction. It doesn't seem to bother him that empowering staff while laying them off in large numbers might prove difficult to pull off as a package. Peters encapsulates in his own work one of the problems that bedevils the guru industry as a whole: what the gurus say in one breath, they boldly contradict in the next.

No guru presentation is complete without practical suggestions about how you, too, can become a billionaire. In recent times, Peters has taken to wrapping up his show with two "practical" suggestions: go after women and go after old people. Women are getting richer, he points out, and the population of old people is growing faster than rabbits in Australia. Exactly how many billions Peters' listeners will coin from such dazzling insights into modern demographic trends remains to be seen.

The impracticality of the gurus' practical recommendations stems from the very conception of the project in which they are involved. Recommendations that are aimed at almost every manager of almost every business are bound to be without content or foundation. "We've reached the limits of incrementalism," the gurus Hamel and Prahalad intone in their 1994 hit, *Competing for the Future*.[23] But who is this "we"? How can the authors possibly know that there aren't some of us out here who might just benefit from a little more of this incrementalism (whatever that is)?

The failure of gurus like Peters to provide substantial research becomes glaringly evident in their tense relationship with the business schools. Peters may be the "guru of gurus of management," at least in the estimation of his own blurbs, yet there is probably no program in management education in the world (outside of Peters' own "MBA in a box") that teaches his work—although some apparently do use it as an illustration of how *not* to perform research. When Jim Collins hearkened to the siren call of gurudom, it was somehow important for him to stop teaching at Stanford. The case of Drucker is even more curious. From time to time, even the business school leaders laud Drucker as one of the great management thinkers of all time. Yet one searches mostly in vain for substantive scholarly citations of his work. The clearest sign that there was no real research to begin with in *Excellence*, in Drucker's 26 books, or in the guru literature in general is that no real research has followed.

In the field of popular science, it is interesting to note, by way of contrast, that the crowd-pleasing books are often written by—or at least in close collaboration with—notable scientists. The management gurus, however, write with complete indifference to or even *against* the academics. They play the role of the ancient Greek sophists to all those Platos in the modern academy. They thrive on the scorn of the professors and their elite friends. Their aim is to deliver the secrets of power—the gurus call it "excellence"; the sophists called it "virtue"—to the common man. (Interestingly, Peters and Waterman's original title for their book was *The Secrets of Excellence*, but McKinsey bigwigs nixed that over the worry that it made it sound as if they were giving away client data.) On the basis of their vaunted experience in the rough-and-tumble of life in the cubicles, the gurus—no less than the sophists—champion the pragmatic, humanistic, relativistic dimensions of knowledge. As it turns out, the gurus know what the public wants. In 1984, not long after *Excellence* came out, four of *Business Week*'s "Top Ten Business Books of the Year" were authored by academics. By 1991, only one from the same list came from the professors, and in 2001 the score was again one in 10.[24]

The divorce between popular and academic management theory represents a devastating indictment of both fields. The fact that Peters alone has outsold the combined faculties of most business schools gives good reason to think that the research the business schools are producing isn't particularly relevant for managers. (And if it isn't relevant for managers, it isn't even the research it pretends to be.) The inability of Peters and his fellow gurus to make recognizable contributions to the chief repositories of knowledge in our society, on the other hand, undermines their pretensions to expertise. The gurus, in fact, seem to provide a clear instance of Gresham's Law in action. Gresham says, in essence, that the bad money always drives out the good. In a market where popularity is everything, there is always only bad management theory.

Peters may show nothing but scorn for the jargon of the management rationalists and bureaucrats, yet—perhaps out of a perverse desire to emulate his dreaded foes—he, like most gurus, has come up with a jargon of his own that is no less obtuse. He lambastes 500-page reports that clog up organizations, yet he churns out 800-page books with frightening regularity. (Before the editors got to it, *Liberation Management* weighed in at 1,962 pages.)[25] Peters mocks MBAs; yet with his bustling consulting company, his suitcase full of handy management techniques, and his bombastic disquisitions, he is in some ways the consummate MBA (not to mention that he does have that degree from the Stanford Business School).

Given all the contrary evidence about the quality of their research and the durability of their findings, the question one should ask of the gurus is this: Why do they still cling to the pretense of expertise? Why don't they admit that they just pulled it all out of the hot air in their heads? In his multimedia performances, Tom Peters, to his credit, does sometimes appear to confess that he is indeed "winging it." Among all the gurus, he is the most self-aware, and in a strange way the least deserving of criticism for failure to achieve a standard of research to which, at least in recent years, he manifestly does not aspire. The trouble is, he is usually so far into his routine by the time he lets the audience in on the secret that few people take him seriously on the point. He is like the great Wizard of Oz, except his listeners imagine that stepping out from behind the curtain is just another one of his tricks.

The gurus hold on to the pretense of management expertise because that is the idea that fuses their work into a meaningful whole. However much they disdain the academics, the gurus subscribe to the myth that Taylor concocted and that has sustained the business of management ever since—the idea that management is a specialized body of knowledge or expertise that evolves over time and is the preserve of a certain class of professionals. Indeed, the gurus are today's chief propagandists for this new, modern religion. Drucker, with his usual self-confidence, has allowed himself to be identified as "the man who invented management," or, at least, who "established management as a discipline and as a field of study."[26] In fact, neither he nor his successors established a discipline; they merely asserted the *idea* of a discipline. (And, for what it's worth, it was Taylor, not Drucker, who had the idea first.) If one is to appreciate the gurus properly, to understand why they have risen to prominence and what their work actually portends, one must approach them not as the experts that they claim to be, but as the spiritual leaders that they really are.

The Trial

My day in court turned out to be three days in a dowdy conference room in midtown Manhattan, with half a dozen lawyers sitting around a square, walnut-veneer table under the light of a few dirty windows partially blocked by malfunctioning shutters. I had earlier cherished the hope of arguing my case before a jury of my peers, like Gregory Peck playing Clarence Darrow in what I imagined would become a forum on justice in the workplace. But I was deprived of my soapbox by the clause in the firm's shareholders' agreement specifying that disputes would have to be settled before the same arbitrator who had overseen the dispute between the firm and its Chicago parent four years previously.

The arbitrator was a charming, 70-something woman who ruled the room with an authoritative smokers' rattle. She sat next to a young associate of hers on one side of the square. I sat to her left with my two lawyers, Neil and Clay. Opposite us were three lawyers for the firm, led by a troll-like young man who seemed to have a permanently unhappy expression on his face.

From a legal point of view, my case was not exactly material for the Supreme Court. Indeed, the case should have been settled, and no doubt would have been, had fighting it not formed part of a wider legal strategy that the firm chose to pursue. But it did produce an entertaining spectacle, and in its own small way it raised some curious issues about justice in the modern workplace.

Among the many former partners of the firm who undertook legal action against the firm around the time of the "purge," I happened to be the first to get a hearing. This was in part because the firm had botched my dismissal in a unique way; in part because Owen was still in the process of playing the remaining partners off one another, using the prospect of a sale as bait; and in part because I had better lawyers and I pushed them to act as quickly as possible. Being first in line ultimately proved to be another stroke of incredibly good fortune. But in the short term it lent my case a unique importance in the eyes of the firm. As I learned late in the process, the firm was closing in on its encounter with its extraterrestrial friends in the Internet consulting world, and the remaining partners were keen to avoid setting a precedent that might have allowed purged partners to share in the spoils of the sale of the firm.

Under the direction of Patrick, who had now become the firm's chief litigation officer, the firm's lawyers interviewed more than a hundred individuals in the firm who had worked with me on a regular basis in the past. The lawyers urged the employees "to help out the firm," as one associate later told me, by testifying to my alleged incompetence and depravity. They did not find any takers. The firm's lawyers also devoted many billable hours to combing through all of my time sheets, credit card bills, and telephone records for the previous year, hunting for further evidence of my turpitude. My case also allowed the firm's legal team to indulge themselves with an all-expenses-paid trip to Spain, where they interviewed many people who had worked with me there. In the week before the hearing, the firm's team and its key witnesses held an off-site workshop to prepare for the grand event. I do not know how much the firm spent in total on my case, but from appearances I can only guess that it totaled significantly more than a million dollars.

In support of my case, my lawyers had already deposed half a dozen fellow consultants with whom I had worked in the previous year. We were permitted to approach these individuals and arrange depositions only through their lawyers. The Troll, who "represented" all of those employees who did not have lawyers of their own, naturally did his best to "prepare" my witnesses. He made sure that they were available only on tape, and not in person, for the hearing. Despite the obvious risk to their careers, all of my witnesses performed honorably and admirably, testifying to the fact that I had been working productively up to the moment I departed the firm.

As the hearing began and the lawyers delivered their opening statements, it became clear to me that the firm's massive investment had not enhanced the merits of its case. The Troll evidently could not make up his mind whether the firm had fired me for good reason or I had voluntarily abandoned the job for no reason, so he chose to argue it both ways. He ignored the central legal point: that, even on the implausible view that the firm had fired me with cause, it had failed to follow any of the procedures for doing so specified in the shareholders' agreement. What unified his position, I came to understand, was not logic, but a theme. The theme was that, no matter how you sliced it, I was scum. This, of course, is standard practice within American courtrooms, as it is increasingly in American politics: if you have nothing else on your opponent, go after his "character."

In his presentation, the Troll attempted to bring some theater to the somber room, but his talents as a thespian were limited to the expression of only one emotion: righteous outrage. He licked his fingers compulsively every time he was about to touch a piece of paper.

"We could use a little less emotion," the arbitrator said to him tartly at one point.

The first day of my hearing passed in a pleasant way. I was the sole witness, and I spent a day telling my story first in answer to my lawyer's questions, then in cross-examination by the Troll.

The second and third days of the hearing were devoted to the firm's theory that I was repugnant. The first witness was a female partner from New York whom I had seen during one two-day conference over the previous two years. She offered a very harsh assessment of my performance during those two days. I was delighted to learn, some months later, that she, too, was eventually engaged in litigation against the firm.

The firm's next witness was the Prince of Darkness. I had last had an extended conversation with the Prince some two or three years previously. He looked much fatter than I had remembered, and his skin seemed to have a sweaty and unhealthy glow. Just as he was sitting down to testify, his cell phone rang. He walked off toward one of the windows in order to carry on a very important conversation. The arbitrator dropped her jaw in mute horror. The Troll got up and tried to wave the Prince back to his seat, but the conversation was evidently more important than our proletarian proceeding. When the Prince finally sat down, it became clear that the purpose of his testimony was to convey his "evaluation" of me based on two- or three-year-old conversational data. My lawyers successfully objected that this was ancient history and irrelevant to the case, so his brief testimony amounted to nothing, and he was escorted away.

The Troll then wheeled in an officious young partner who had been promoted well out of his depth in order to oversee the "partner evaluation committee" that had emerged from the firm's "strategy review" as one of the "firm-building initiatives." This new evaluation process, the young man informed us, had been created "out of fairness" to all partners, including those who had left the firm, since there had been no formal evaluations during the previous year.

The Troll licked his fingers and then ceremoniously handed the witness a document that contained the fruits of the august committee's labors. The young partner obligingly went down the list of partner evaluations and noted that I had received the absolute worst performance rating in the history of the universe.

My lawyer subsequently asked him to read the date at the top of the page. The evaluations had, in fact, been produced two and a half months after I had left the firm and commenced litigation. The young man also had some difficulty reconciling the "evaluation" with the fact that, on the basis of earlier reviews, I had been receiving respectable increases in my (theoretical) bonuses in the prior years.

Patrick, to whom I owed a debt of gratitude for having made my exit strategy possible in the first place, was the firm's most relevant witness. He had by this point become almost a model witness, since he was involved in a large number of other disputes with the firm's former partners. He made a point of addressing the arbitrator by her first name, thereby insinuating a level of warm collegiality established after so many healthy interactions.

When asked why he had stopped paying me, Patrick at first maintained that he had done so because I had started working "part-time." With the Troll's guidance, he used the flurry of proposals I had made about the possibility of becoming a part-time partner—proposals that Patrick had utterly ignored at the time—to suggest that I had unilaterally changed my status from partner to part-time freelance consultant and thus had voluntarily handed back all of my equity in the firm at no cost.

When Neil read back the clauses that I had been careful to insert in each one of my proposals to the effect that, if the firm and I could not come to an agreement about a change in my status, then I would happily continue working as a normal, full-time partner, Patrick calmly replied that he "interpreted" my proposals as a "statement" that I had planned to work part-time.

Neil showed Patrick a letter that Santiago had written to him in my final month at the firm pleading that he resume my salary and noting that I was working "full-time." Patrick agreed that that was what the letter said, and then affirmed once again that I was working part-time. Neil then asked why, if he thought I was working part-time, had he chosen to pay me nothing. Do part-timers work for free? Patrick suddenly decided that I had not been working at all. "I had no idea where he was," he said. On the table in front of Patrick rested the phone log of 26 calls that I had placed to his assistant and the letters I had faxed him upon learning that I was not being paid.

From Patrick I learned a lesson that has no doubt been absorbed by many political leaders in recent years. If you're going to lie about the fact that there is an elephant in the room, do it while you're standing right next to the thing. If you try to hide the critter or distract people's gaze from it, they will immediately know that you are lying. But if you come right up to it and give it a pat on the shoulder, they'll start to think that maybe the elephant is lying.

Patrick's muddled claims about my part-time status nonetheless did contribute to a more significant issue raised by the firm's most interesting witness, Santiago. For the purposes of the firm's case, Santiago had become my "manager." Although I had more equity in the firm—I was generating 70% of the revenue in his country, and I had never felt under any obligation to report to him on my activities—he was the nominal head of the Spanish office, and according to the logic of the M-Form corporation, since I had most recently been working with Spanish clients, he was my "superior."

Santiago could not bring himself to go along with the firm's theory about my awfulness. He was, in any case, constrained by the fact that, in the course of his pleas to get my salary resumed, he had written to the New York partners saying that I had "performed outstandingly well." He was also forced to acknowledge that, just before the firm decided to cut me off, our client in Barcelona had insisted on naming me in its contract with the firm as the partner in charge of a 2 million–euro follow-on project. Ignoring the Troll's pained grimaces, he even added in his testimony that, as my "manager," he "was very satisfied" with my performance and that I "did very good work." But he did also say that he often did not know where I was and that, when he wasn't writing letters reminding the firm that I was working full-time, he thought I might have been working part-time at least part of the time.

He had a point, and in many ways it opened up the most (or perhaps the only) interesting topic in the otherwise farcical proceeding. In a narrowly epistemological sense, of course, it was true that he often didn't know where I was, just as I often didn't know where he was, so he was correct in saying that I might have been working part-time, just as I could have said the same about him. In the consulting business, as in many other white-collar, semiprofessional, postindustrial occupations, there is no clock to punch; and even if there were, it would often show seemingly erratic schedules. Not only is there no clock; there is often no office. I frequently worked from home, if not from airplanes, hotels, or, better still, the cafés on the beaches of Barcelona.

At one point during my cross-examination, the Troll, trembling with rage, handed me a fax I had received in the course of my work and asked me to read the header: "m- s- home."

"You were at home so often that they already had your fax number on auto-dial," he screamed, spittle flying from his lips. He reached such a pitch of indignation that the arbitrator herself called out, "Objection! That is exactly what I do not want any more of. How about taking a five-minute break." She got up in disgust and went outside for a smoke. I thought the Troll had made the point quite nicely. I was doing so much work at home that the assistants had programmed my number on auto-dial.

But Santiago had put his well-manicured finger on a still more impor-

tant issue. Setting aside the epistemological complexities about the meaning of *full-time* in a postmodern line of work, there is a sense in which the
term could be taken to mean "fully committed"—that is, "giving it all
you've got." And it was certainly true that I was not giving my job all I
had. I was not one of the gurus' good children. I did not wake up in the
morning wondering what I could do for the glory of the firm, nor did I
go to bed reviewing my accomplishments of the day for the firm. On the
contrary, I invested enough of myself in my job to justify my artificially
lowered income and to honor the interests of co-workers and clients, but
not a drop more.

My situation was, in fact, fairly typical in the working world. In 2005
the consulting firm Towers Perrin asked tens of thousands of workers
around the world to indicate their level of agreement with statements
such as "I really care about the future of my organization" and "my organization inspires me to do my best." They concluded that "the vast majority of employees across all levels in an organization are less than fully
engaged in their work."[27] To anyone who has spent any amount of time
in the world, this result must seem entirely unremarkable. Indeed, most
sane people would probably think it rather creepy if a vast majority of
people were willing to express unadulterated love for their organization.
What is noteworthy, however, is the gurus' response to this basic fact
of working life: "85% of those at work . . . are giving less of themselves
than they could," Gary Hamel shrieks in horror in his comments on the
result.[28] In guru land, the failure of employees to give 100% (and more!)
to the greater glory of the organization seems an incomprehensible evil.

During the hearing, the firm and its lawyers pressed on these questions about what might be called "input" largely out of necessity, since by
any reasonable measure my output was quite respectable. But the focus
on input also reflected a curious paradox about the cultural world that
the management gurus have created (and that, curiously, seems to shape
the legal world as well). .

On the one hand, any guru worth his multimillion-dollar salt will tell
you that output is the only thing that matters on the job. It's not hours
at the desk but number of customers satisfied that counts, they will say.
This is the point of Drucker's most enduring fad—MBO, or "Management By Objectives"—just as it is the essence of many of Peters' bromides

about being "value-driven" and so on. And yet, among those who labor under the spell of the gurus, nothing is so greatly prized as sheer "input." Indeed, inasmuch as work is all about "fun," "passion," "persistence," and "heart," as Peters jubilantly informs us, then it is input that becomes the touchstone of success at the job.

My position as one who was working merely for the money and who shared none of the career aspirations of most of my peers was not enviable, but it did give me a certain perspective on the working habits of those around me. What I observed is that the children of the gurus generally supply a level of input that is not correlated with or justified by their level of output. They "work" much harder than they need to. Scare quotes are necessary here because "work" just means that they squander hours at the office accomplishing nothing of value. Indeed, when they are not rearranging the family photos or playing computer games, they often use their extra hours at the office to complain about how many hours they work, or to indulge in fantasies about what they will do when they at last escape work. Then they turn around and compete with each other to spend still more fruitless hours at the office and deride those who decline to join them in this bonfire of utility as "slackers." All of this led me to formulate a principle—which I chose not to articulate during the course of my hearing—that we would all get much more done if we stopped working all the time.

The question Santiago raised and put at the center of my hearing concerned the nature of the contract I had undertaken when I had agreed to work full-time for the firm. Had I signed away all of my energy and initiative and everything else I had—a.k.a. my soul? Or had I simply made a deal to supply certain services in exchange for certain compensation? This, of course, is the same line of questioning that first arose in memorable form on the pig-iron fields of the Bethlehem Steel Company, in the work of Frederick Winslow Taylor. The gurus, with their talk about "heart" and "passion," who hovered over the discussion, were clearly pressing the case for the "soul." Although I refrained from putting the matter in quite these words at the time of my proceeding, I was and remain opposed to the idea of selling souls.

Toward the end of the hearing, we learned that Roland, who had graciously offered to testify on my behalf, would be offering his testimony in the following week owing to a scheduling conflict. He did give his very helpful testimony by conference call, for which I was grateful. At the hearing, however, the Troll moved to close the record without allowing me the benefit of Roland's testimony.

"I would like to avoid a situation, frankly, where the other side gets a week to converse with [Roland] about what has been testified here and the risk of testimony being tailored accordingly," he said. I took this to be a textbook case of projection: he was alerting all present to his own approach to handling witnesses.

"I am not in the business of telling witnesses what to say," Neil replied coolly. "I have never spoken with [Roland] and I don't expect I will speak with him before he testifies, whenever that may be."

"I think it was unfortunate that [the Troll] thought the lapse of time would be used in this way," the arbitrator said wearily, looking in need of another cigarette. "I am not going to impute on anyone in these proceedings anything other than the most honorable conduct."

Her choice of words was apt. It was fair enough not to *impute* dishonorable conduct on anyone. But it would have been another thing entirely to *infer* it, from the testimony offered. At this point, after months of discovery processes, hundreds of pages of briefs, hours of depositions, and now three full days of hearings, the firm's strategy of driving up my legal costs was starting to have its intended effect. Owing to the strange circumstances of my departure, not only was I running short of cash, but it was also unclear whether I had health insurance, as the firm had not allowed me to make any arrangements for an extension of benefits. The only thing I had in the bank was the hope that this arbitrator would draw the correct inferences.

How to Become a Management Guru
in Five Easy Steps

mong the most significant accomplishments of the Bill of Rights of the US Constitution was the creation of what might loosely be called a free market in religion. In the first decades after the creation of the constitutional guarantees concerning the freedom of religion, the old monopolies—the previously established churches—shriveled, while new entrants—mostly, the evangelical sects—captured 70% of the market. At the same time, the total market for religion expanded dramatically. The new breed of itinerant preachers who fanned out across the continent in effect conducted a grand experiment to test the varieties of religion that will sell in a democratic society. Forced to compete not just with each other but with alternative entertainments, such as whiskey and the theater, America's godfathers became pioneers in the techniques of mass marketing. Ultimately, many of them gravitated toward a particular formula that, with variations here and there, continues to serve as the most effective basis for disseminating a popular religion.

The industry that Tom Peters founded succeeded largely by sticking to the formula devised by America's pioneering preachers. In a sense, Peters brought management theory back home, by reuniting it with a much broader and deeper spiritual tradition that dates from the earliest days of the American republic. To be sure, the management theory before Peters had always had religion, but its religion was a hieratic one. It came down from a priesthood on high—from popelike figures such as

Frederick Winslow Taylor and Elton Mayo. Peters' achievement was to transform the religion of management into a demotic one—a people's religion. Herewith, then, are the five easy steps to establishing a popular management religion.

1. We are all going to die! Starting with *Excellence* and continuing to his present seminars, Peters cannot find enough unnerving adjectives to describe the present time. He calls it "frightening," "dangerous," "disruptive," "crazy," "topsy-turvy," "uncertain," and "dire." In his first book, the immediate blame for the madness goes to the satanic Japanese, whose superior management skills have made life hell for American business. In later books and seminars, as it becomes clear that the Japanese are not going to be feasting on our babies after all, Peters spreads the blame more widely, citing globalization, technological innovation, a general increase in competitiveness, and the growing fickleness of consumers, especially the young. In the 1980s, the world is in "chaos"; the 1990s become "the nanosecond nineties"; and the 2000s, "the terabit twenties." "The only thing we can be certain about is uncertainty," Peters proclaims. As a matter of fact, one other thing that we can be certain about is that, whatever year it happens to be, Tom Peters will describe it as the scariest time of all.

We can also be certain that, in Tom Peters' world, the past is a different place. Twenty years ago—whenever that may be—life was calm, predictable, and even a little boring. For Peters, the paragon of this somnambulant past is his father's city gas company, where decade after decade the same people shuffled the same papers all day long.

For all gurus all the time, the story is the same. Every year is 1491 in America—to use the most vivid metaphor in Charles Handy's ample stockpile. We are perpetually suspended at a moment in time that divides a placid past from lots of pillaging and beheadings by some very aggressive foreigners. In 1994, Gary Hamel and C. K. Prahalad named the "inconstant environment" as the first challenge facing management.[29] Thirteen years later, the same Hamel begins his newest book with an observation about "how little the practice of management has changed over the past several decades."[30] But "sometime over the next decade," he warns, "your company will be challenged to change in a way for which it has no precedent."[31]

Peter Drucker, who in this respect had the misfortune of being productive too long, is perhaps the most obdurate proponent of the view that there is no time as vexatious as the now. In the spring of 2001, Drucker insisted that we were "in the throes of a transition period."[32] But according to his 1980 book, *Managing in Turbulent Times*, the age of turbulence is already upon us, and the era of "predictable times" is confined to "the 25 years between the Marshall Plan and the OPEC cartel" in 1973.[33] In 1969, however, while the world presumably relaxed in this idyll of predictable times, this same Drucker argued in a book titled *The Age of Discontinuity* that the Age of Continuity has come to an end.[34] Go back another decade into this Age of Continuity, to the flat-earth year of 1959, and Drucker was writing, "At some time during the last 20 years [1939–1959], we imperceptibly moved out of the Modern Age and into a new, as yet nameless era."[35]

The gurus' obsession with the instability of the present is to some extent the expression of a timeless insight about what it is like to live in a dynamic, capitalist economy. In the first decades of the twentieth century, the Austrian economist Joseph Schumpeter described in vivid language the "gales of creative destruction" that regularly topple the old order and reward innovation in a market economy.[36] In 1848, Karl Marx famously wrote that, under capitalism, "All fixed, fast-frozen relations . . . are swept away, all new-formed ones become antiquated before they can ossify. All that is solid melts into air, all that is holy is profaned."[37]

That life in a capitalist economy involves constant change can hardly be denied. But are the gurus right that the present time is so much more unstable than the past? By many measures, economic life in the developed world is actually less "turbulent" than it ever has been. In the United States, the volatility of GDP growth decreased from 3.0% in the period 1946–1968 to 1.2% in the period 1985–2006; the volatility of inflation decreased from 3.2% to 0.6% over the same two periods; and the volatility of corporate profit growth decreased from 16.7% to 12.8%. The economic perturbations of the last half century are like a summer day's surf compared with the tsunamis of the Great Depression and the periodic panics of the nineteenth century. Technological change today can make heads spin with glee; but today's new technologies are hardly more destabilizing than the railroads, the automobile, the airplane, steamships, electricity, telephones, mass production, antibiotics, and radio were in their day. Globalization, too, is undoubtedly a force to be reckoned with; but the process has been going on for centuries, and in the grand scheme it may now be less disruptive than the creation of a continental market was in the United States in the late nineteenth century.

To dispute the gurus on questions of fact, however, is a fool's game. When Peters and his fellow gurus contrast the innocent past with the present danger, they are not describing phenomena that can be observed in real time. They are invoking a certain emotional state of being. They are expressing our fear of change—and, ultimately, our fear of death. The pressure from which they seek refuge has its ultimate source not in managerial experience per se, nor even in a particular economic system, but in our own mortality. They are, in fact, taking the first step in the long-established formula for success in any democratic religion, which is to tie this fear of death and destruction to our particular time (whenever that may be), and so to link our existential anxieties with a claim about the peculiar wickedness of the age.

The gurus, like their evangelical predecessors, understand instinctively how to exploit a fundamental flaw in the human intuition of time. Reason tells us that time is a continuum, and that yesterday, today, and tomorrow are in reality no different from one another. But the primitive, chthonic mind disagrees. It tells us that yesterday is very unlike today, which is nothing at all like tomorrow. The past is innocent and stable, like childhood, like the Garden of Eden, or like the father who went off to work every morning with the same briefcase in hand. The present, which really exists only as the immediate future, is a source of perpetual instability, fearsome threats, and relentless anxiety. The far future (see step 3 below) resolves this instability in the form of calamity or rapture, permanent doom or eternal salvation.

The gurus understand that to invoke this particular state of being, this anxiety before the present/immediate future, has a salutary aspect. It is a way of predisposing us to action. It shakes us out of complacency and brings focus to our energies. What the gurus may not always be willing to say is that invoking this state of being also happens to be a highly profitable move for the gurus themselves. As America's evangelists understood, fear sells. Bad news for you is good news for the gurus. Management theory has its feet glued to superstition, and superstition floats only on an ocean of fear.

2. The bureaucracy is killing us! In *Excellence*, Peters and Waterman make clear that the greatest obstacle to our future happiness is to be found right here at home, in those glass and steel midtown office buildings. "The numerative, rationalist approach to management," the authors declare, "is right enough to be dangerously wrong, and it has arguably led us seriously astray."[38] Their chief bogeyman is Frederick Winslow Taylor (though Max Weber, the German sociologist who made the mistake of pointing out the obvious truth that bureaucracy is a better form of administration than rule by tribal elders or charismatic dictators, often comes in for abuse too).

In *Excellence*, this critique of rationalism sounds a reasonable note. It might easily be mistaken for the musings of a pair of detached observers who wish to alert us to the many dysfunctionalities that inevitably beset large organizations as they tackle complex tasks or to the irrationality of rationalist number fetishists. In Peter's later work, however, the veneer of sanity melts before the underlying rage. "R-I-P. Rip, shred, tear, mutilate, destroy that hierarchy," he writes in *Liberation Management*—a book whose title consciously evokes liberation theology.[39] In *Re-imagine*, his 2003 effort, he announces "an Unabashed Commitment to Destruction"[40] and asserts that "a cool idea is by definition a Direct Frontal Attack on the Holy Authority of Today's Bosses."[41]

As one follows Peters through the decades, it becomes clear that the assault on bureaucracy isn't a program but an expression of feeling. It isn't ultimately about changing things; it's about getting something off one's chest. The specific thing on the chest is the feeling that Nietzsche identifies as *ressentiment*—the resentment of the powerless before power. In 2003, while predicting for the umpteenth time the imminent "death of bureaucracy," Peters becomes mildly self-conscious of his own position: "I . . . have been screaming and shouting about bankrupt business practices for 25 to 30 years . . . mostly to no avail."[42] He therefore begins every chapter in the book with a "rant." The rants don't accomplish much—as Peters says of his predecessor McGregor, "Everybody knew that what he said was true, and everybody continued to treat their workers like shit"[43]—but they sure do make one feel better.

Peters' descent into ranting exposes a fundamental paradox concerning the audience for the guru literature. The guru business, in general, pretends to direct its grand pronouncements at the CEOs of the world. When the *New York Times* recently surveyed actual CEOs about their bedtime reading, however, it found that very few bothered to read the gurus. The dirty little secret of the business is that its audience is made up almost entirely of middle managers and wannabes. "You rarely found big company people there," says one of Peters' associates about the "Skunk Camp" workshops hosted by the Tom Peters Group. "It was middle managers from Domino's Pizzas and the like."[44] "The average seminar participant I work with comes dressed in a drab suit, uses drab language—and noticeably quivers when I suggest that the most likely path to career salvation for the beleaguered and endangered middle manager is to try to get fired," says Peters, who understands that insulting his audience—within limits—is also a critical part of winning their trust.[45]

In this respect, the guru business is the flip side of the strategy business. Both emerge from the same socioeconomic transformation—the rise of the M-Form corporation and the creation of the new middle-management class. Whereas the strategy business approaches this new reality from the top down, however, the guru business comes at it from the bottom up. It is important to remember, of course, that the "bottom" here is the middle. Peters and his fellow gurus never address themselves to the kind of workers who wear overalls and join unions. His people are the cubicle people.

A key factor in Peters' success is his remarkable talent for identifying himself with his chosen audience. "Obeying the rules is obeying *their* rules,"[46] he fumes, making clear with his choice of pronoun whose side he is on. At one point he writes himself an imaginary tombstone: "He would have done some really cool stuff, but his boss wouldn't let him."[47] (Peters, of course, has not had to worry about nasty bosses since he walked out of McKinsey in 1981.) His "overall rant" is that "people . . . in enterprise, in government . . . are thwarted . . . at every step of the way . . . by absurd organizational barriers and by the egos of petty tyrants (be they corporate middle managers, or army colonels, or school superintendents)."[48] Decades have passed since his days in the navy and in The Firm, but the bitterness is still very much near the surface. In a sense, Peters gets paid to bash bosses.

Other gurus attempt to follow Peters into the psyche of the bureaucratically oppressed, though often with less panache. Drucker, who scurried away to the safety of freelance writing and consulting after his own brief experiences working inside the machine, famously said that 90% of management is making it difficult for people to get things done. Peters, never willing to be outdone in hyperbole, declared that this was an underestimate. All of the gurus preach a rebellious attitude appropriate to the little man, but Peters beat them all to the extreme edge with *Liberation Management*, the point of which is to liberate us from management altogether.

Peters' assaults on bureaucratic power and rationalist expertise form part of a much older and wider tradition of anti-intellectualism in America. His work draws much of its energy from the anger directed at a despised and feared elite that boils just underneath the surface of American life. Peters takes on pointy-headed MBAs in the same spirit with which preachers and populists have always railed against eggheads from Harvard and Yale. "Never ever ever in your life hire someone with a 4.0 grade point average," Peters admonishes audiences, many of whom undoubtedly work for MBAs. "The pursuit of high ethical standards might be served well by the elimination of many business schools," he adds.[49] One can picture him as a latter-day version of the Russian anarchist philosopher Mikhail Bakunin, shouting out from his stage in a corporate conference center, "To be the slaves of pedants—what a fate for humanity!" The deep-seated hostility to rational inquiry that pervades the so-called research offered by Peters and his fellow gurus is ultimately a reflection of this long-standing anxiety about intellectuals and experts in our society.

As an antidote to the power of the intellectuals, Peters, like many of his populist predecessors, champions homegrown smarts and authentic experience over book learning. In his first books, Peters gets out the message that "far too many managers have lost sight of the basics."[50] Later, from the comfort of his alpaca farm in the Green Mountains, he tells us that "Vermont farmers have a lot to teach us"[51]—just as, in an earlier century, Jean-Jacques Rousseau, from the safety of his rural retreats, informed us that humankind is born innocent but lives everywhere in the chains of a corrupt corporate bureaucracy, and that there is more wisdom to be found among the peasants of the Savoy than in all the salons of Paris.

The anger that Peters and his fellow gurus tap has a real foundation in experience. Life in a corporate bureaucracy involves many injustices. The attack on managerial elites that Peters represents is, at its best, an expression of the democratic and egalitarian instincts of American culture, and it can serve as an important check on the excessive concentration of power. As Hofstadter points out in his history of the topic, however, anti-intellectualism tends to rise in proportion not to the weakness of the elites it despises, but to their strength.[52]

3. There is good news in America! One of the fundamental principles of both democratic religion and the film business is the absolute necessity of a happy ending. To balance the fear of the present and the loathing of bureaucracy that he so ably invokes, Peters knows he must dispense an even greater dollop of hope. "We often view ourselves as victims of heartless organizations . . . as hapless and helpless 'cubicle slaves,'" he says. "We must remind ourselves that the White-Collar Revolution will erase all that. We must understand that in the New Economy all work is project work—and that every project must be a WOW (special) project."[53] "Never underestimate the market for hope," adds fellow guru Gary Hamel.[54] The back cover of *Excellence* screams with hope: "There is good news from America. There is an ART OF AMERICAN MANAGEMENT—and it works!"[55]

But realizing the promise of the "White-Collar Revolution," Peters makes clear, is not just a matter of testing out a few new tips and tricks. True to his crypto-evangelical roots, he demands from his listeners a total conversion experience. "Turn your whole-damn-enterprise Upside Down—Right Now!" he shouts.[56] There are no shades of gray in Peters' world. (Or brown—"Pity the poor brown," he says.[57]) He makes an emphatic distinction between those who get it and those who don't, between the saved and the damned. "You'd have to be an outright fool not to see that we're in the midst of something big . . . VERY BIG!" he says.[48]

Though the other gurus may not always agree with Peters on exactly what this very big something is, all follow his lead in demanding total conversion to their favored doctrine. Indeed, in order to make their proposed solutions seem all the more valuable—and to ward off critics who might accuse them of peddling phony miracle cures—they invariably insist that the medicine will taste awful and be hard to swallow. Total transformation, they gravely inform us, is never easy.

Following the pattern established in evangelical and self-help narratives, the gurus' offer of salvation has three distinguishing features. The first is that it is always imminent. Judgment day is not tomorrow, perhaps, but the day after tomorrow—and in any case will not occur later than the decade after this one. The important point is that it is close enough for listeners to touch, but not so close that it can be confused with the wicked world of the present. The second is that it involves a social transformation that goes well beyond an increase in profits and productivity. "We are in the midst of redefining our basic ideas about what enterprise and organization and even being human is," Peters enthuses.[59] The third is that it usually takes place—or at least gets its start—in that land of boundless promise: America.

Perhaps the best example of this pattern of salvation stories, especially on the first two points, comes from Peter Drucker—who once again lived too long for the good of his own credibility. In his very first book, *The Future of Industrial Man*, Drucker identifies the fundamental problem that all of his future visions of salvation are intended to resolve. "In the modern corporation," he writes, "the decisive power, that of the managers, is derived from no one but the managers themselves controlled by nobody and nothing and responsible to no one. It is in the most literal sense unfounded, unjustified, uncontrolled and irresponsible power."[60] The corporation, Drucker acknowledges, is a social, political, "and even moral" institution; yet, within a democracy, the power vested in the hands of management of a corporation appears to lack a legitimate foundation. He fears that such an illegitimate source of economic power will prove unsustainable and socialist governments will take over the economy. The aim of Drucker's work henceforth is to secure the foundations of the corporation as a socially responsible form of power in the modern economy (and thereby forestall the necessity for a socialist revolution).

In his work from the 1940s and '50s, Drucker hints that General Motors established the prototype of an organizational form that, with the benefit of a few nudges in the right direction, will soon resolve the problem of the social legitimacy of management power. According to his analysis, GM is much more than a car company; it is a new way of life. The decentralized, professionalized M-Form organization, he optimistically forecasts, will dissolve conflicts between the corporation and society and between labor and management.

In his work from the 1960s and '70s, upon acknowledging that his earlier hopes for big-business socialism are somewhat exaggerated, Drucker decides to pin his expectation for an imminent social transformation on what he calls "pension fund socialism." Workers and capitalists will at last lie down together, he argues, because, by virtue of their pension fund holdings, workers will become capitalists. These new worker-capitalists will manage the economy in a manner that respects workers' rights and brings legitimacy to the economic order. In view of later developments (such as, for example, aggressive buyout funds that take their money from pension funds), Drucker's forecast for pension fund socialism now falls somewhere between hollow and silly.

In a celebrated article from 1988 grandly titled "The Coming of the New Organization," Peter Drucker shifts the focus of his future fantasies yet again. This time, the problems of conflict and control will dissipate as fundamental changes in the nature of work result in the spontaneous generation of the eponymous "new organization." Sticking to his preferred forecasting period of two decades, Drucker announces that "the typical large business 20 years hence will have fewer than half the levels of management of its counterpart today, and no more than one third of the managers . . . it will bear little resemblance to the typical manufacturing company, circa 1950, which our textbooks consider the norm. Instead it is far more likely to resemble: the hospital, the university, the symphony orchestra . . . it will be what I call an information-based organization."[61] What makes this particular prognostication sadly touching, in Drucker's case, is that if we look back into his earlier work, it becomes evident that the "new organization" has always hovered over his thinking as an ideal. "The business enterprise of today is no longer an organization in which there are a handful of bosses at the top who make all the decisions while the workers carry out the orders," he writes in 1959. "It is primarily an organization of professionals of highly specialized knowledge exercising autonomous, responsible judgment."[62]

Drucker's resurrection of the "new organization" in the 1980s, in fact, was a desperate attempt to throw himself on the back of the truck that Peters was driving. Just about every guru at the time understood that the key to success was to offer a plan of salvation along the antibureaucratic lines articulated in *Excellence* and further pursued in *Liberation Management*. "Tomorrow's effective 'organization' will be conjured up anew each day," exults Peters.[63] What he perhaps failed to anticipate was that his fellow gurus would be conjuring up a new name for the new organization each day too. Rosabeth Moss Kanter— a Harvard Business School professor who some have suggested is Tom Peters' alter ego in polite society—championed the "integrative organization," an "informal" and "knowledge-driven" form of life that is apparently rid of bureaucratic evils.[64] Other gurus proposed, for example, the adaptive organization, the informed organization, the knowledge-intensive organization, the learning organization, the network organization, the organic organization, the hybrid organization, the postentrepreneurial organization, the postindustrial organization, the postmodern organization, the poststructuralist organization, the self-designing organization, and the shamrock organization.

All of these variants of the new organization are distinguishable from one another primarily by what Freud called the narcissism of petty differences. They are new bottles for a wine that was very old even when Elton Mayo brought it into the business schools back in 1929. They describe a world without power, where productive collaboration happens in a spontaneous and uncontrolled way. As Peters puts it in his inimitable style, they are about "boss-free implementation." Alas, except for occasional sightings in faraway corporations or in carefully constructed laboratory experiments, such as the Hawthorne T Room, the new organization exists always only in the safety of an imaginary future.

In the 1990s, as the hysteria about the new organization faded, Drucker came up with another peg on which to hang his undiminished hope for a socially legitimate form of managerial power. "The right answer to the question, Who takes care of the social challenges of the knowledge society?, is thus neither the government nor the employing organization," he wrote in 1996. "It is a separate and new *social sector*."[65] Although the social sector to which Drucker refers here has grown in recent years (thanks in part to rising inequality and changes in the tax code), the notion that this sector will lead us to salvation (or that its management is free from the issues that beset the for-profit sector) is no less utopian than that which came before.

The continuous recycling of the gurus' visions of a future free from bureaucratic constraints makes it quite obvious that these never really refer to a point on the space-time continuum as we know it. They are not predictions of some future outcome based on a dispassionate observation of present trends. At best, the gurus' visions express an ideal. Mostly, however, they serve as a necessary end point in the narrative structure of management thought. They are the prize at the end, the reward for travails, a bottle of hope—call it "liberation tonic." They exist as an inescapable consequence of the processes of natural selection at work in the evolution of the guru industry. Among gurus as among spiritual leaders, only the hopeful survive.

4. **"You have the power!"** A listener approaches Peters after one of his presentations and says, "I can't implement any of this stuff. I don't have the power." Given that his sermons are nominally aimed at CEOs but land in the ears of middle managers of pizza delivery companies, this kind of disconnect must happen all the time in Peters' seminars. So how does Peters respond? "I flip out. This issue is different. *It's up close and personal!* It gets right to the core of how I've lived my life ever since I was a 'powerless' junior officer in the Navy in 1966 . . . ever since I was a 'powerless' new-kid-on-the-block at McKinsey & Co. in 1974. In each case, I reveled in my powerlessness."[66]

Those who, like Peters, aspire to help others help themselves long ago discovered that the secret to their own success lies in convincing others that they already have all the power they need to achieve their goals. A recent best-seller title in the self-help genre, *The Secret*, illustrates this point in extreme form. The secret in question turns out to be that we all create our own reality all of the time.[67] Whether you get cancer or win the lottery, it's all your own doing. Norman Vincent Peale, one of the pioneers of the modern American self-help genre, says, "There is enough power in *you* to blow the city of New York to rubble. That, and nothing less, is what advanced physics tells us."[68] And that, pretty much, is what Tom Peters tells us too. "'Getting things done' ultimately is not about 'power' or 'rank,'" Peters hyperventilates. "It's about PASSION and IMAGINATION and PERSISTENCE."[69]

Rosabeth Moss Kanter, Peters' respectable doppelgänger, cloaks a similar point in language more appropriate to the academic setting in which she finds herself. In her 2006 effort, *Confidence: How Winning Streaks and Losing Streaks Begin and End*, she defines confidence as "consisting of positive expectations for favorable outcomes" and argues that success and failure are "self-fulfilling tendencies" resulting from an abundance and lack of confidence, respectively. Peter Drucker, in his somewhat more clumsy way, suggests that attitude is everything. He, too, assures us that middle management will inherit the earth: "The man . . . who stresses his downward authority is a subordinate no matter how exalted his title and rank," he says. "But the man who . . . takes responsibility for results, no matter how junior, is in the most literal sense of the phrase, 'top management.'"[70]

In his books and presentations for the middle managers of the world, Peters regularly tosses out vignettes about Churchill, Gandhi, and Einstein. The message is that you, too, can make history.[71] The other gurus are no less unbounded in their expectations for the opportunities for heroism that present themselves to the managers of the world. Drucker's first major book of advice, *The Practice of Management*, from 1954, is subtitled "the most important function in American society." Workers will perhaps be alarmed to discover in its first line that "the manager is the dynamic, life-giving element in every business." Many management guru books are simply excuses to retell stories about how heroic managers triumphed against all odds to build massively profitable corporations. The figure of the manager-hero is as central to the appeal and to the efficacy of the guru literature as empowerment is to evangelism and self-help.

We are all CEOs now, the gurus say. Presumably it's just our paychecks that have to catch up. It is often helpful, for motivational purposes, to urge people to take charge of their own lives, realize their potential, and so on. The wisdom of the gurus becomes problematic, however, when it is confused with an analysis of the actual distribution of power in our society.

5. Just look at me! In most cultures, the guru is a special person. He benefits from unique access to the mysterious forces of chaos lurking just under the deceptive surfaces of our world. Thus, he has the ability to intuit the movements of the cosmos and so to foretell our destiny. He doesn't have to prove what he says—he has the luxury of using what the medieval theologians called "the argument from authority." The guru, in fact, ceases to be a simple human being and becomes a representative of his own brand. He may grow out his hair, dress up in underwear, retire to the hills, or otherwise cultivate eccentricities. Everything he does and says carries a symbolic weight. He does not speak in sentences, but in pronouncements. Sometimes he speaks in tongues. He is a master of twists, loud nonsense, and non sequiturs: "I'm a writer. I love words. One of the words I love is 'quests,'" Peters says on one videotape.[72]

"You know when Tom walks into a room. There's a buzz. All eyes are on him. He has a presence which is compelling and exciting," one of Peters' former associates confides to his biographer, Stuart Crainer. "People carried his books like the Bible. They were highlighted in different colors. They were well-thumbed and dog-eared through re-reading. There were fanatics who hung on every syllable. It was amazing to watch. It was like a religious cult."[73] Another associate says he was astonished at "the reverence with which people thought of Tom." For many of his devotees, Tom was like "the Pope."[74]

In America, where salvation has almost always been measured in cash value, the surest sign of the guru's special position in the order of things is his own material success. Tom Peters has certainly demonstrated that he is special. With a calendar of 60 or so money-spinning seminars a year, millions of books in print, an award-winning blog, a staff of 25 employees, and that 1,600-acre farm in Vermont to his name, Peters has collected many blessings from his message of corporate liberation. His competitor Jim Collins, like a number of other gurus, has also received huge down payments on his heavenly rewards.

The naysayers, as is their wont, will wonder whether the guru has any qualifications for the job other than his own success. Peters' actual experience in management, they will point out, is hardly one to inspire confidence in his advice. His longest period of employment was the six years or so (with significant interruptions for personal reasons) that he spent in the bubble universe of McKinsey, where the likelihood is that he never had to manage more than a couple of bright MBAs and a secretary at any one time. His own firm, the Tom Peters Group, is notorious for lackluster management and lackadaisical customer service. "My own experience is that TPG largely fails to practice what Peters preaches," writes Crainer. "Calls do go unreturned. There is the impression that the company is simply a means of screening Peters' calls."[75]

As Peters understands, however, the authority of the guru does not stem from knowledge, degrees, or experience. It has its foundation in a personal narrative. The guru's story is one of triumph over adversity. It is his own passage through the dark night of the bureaucratic soul and his subsequent redemption and ascension into consulting heaven that cement his bond with his audience. His listeners need to know that he has suffered as they have, that he has witnessed the madness firsthand, that they're not crazy—it's just that the world that has gone nuts. His own rise from the boiler room of a navy warship to the commanding heights of the guru economy offers hope to us all.

There can be no doubt that for some people, the five-step spiritual path followed by gurus like Tom Peters leads to fulfillment. For many, however, the religion of the management gurus is a form of false consciousness. It masks the political nature of many of the problems that concern them and thus draws them away from a proper understanding of their self-interest. Although it promises freedom, it in fact delivers a more refined form of servitude. As the semiestablished church of our times, its global effect is to perpetuate rather than to challenge managerial authority.

Fads in Management Theory: The Wheel of Suffering

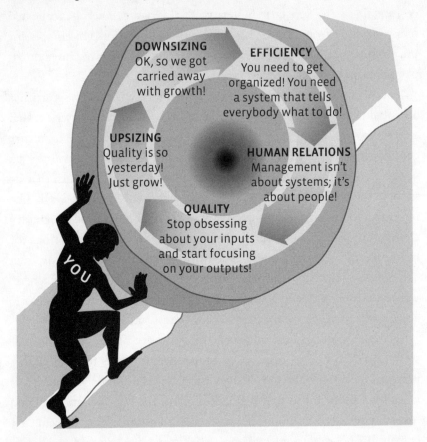

The fact that capitalist economies undergo constant, destabilizing transformation has been well known since Marx's day. The important and essentially political question that looms behind this fact is how the risks and costs of such change should be shared among workers, employers, and the state. In the three decades since Peters brought management to the masses, the risks and costs of transformation have, on the whole, shifted down the social spectrum, even as income has pushed upward. The disempowerment of the lower classes has grown in direct proportion to the growth in the rhetoric of empowerment preached by the gurus. Peters himself alludes to the problem with a cavalier shrug: "Are most of the people who attend my seminars middle managers? Yes. Why do they come? Beats me. Middle management, as we have known it since the railroads invented it right after the Civil War, is dead."[76]

To their credit, Peters and Drucker, unlike a number of the other gurus, do at times indicate an awareness of the political dimension of the issues they tackle. In *Re-imagine*, Peters notes in passing that in order to meet the challenges of the new economy we must have "a new social contract".[77] "We need radically different public policies to make this new opportunity viable. For example, health care benefits that are universal and not attached to the company. Hearty and perpetual re-training opportunities, supported in part by the government. Pensions that are self-managed and independent of one's employer."[78] Peters describes himself as a "card-carrying" member of the ACLU, is active in Democratic Party politics, and once considered running for Congress. Drucker, of course, raises in his earliest work the general question about the legitimacy of management power, and he is critical throughout his career when he perceives abuses of this power. He is particularly scathing in his criticism of CEOs who reap ungodly sums in exchange for firing large numbers of workers and otherwise distributing risk downward.

In the general scheme of guru literature, however, such moments of political agitation are really just lapses from a program of ideological cheerleading that tilts heavily in the opposite direction. The real thrust of the gurus' chaos talk is in fact to transmit the risks of capitalism directly down to the lowest orders of middle management and below. It is a way of blaming the Japanese (or whomever) directly for problems that are at least partly political and then asking workers (including middle managers) to assume responsibility for responding to these problems. Peters' self-help ideology does not permit him to see in this downward shift of risk the abdication of corporate or government responsibility. Instead, he hails the beginning of an era of "Renewed Individual Responsibility." The central tenet of self-help—that "you have the power"—may be quite useful as a motivational tool; but it can also stand in the way of acknowledging that some risks are best borne not by the individual, and that some ills are best addressed by collective political action rather than individual heroism.

In keeping with the long tradition of management thought since Taylor, the utopian proposals of the gurus rely on management itself to solve the problems of management. In *Chaos*, for example, Peters urges his readers (all notionally CEOs) to "provide a guarantee of continuous employment to your permanent work force," which he defines as the workforce required to meet 90% of demand.[79] If managers would just be nice, it seems, our problems would vanish.

Drucker is so convinced of the innate goodness of management that he tends to see the underlying political and economic conflicts as merely matters of public misperception. "There has never been a more efficient, a more honest, a more capable and conscientious group of rulers [than managers]," he says in his first book.[80] In 1974, noting that the workers of the world were not yet seeing things his way, he adds, "The fact of increasing income equality in the US is quite clear. Yet the popular impression is one of rapidly increasing inequality. This is an illusion; but it is a dangerous illusion. It corrodes. It destroys mutual trust."[81] He goes on to cite the whopping $500,000 salary of the CEO of a large corporation as an example of income inequality run amok. Today, it would appear that Drucker was the one suffering from a dangerous illusion.

The gurus, in fact, make a caricature out of the specious, voluntary professionalism that has characterized management thought since Taylor's day. In his discussions of the "new organization," Drucker conveys the impression that the problems of authority in the workplace will wither away once managers begin relating to one another and to workers as the professionals they are. "We use the word 'PARTNER' until we want to barf!" adds Peters, trying to convey the notion that managers should treat everyone not as instruments but with respect.[82] These are fine sentiments, no doubt, but they refer to a profession that exists in name only, a profession that lacks almost all of the structures and policing mechanisms found in the other professions. Far from serving as a check on management power, the gurus' ideas about professionalism and "putting people first" often serve as rhetorical instruments for the extension of management power.

"The excellent companies require and demand extraordinary performance from the average man," the authors of *Excellence* declare.[83] Read this pronouncement one way, and it sounds like a stirring call to bring out the best in people. Read it in another way, and it is a program to encourage companies to extract more labor from their workers than perhaps they have a right to expect. It is not so different, in the end, from demanding an extraordinary 47½ tons a day from the pig-iron loaders of the world. In the wake of *Excellence*, there is scarcely a CEO in the world who does not understand that "culture" is a valuable device for inducing employees to accept the idea that they should work harder for less pay.

Although Peters is paid to bash bosses, it should not be forgotten that in many cases it is the bosses who pay him to do this. The "cash cow" of the guru industry is the lecture and seminar business, and it is corporations, not individuals, who fund these events. CEOs may not read or care much for the gurus, it seems, but they are quite willing to subject their subordinates to the gurus' guidance. And these CEOs have reason to believe that they are getting a good deal. If religion is the opium of the people, as Marx suggested, then management theory should probably count as a kind of amphetamine. It causes agitation and hyperactivity. It does have the unfortunate side effect, however, of making people feel much more efficient than they actually are.

There are few better examples of management theory's medicinal nature than Tom Peters himself. Three decades after he had his chat with the god of organizational effectiveness, Peters hasn't let up. He travels the business world at a manic pace; and, to judge from his writings, the traveling only makes him madder. When he checks into a hotel, he immediately assesses whether every detail is to his satisfaction. He feverishly applauds the small triumphs of customer service—the threaded needle in a hotel sewing kit; the concierge who remembers his name. He has trouble getting over bad service. When a television repairman fails to show up to fix the set in his hotel room, the episode merits a scathing indictment of managerial incompetence around the world.[84] Peters' books are a litany of confrontations with infuriating local phone companies, snooty airlines, and all the other horrifying bureaucratic monsters that populate the nightmares of the modern consumer. He is a permanently dissatisfied customer, the screeching spokesman for the little guy against the machine.

Reminiscing about his first success, *Excellence*, Peters says, "There's an almost Zen-like quality to the book. In fact, it makes the point that, when it comes to managing and controlling people, only by not try-ing do you succeed."[85] Yet there is a most un-Zen-like quality to Peters. For more than 25 years, he has run a publicity-seeking campaign that would have bored less-driven writers speechless, if not sent them into cardiac arrest. His to-do lists spill out in batches of 50 or 100 at a time. He writes a blog that spins away all the loose ends of his public image. He is a control fanatic. And yet, on stage and in the unending stream of consciousness that forms his oeuvre, it becomes apparent that the one thing he is unable to control is himself.

This most un-Zen-like spirituality emerges directly from Peters' reli-gion of management. When Peters froths over details like the sticky labels on Rubbermaid products that peel off easily or the car salesman who puts fresh flowers in his used cars, he isn't celebrating a few rather trivial improvements in customer service; he is hunting for signs of character and spiritual commitment that transcend the product or ser-vice on offer. When he insists that business is not about profits, but "about heart" and "about beauty," he is declaring his longing for a cor-poration that is more than a corporation. He wants to feel the love of his telephone company, to find proof that it cares for him for more than just his business. When he says that "life at work is cool," he is really still searching for a job that is all fulfillment and no job. He is, in the final analysis, in search of something that isn't there. His dissatisfaction is guaranteed.

"We are the only society in the world that believes it can keep on getting better and better," says Peters, in one of his postmodern, self-referential moments. "So we keep on getting suckered in by people like Ben Franklin and Emerson and me."[86] One could debate whether the author of *The Pursuit of WOW!* overreaches by putting himself in the same sentence with such luminaries, but he is surely correct to point out that there is something very American in the manic spirituality that he and his fellow gurus promote. The blend of corporate mysticism and transcendental consumerism he offers has its roots planted in the pragmatic, optimistic, can-do American work ethic. But, like the Taylor-ist philosophy from which it springs, it is also a work ethic gone mad. It begins with the idea that work can be meaningful and stretches it to the point where there is no meaning outside work. It becomes a deluded form of optimism, a feverish activity that masks an underlying anxiety about the meaning of life, a form of self-alienation so complete that the self disappears entirely into its consumer preferences and transactions. It has populated the country with people who, like Peters, seem unable to go home at night.

The Promised Land

Two months and several dozen more pages of legal briefs after the hearing, the arbitrator delivered her verdict. It arrived in the form of two pages of double-spaced, large-font text that looked as if it came straight from a vintage typewriter. The two pages consisted almost entirely of bullet points detailing my "award."

In the award, the arbitrator granted me everything I believed I was owed when I departed the firm. I was entitled to my missing salary, my unpaid bonuses, my equity interest in the firm at book value, my retained interests in the event of a sale of the firm, and my full interest in the founders' fund, both for the "vested" years I had worked and for the "unvested" future years, even when I would not be working for the firm. In calculating the value of the unpaid bonuses, the arbitrator also saw fit to grant me handsome annual pay raises all the way through to my last day at the firm.

The arbitrator, however, declined my request to have the firm pay for my legal expenses. She also did not find the firm guilty of any violations of labor law (I had thought that having people work without pay was sure to be illegal). On the whole, nonetheless, so far as my interests were concerned, the outcome seemed fair and just. I was awarded what I would have received had the firm chosen to honor its commitments to me, less a tax payable to the lawyers and arbitrator—which was perhaps not an unreasonable penalty for my poor judgment in having gone into business with the firm in the first place.

Although I viewed the award as a triumph, the firm's managers viewed it as merely a piece of paper. And paper was not a commodity in which they placed much value. They at first chose to ignore the award, preferring instead to incite me to file yet another suit. After an intervention by the arbitrator, they belatedly coughed up the missing salary, bonuses, and equity at book value. But when I tried to collect on the founders' fund—which I thought of then as the most important part of the award (at least symbolically, since the future growth of the firm was looking grim)—the firm's managers flatly refused to heed the terms of the arbitrator's decision.

The founders' fund issue was soon eclipsed by a more important one having to do with the "retained interests." The deal between the firm and its extraterrestrial acquirers had at last been consummated, and the newly merged entity was in turn acquired by another highly touted Internet consulting company. But the remaining partners of my old firm hadn't yet finished rewriting the rules in their own favor. They structured the all-stock deal with their savvy Internet buyers in two installments, one payable immediately and the other, somewhat larger one a year or so later. They then amended the retained-interest part of the shareholders' agreement of our firm to exclude the claim of departed partners, such as me, on the second installment. I began legal action to fight this latest machination, but in the end there was not enough time to pursue it to its conclusion.

As a result of my successful arbitration, I was fortunate in that, unlike many other purged partners, I had a legally unambiguous claim to my retained interests, such as they were. Perhaps because the firm was now becoming part of a public entity, it lost some of its flexibility to operate free from ethical and legal constraints, so it arranged to transfer to me my slice of the first installment of the all-stock sale.

In the weeks before I received my shares, the dot-com bubble reached its frothiest peak. There was madness in the air, as pundits proclaimed the realization of the dream of a people's market, where hipness and excellence and capital would fuse in a great festival of democracy. For the lucky few with a stake in the festivities, it seemed more like a giant shell game, with huge wads of undeserved cash rolling from shell to shell, someone sure to turn up a winner. The stock in the combined company in which I now owned a tiny percentage soared, and several analysts put their 12-month target prices for the stock at two or more times its already wildly inflated value. "Gee, maybe you should hold on to them when you get them," my friendly broker said. Friends asked me if they should buy.

I told everyone who would listen to keep their wallets in their pockets. I knew very little about the rest of the acquiring company's business, but, to paraphrase Groucho Marx, I did not want to invest in any company that invested in my company. The acquisition had done nothing to halt the firm's disintegration. Résumés were flying out of the windows of the firm's fancy new headquarters like so many snowflakes. Within one year of the acquisition, two-thirds of its employees were gone. The partners, as far as I could tell, were planning to wait around only long enough to collect their shares. It seemed that at any minute the shell game would come to its ugly denouement.

In the weeks before receiving my shares, as the share price crested and then began to drift downward, I began to short the company stock by buying put options. The nanosecond I received my shares, I sold them all, which, combined with my short positions, allowed me to pocket a substantial and grossly undeserved reward for my years of labor. If justice reigned in the world's financial markets, I would have been lucky to escape from the experience with a clutch of worthless business cards. Thanks entirely to the exuberant irrationality of the investing public, however, my career as a management consultant came to a close with a profit comparable to what I might have earned in a more respectable firm over the period.

Three weeks after I received and disposed of my holdings, the shares in the combined strategy- and web-consulting company had lost half their value. Some months later, they were trading for a dollar or two. One year to the day after the transaction, the shell of my old firm, a Cayman Islands entity that existed mainly as a vehicle for paying off debts and funneling stock to the remaining partners of the firm, declared bankruptcy. Shortly after that, the combined Internet consulting company, which had at its peak boasted a total value of several billion dollars, became insolvent too. The second installment on the purchase of my firm—the installment that the remaining partners had taken pains to hoard for themselves— was valueless by the time it came due.

As I pulled away from the wreckage in my small but sturdy lifeboat, I was astonished to discover that I was almost alone in surviving the events in sound financial condition. Many of the "purged" partners, I gathered, had been unable to secure legal judgments in time to collect their shares. I heard through my lawyers, who got it from the Troll, that Owen, whose shares at their peak must have had a paper value in the neighborhood of $40 million, had held on to his stake even as the Internet company sank into nothingness. Patrick and many of the other remaining partners had apparently gone down with him.

The bankruptcy of the firm's shell company, in fact, resulted from the remaining partners' inexplicable decision to use shares in the parent company to cover the shell company's liabilities. The bankruptcy canceled the debts the company owed—debts payable to me, among others—which resulted in a possible windfall paper profit for the firm's remaining partners, which in turn triggered an enormous potential tax liability. As one anonymous partner lamented to the press, "Not only has the sale . . . not been a money-making proposition for most of us, but it has put certain people in a position where they could potentially be facing personal bankruptcy."

The firm's remaining partners had, in effect, doubled-down their bets on the descent. I can only conclude that their delusions about the worth of any project in which they happened to be engaged were impermeable to reality. In those last days of the firm, I pictured Owen, strapped to his sinking whale, waving the others to follow him down, promising to build something bigger than himself somewhere at the bottom of a sea of financial irregularities.

The collapse of the firm I helped to found is at some level a tawdry tale that illustrates nothing more than that the world has a number of bad apples scattered among the good. But there are some useful lessons in it nonetheless. At least some part of the trouble arose not from the apples but from the orchard—that is, from an approach, a system of thought, and a set of values that brought out the worst in the bad and left out the best in the good.

The fall of my firm did not reflect well on the formal apparatus of managerialism in our society—the elite business schools, the top-tier management consultancies, and the learned discipline of management theory. My firm was made up of management consultants with the best pedigrees, most with MBAs from the finest universities, all ostensibly paid to supply humankind with their expertise on management. But we couldn't manage our way out of a shoe box. And the best training that money can buy could not save us from ourselves. Indeed, the rhetoric of management served all along to obscure the ethical contradictions at the base of the firm's existence. Everyone involved was "maximizing shareholder value" all the way to the end of the party. Most managers, consultants, and MBAs, to be sure, are good people and do good work. But the alarming reality is that these comforting facts obtain despite, rather than because of, the education these folks receive and the ideology they share.

The popular doctrines of management gurus fared worst of all in the microcosm of my old firm. The firm reveled in the gurus' advice to "nuke the hierarchy" and promote the soft power of shared values and culture. But it was this very absence of structure that enabled the rise of an unchecked power within the firm. The firm declared its allegiance to people, not institutions; and yet it was this misguided and manipulative humanism that led to a cult of personality and that fueled the delusions of grandeur of its leaders. The firm promised to "break all the rules," just as the gurus demand—and then it went on to break a few too many rules. Above all, the firm held out the ideal of professionalism as the glue that would keep all the pieces together; yet all it offered was the specious professionalism of the gurus, a purely voluntary code that recognizes no standards and accepts no enforcement other than the goodwill, self-interest, and arbitrary whims of the so-called professionals themselves.

From the comfortable distance of an intervening decade, the story of my own, miniature Enron may seem to be very much of its moment. The firm enjoyed its 15 minutes in the public eye because, like a number of other enterprises in that strange time, it indulged the glittering fantasy of the gurus, a fantasy in which a priesthood of hipsters operating in the pure freedom of an open market would exploit a miraculous new technology in order to bring about a new form of human existence. And yet the story ultimately rested on the kind of hope that, in its more sober form, has long been one of America's most important contributions to the world, and, in times of extreme enthusiasm, becomes an excuse for self-delusion and deceit. The moment to which my story belongs has, in fact, repeated itself many times in the American past, and it will undoubtedly recur many times in the not-too-distant future.

The Future of Management Education

The time has come to recognize that higher education in management rests on a fatal fallacy. The idea behind the contemporary business school is that preparing future business managers means training them in a discipline called Business Management. After 100 years of fruitless attempts to produce such a discipline, it should be clear that it does not exist. Preparing managers to manage, in fact, is not different from preparing people to live in a civilized world. Managers do not need to be trained; they need to be *educated*. And for that purpose, although a certain amount of study of business-related subjects may prove useful, the business schools as they are presently constituted are at best superfluous.

Albert Jay Nock, a cantankerous libertarian and man of letters who belongs even less to any of today's political categories than he belonged to any of those of his own time, surveyed the American educational system in 1937 as an old man and noted with dismay how it had changed since his youth: "The difference seemed to be that while education was still spoken of as a 'preparation for life,' the preparation was of a kind which bore less directly on intellect and character than in former times, and more directly on proficiency. It aimed at what we used to call training rather than education; and it not only did very little with education, but seemed to assume that training *was* education, thus overriding a distinction that formerly was quite clear."[1] In the 70 years since Nock wrote those words, that vital distinction between training and education has only further atrophied.

To be sure, training has its uses. We want our dentists to be taught how to use their drills, and we want our accountants to know the difference between a credit and a debit. Some of the training that business school students receive—in subjects like accounting, corporate finance, and marketing—undoubtedly has its uses. But in today's rapidly changing markets, training can be outdated by graduation day, and workers must be retrained on the job. Training at its best can be a substitute for experience, but it is no substitute for an education.

Many of today's managers are well trained enough, but their training does little to improve their level of education. If Henry Adams came back to life, he would recognize them instantly. They are "a crowd of men who seem . . . ignorant that there is a thing called ignorance; who have forgotten how to amuse themselves; who can not even understand that they are bored."[2] This lack of education does more harm to society and to individuals than do any deficiencies in training.

In 1988, Porter and McKibbin issued a study of business schools that argued for a kind of "softening" of the curricula. The study echoed a widespread criticism that business education is too "hard"—biased in favor of theory and quantitative analysis. It advocated multidisciplinary, experience-based approaches and a renewed emphasis on subjects such as leadership, communication, and ethics. Though the findings were said to be novel, in fact the study assembled a collection of criticisms dating back at least to the first years of the business schools. Almost two decades before Porter and McKibbin's study, in a memorable article in the *Harvard Business Review*, the professor and former manager J. Sterling Livingston criticized the formal training offered in business schools as fundamentally irrelevant to businessmen.[3]

Undoubtedly, these criticisms have some merit. But the record makes clear that they represent perennial expressions of frustration rather than a real program of change. In 2005, Bennis and O'Toole essentially repeated Porter and McKibbin's findings in their critique of the business schools. In 2008, another scholar surveyed the top 50 business schools and concluded that, despite the highly favorable reception of the study's recommendations, "at many schools, the ideal curriculum remains far more a normative construct than a positive reality."[4] In my view, the calls for the creation of a softer and more "relevant" curriculum are well-meaning but misguided. They take for granted the same instrumental, training-oriented approach of business education that is the ultimate source of the problems they identify.

The business schools will, in fact, never escape this dialectic between hard and soft learning—or between rigor and relevance—because it follows inevitably from the flawed premises of their existence. The so-called soft skills are in many ways the proper focus of an education, and they are (or were, at least until recently) the substance of a good, liberal arts education. But these skills inevitably accumulate by indirection, through the unpredictable interaction of a wide range of educational experiences. They aren't the kinds of things that can be simply handed over the table in a training presentation. If a business-specific training program isn't hard, there is nothing to transfer. But if it isn't soft, it isn't relevant for most managers. A similar quandary arises from the much-desired objective of teaching "multidisciplinary," or "integrative," thinking. Such thinking presumes access to a wide—and perhaps, in principle, unlimited—range of material. But how can a narrow collection of training programs in subjects that even most businesspeople find arcane be expected to supply the foundation for such a synthesis?

The instrumental approach to business training also does a disservice to the "hard" subjects that are supposed to be its strength. The real flaw in most academic research in business subjects is not, as the critics have it, that such research is not relevant; it is the very expectation that it should be relevant. There is a terrific amount of knowledge to be gathered and studied concerning business management, above and beyond that which now emerges from economics departments, and there is no reason to limit it to that which can be usefully imparted in introductory courses to large numbers of prospective managers. In fact, there is no reason to limit its audience to managers at all. Business research may ultimately prove more useful for public policy makers, for voters, for students of other disciplines, for members of the financial community other than managers, and even for managers, insofar as, more than managers, they are thinking people and citizens.

If business schools would drop the pretense of providing practical training and engage in disinterested, critical study of business and management practices and culture, they might actually make a significant contribution to society. Although it seems indisputable (to me at any rate) that there are too many MBAs in the world, it does not follow and is probably not the case that there are too many PhD's in business subjects. Indeed, the depth and quality of that research should be expected to improve as the market for MBAs shrinks.

The most important source of the problems with academic research in business management is not that it is too far from its "customers," but that it is too close to them. It is too close to its students, who will always demand that its results be reduced to easily digestible banalities. It is also too close to the corporations that sponsor its research programs, hire professors as consultants, contribute to endowments, and exert pressure through recruiting policies. (If any political party funded political science departments in the way that corporations fund the business schools, we would naturally consider their research to be little more than propaganda.) The same problem of excessive "closeness to the customer" characterizes the modern business press. By bringing transparency and critical analysis to bear on management practices, the press, like the academy, should play a crucial role in checking the power of management. But how can it fulfill its obligations to do so if it is, on the one hand, beholden to its corporate sponsors and, on the other hand, slavishly pandering to the celebrity cravings of its audiences?

The descent into market-based idiocy has undoubtedly accelerated since *Business Week* and *U.S. News & World Report* began ranking business schools (or more precisely, MBA programs) in 1988. These rankings now serve as the singular metric by which schools, students, and recruiters assess schools.[5] The fanatical obsession with rankings may have spurred some useful competition among business schools, but it has had the effect of further eroding whatever small claim they had to be offering a serious education. Because the rankings give weight to student assessments and demands from practitioners, they inevitably force business schools in the direction of developing a noncontroversial, user-friendly, vocational program. At the end of the game, the business schools will be all business and no school. "Customer satisfaction" is a good way to sell shoes; but it is a bad way to relieve ignorance. It is fundamentally stupid to base the content of an education on what the as-yet uneducated person decides is best.

The prevailing, instrumental approach to business training makes it unlikely that such training will ever contribute to a moral education. Suppose we created a school that promised to train students in a few minor disciplines that were about as useful as techniques for counting grains of rice, along with a few major disciplines whose scientific cred- ibility was on a par with astrology, so that they learned to disdain the disinterested search for knowledge; suppose we planned to teach them the importance of using euphemisms and jargon so that they knew they would never really have to tell it like it is; suppose we based our whole program on the notion that success in all things is measured only in nar- rowly financial terms; suppose that, just to make ourselves feel better about it all, we organized an extra course on "ethics," where we expected students to memorize phrases like "the categorical imperative" that they would never use again; and suppose, finally, that we then let prospective students know that their ability to secure admission to our school and pay the hefty tuition represented a crucial step in advancing their careers. Who would come to our charming little institution? What would they learn? What would they do upon graduating?

There are those who will say that, if the schools award 140,000 gradu- ate degrees in business every year, it's because that is what the market demands. If senior executives receive tens or even hundreds of millions of dollars for their managerial services, it's because that is what the mar- ket will bear. If management consultants and management theorists find lucrative work, it's because there is a market for their services. Manage- ment, they will say, is a kind of technological expertise that pertains to individuals by virtue of their training or their talent, and as long as it trades freely in an open market, everything is as it should be. All we have to do to ensure that management does what it is supposed to do, they will add, is to align it with the market by rewarding it for maximizing shareholder value.

This fusion of management theory and free-market ideology in the shareholder-value-maximization model of management represents the most recent and perhaps the ultimate stage in the evolution of management thought over the preceding century. It rests on a fusion of the guiding idea of Taylorism (that management is a kind of technological expertise), the vision of the human relations movement (that this technology extends to the total control of human collectivities), and the premise of the strategy discipline (that the technology of management confers mastery over markets themselves). It has become the foundational doctrine of the business schools and the defining economic dogma of our times. It makes sense of the many extraordinary happenings in the corporate world today. But it is seriously flawed and often maleficent.

The shareholder-value model at the center of modern business education, like the doctrine of scientific management that it has replaced, takes for granted that the aim of management can be expressed in a single, scalar metric. But in fact, as Taylor's failures made clear long ago, in an imperfectly knowable world, at some point such a metric will invariably be at odds with the goals that motivate it. The shareholder-value metric, it is now abundantly clear, often induces managers to engage in destructive, short term–oriented actions at the expense of a firm's long-term goals; it favors excessive risk taking, since managers typically have much to gain on the upside and little to lose on the downside; and it gives managers credit and blame for events over which they have no real influence. The general principle of aligning shareholder interest with management is not a bad one, but the idea that a singular metric can seal a bond that is by its nature ethical is dangerous. Managers have a responsibility to work on behalf of shareholders, and it is a delusion to think that an incentive scheme based on any predetermined metric can substitute for this essentially ethical obligation.

The shareholder-value dogma is crippled also by the utopian assumptions that have characterized management thought since Taylor. By pretending to dissolve conflicts of interest with a simple calculus of metrics, the shareholder-value model ignores the realities of power. A glance through the recent history of executive compensation, with its complicated tales involving the backdating of options and the payout of prenegotiated severance packages, shows just how easy it is for managers to manipulate incentive schemes. Such schemes merely serve as cover for an autocratic model of corporate governance that, in keeping with the preceding tradition of management thought, contradicts the political wisdom of the framers of the US Constitution.

To be sure, a truly free market in management services—one where judge, jury, and advocates are embodied in distinct individuals—is a fine ideal. The problem with the shareholder-value model is that it achieves by stipulation what is often not achieved at all through decades of concerted effort. The model works only on the supposition that the market for managerial services is highly liquid and efficient. But markets are not born free; they are made free. As economists such as Joseph Stiglitz[6] have pointed out, in an imperfectly knowable world markets achieve the level of freedom and efficiency described in classical economic theory only when a number of restrictive conditions are met—conditions that in many cases must be established through government intervention, in the form of laws and regulatory bodies.

The managerial market, where information is almost by definition imperfectly distributed, is very far from a free and efficient market. In 65% of large, public corporations in America, the CEO is also the chairman of the board.[7] There probably isn't a major US corporation that does not have the CEO or former CEO of another corporation on its board. The consultants and auditors that managers and board members hire to provide a putative outside check report to the same people they are supposed to be checking on. If someone does catch the board members in a mistake, in any case, the universal use of directors' liability insurance means that they need never worry that they will have to pay for malfeasance. As in Taylor's vision of a scientifically managed world—or in Plato's republic, for that matter—the people who play the game are the same ones who write the rules. We should hardly be surprised that they almost always turn out to be the winners.

Perhaps the costliest error built into the shareholder-value model taught at business school is the misunderstanding that it fosters about the sources of economic prosperity. The reigning dogma assumes that economic success is entirely a property of individuals—superhero, business school–trained managers who can step into a large organization and make it sing. But in fact, although individuals do differ in their managerial abilities, many of the factors that produce managerial success are the properties of collectivities, not individuals. Within an organization, it is the general *ethos*, in the classical sense of that term—the level of mutual trust, often established over years or decades—that makes successful collaboration possible. The balancing of different skills and often even contrary points of view within a group, too, is typically a major factor in success. Perhaps the most important factors are those that lie outside the organization altogether—the legal, cultural, and ethical infrastructure of wider society on which organizations depend.

The evidence for the collective nature of much of managerial success is so obvious that the fact that it is overlooked merely highlights the dogmatic nature of the managerial ideology that dominates business education. If economic success were entirely a property of individuals, one would suppose that CEOs who move from one company to another would almost always match their prior performance. But in fact they rarely do. According to the theory, we should be able to alleviate world poverty by packing corporate superstars off to Central Africa and other places where their alleged managerial talents could do some good. But we know very well that if one were to take many of these executives so far outside their comfort zone, they would accomplish little beyond running up large hotel bills.

There is a difference between management in a fully modernized country and management in a developing country. (Trust me; I've worked in Mexico.) But—and here the management thinkers get things very wrong—the crucial difference is not that the poorer countries lack some special bundle of techniques, like the game theory oligopolistic pricing models and other fancy toys distributed in the business schools. Indeed, in many developing countries there are plenty of MBAs, trained at elite American universities; whereas a number of economically successful countries—notably Japan, Germany, Singapore, and China[8]—make do with few MBAs and no major business schools of their own. The difference between the rich and the poor is that, aside from the differences in economic capital stock, the social environment in the poor countries is lacking in the trust, transparency, and shared values that allow management to do its job. Good management arises not from the dispensing of business school diplomas, but from a universal respect for the law, a common set of values and expectations, a skilled population benefiting from good public education, and the legal framework that supports salaried employment. Where this ethical foundation of good management is lacking, managerial wizardry will achieve little. Where it is present, such wizardry comes cheaply and naturally.

At the bottom of the shareholder-value dogma lies a conceptual failure that is characteristic of market fundamentalism in general: the failure to recognize the value of a set of public goods. In many individual instances, the shareholder-value model has induced executives to engage in asset stripping—destroying the long-term productive potential of a corporation for the sake of short-term stock market gains. At a more general level, the dogma implicitly favors a similar kind of asset stripping for society at large—a demolition of the trust on which society is founded. The business schools do worse than train their students in subjects that do not exist; they also prepare them to become destructive members of society.

A recent study by the Aspen Institute appears to confirm that business school is, in fact, damaging to the moral fiber of students. Upon entering business school, the researchers found, students cherished noble ambitions to serve customers, create quality products, and otherwise contribute to the progress of humankind. By the time of their graduation, however, students were convinced that the only thing that matters is increasing shareholder value.[9] Alvin Rohrs, a leader of Students in Free Enterprise, aptly sums up the problem: "We have to get young people to stop and think about ethics and the decisions they're making." "Otherwise," as *Business Week* points out, "today's students may be tomorrow's criminals."[10]

Before one attempts to imagine a world without business schools, it is important to acknowledge that business schools serve a number of functions that have nothing to do with the knowledge they purportedly dispense. Herewith a list:

1. **Recruiting Festival.** My firm, like most consulting firms, was happy to recruit graduates from business schools in large part because doing so is highly efficient. The business schools bring together in one place hundreds of bright, ambitious people who want to fill the kinds of

jobs we offer. For students, conversely, the schools provide a helpful placement service.

2. **Signaling Device.** Why did Hernán Cortés burn his ships after he landed in Mexico? Because he wanted everyone to know that he was here to stay. Conquest or death. Warriors get painful, unhealthy tattoos for the same reason. The tattoos let everybody know that they are in the game for keeps. By virtue of the time and expense involved, likewise, a business degree is a way for students to signal to prospective employers and friends that they are fanatically committed to a career in business (or just to the idea of getting rich).

3. **Status Symbol.** The schools "brand" students as smart, capable, ambitious, and "high status," and this branding itself can (at least theoretically) improve their performance. (In the very many cases in which the schools serve to ease a transition from an earlier career path, one could say that they "rebrand" the product.) Thus, the schools themselves must first be branded. This is the point of the whole ranking system. A guide that details the strengths, weaknesses, and individual character of each business school without ranking them all on a single scale would serve the purpose if the purpose were to supply prospective students with a basis for choosing where to pursue their education. But that is emphatically not the purpose of the rankings, which is to specify (or simply to stipulate) the amount of status that a school offers its students.

4. **Language School.** Business schools teach students to speak the language of business. Come to think of it, this may be a disservice. Still, it's useful to speak like the natives.

5. **Network Maker.** At Wharton, there is a tradition that involves having a drink at each of 10 bars in one night. At Stanford, there are no classes on Wednesdays, giving students plenty of time to hit the university's outstanding golf course. Students may, in fact, get more out of the golf than they do from their textbooks. The sociologists call it "social capital," and it often does pay dividends, in the form of future working relationships.

These nonpedagogical functions of business schools are important. But they don't justify the existence of the schools. We could organize the job fair and get the networking (and maybe even a few tattoos) by sending the entering class of a business school on a cruise to the Caribbean instead. We could get the cultural capital by simply certifying individuals as "having been accepted" to one prestigious school or another, or perhaps organizing prize competitions for the best business school application. Executive MBA programs, which generally take managers out of their jobs in midcareer for a month or two, offer a number of the advantages of business school at a point in most people's careers when they are probably better able to make use of them and without the time commitment of the MBA. Consulting firms often do for their associates what business schools promise to do for students, so perhaps they should offer credentials, such as a Master of Consulting degree, at the end of two years' service. (It is interesting to note that in their in-house, "mini-MBA" programs, consulting firms assume that the intellectual content of an MBA can be communicated in about three weeks.)

One could entertain many fanciful alternatives to the modern business school, but there is one that does not seem far-fetched at all. Liberal arts colleges, graduate schools in the arts and sciences, and other professional schools could, in principle, perform the same functions as the business schools. Indeed, many increasingly do. Their students are just as bright, their brand names are famous enough, the opportunities that they offer for networking should be just as good, and, with some extra investment and perhaps the development of some internal selection processes, their recruitment and placement services could be expected to match those of the business schools. Add a three-week mini-MBA to hone spreadsheet skills, review basic financial analysis techniques, and master some of the business jargon, and their graduates should be ready to take over the world.

None of which is to say that liberal arts programs don't stand in need of improvement, too, in order to fulfill their purpose. Liberal arts programs generally do not do enough to address the scandalous level of innumeracy in our culture. Plato put a sign over the doorway to his Academy insisting that all who entered should first master geometry. In the modern, balkanized university, liberal arts students often express fear if they see anything larger than a three-digit page number. Many humanities departments seem to revel in their ignorance about economic life. The teaching experience in many colleges has atrophied too. In the factory-like setting of the modern university, the genuine mentoring relationships that have traditionally anchored education are too rare.

On the whole, however, liberal arts institutions need not be shy about the virtues of the curricula they supply. Peter Drucker himself suggests that it is through management that "the 'humanities' will again acquire recognition, impact, and relevance."[11] The central insights of management theory are, in fact, the stock in trade of the humanities disciplines. The gurus' tips on organizational politics are all there in Machiavelli's descriptions of Roman and Florentine politics, not to mention Thucydides on the Peloponnesian War or William Faulkner on the American South. There is probably more to learn from studying the defects of King Lear's "management style" than there is from reading articles about Michael Eisner's shortcomings as CEO of Disney. If you want wisdom from a deeply troubled individual complaining that man is born free but is everywhere in chains, then Jean-Jacques Rousseau is a better bet than Tom Peters. The analysis of meaning and the emphasis on understanding context that characterize good teaching in the humanities, too, can count as important preparation for prospective managers.

Management theory, in fact, is already a branch of the humanities—it just may not know it yet. Considered as a contributor to a science of management, on the one hand, Frederick Taylor is bound to disappoint. He teaches us only how to use a stopwatch as a means to infuriate people. Considered as a historical and cultural commentator, on the other hand, Taylor lays bare the ideals that unite and the fault lines that divide our society. He is a philosopher, and his message that the rigorous analysis of work will resolve our social predicaments is one that deserves to be engaged philosophically. The same is true of Elton Mayo. The science of organizations that he promised is a fraud. But he was right in saying that management is all about people and that trust is at the foundation of cooperation. The same is also true of the strategy theorists and the management gurus in general. The science of strategy doesn't exist, but that is no excuse for not making an effort to see the big picture and think ahead. The questions that the management theorists raise and the insights that they offer belong not to a speciously practical discipline of management, but to the history of philosophy, and they should be taught and studied as such.

What makes for a good manager? If we put all of their heads together, the great management thinkers at the end of the day give us the same, simple, and true answer. A good manager is someone with a facility for analysis and an even greater talent for synthesis; someone who has an eye both for the details and for the one big thing that really matters; someone who is able to reflect on facts in a disinterested way, who is always dissatisfied with pat answers and the conventional wisdom, and who therefore takes a certain pleasure in knowledge itself; someone with a wide knowledge of the world and an even better knowledge of the way people work; someone who knows how to treat people with respect; someone with honesty, integrity, trustworthiness, and the other things that make up character; someone, in short, who understands oneself and the world around us well enough to know how to make it better. By this definition, of course, a good manager is nothing more or less than a good and well-educated person.

Selected References

Ansoff, H. Igor. 1965. *Corporate strategy: An analytic approach to business policy for growth and expansion.* New York: McGraw-Hill.

———. 1988. *The new corporate strategy.* New York: Wiley.

Antoniou, Peter H., and Patrick A. Sullivan. 2006. *The H. Igor Ansoff anthology.* N.p.: BookSurge.

Bain, Joe S. 1956. *Barriers to new competition.* Cambridge, MA: Harvard University Press.

Baritz, Loren. 1960. *The servants of power: A history of the use of social science in American industry.* Middletown, CT: Wesleyan University Press.

Barnard, Chester. 1938. *The functions of the executive.* Cambridge, MA: Harvard University Press.

Beatty, Jack. 1998. *The world according to Drucker: The life and work of the world's greatest management thinker.* London: Orion.

Bendix, Reinhard. 1949. The perspectives of Elton Mayo. *Review of Economics and Statistics* 31: 312–19.

———. 1956. *Work and authority in industry.* New York: Wiley.

Bennis, Warren, and James O'Toole. 2005. How business schools lost their way. *Harvard Business Review* May: 96–104.

Best, Joel. 2006. *Flavor of the month: Why smart people fall for fads.* Berkeley: University of California Press.

Birnbaum, Robert. 2001. *Management fads in higher education.* San Francisco: Jossey-Bass.

Bogle, John C. 2005. *The battle for the soul of capitalism.* New Haven, CT: Yale University Press.

Bourke, Helen. 1982. The Australian writings of Elton Mayo. *Historical Studies* no. 79: 216–238.

Brandenburger, Adam M., and Barry J. Nalebuff. 1995. The right game: Use game theory to shape strategy. *Harvard Business Review* July–August: 57–71.

———. 1996. *Co-opetition.* New York: Doubleday.

Braverman, Harry. 1974. *Labor and monopoly capital.* New York: Free Press.

Buckingham, Marcus, and Curt Coffman. 1999. *First, break all the rules.* New York: Simon & Schuster.

Canback, Staffan. 1998. The logic of management consulting. *Journal of Management Consulting* 10 (2): 3–11.

Carey, Alex. 1967. The Hawthorne studies: A radical criticism. *American Sociological Review* 32: 403–16.

Carson, Paula, Patricia A. Lanier, Kerry David Carson, and Brandi N. Guidry. 2000. Clearing a path through the management fashion jungle. *Academy of Management Journal* 43: 1143–58.

Chandler, Alfred D., Jr. 1962. *Strategy and structure.* Cambridge, MA: MIT Press.

Christensen, C. Roland, Kenneth R. Andrews, and Joseph L. Bower. 1982. *Business policy: Text and cases.* 5th ed. Homewood, IL: Richard D. Irwin.

Clark, T. 2004. Controversies and continuities in management thought. *Journal of Management Studies* 41: 367–76.

Clayman, Michelle. 1987. In search of excellence: The investor's viewpoint. *Financial Analysts Journal* May–June: 54–63.

Collins, David. 2000. *Management fads and buzzwords: Critical-practical perspectives.* London: Routledge.

Collins, Jim. 2001. *Good to great: Why some companies make the leap—and others don't.* New York: HarperBusiness.

Collins, Jim, and Jerry Porras. 1995. *Built to last: Successful habits of visionary companies.* New York: HarperBusiness.

Copley, Frank Barkley. 1923. *Frederick W. Taylor: Father of scientific management.* New York: Harper.

Craig, David. 2005. *Rip-off!* London: Original Book.

Crainer, Stuart. 1997. *Corporate man to corporate skunk: The Tom Peters phenomenon.* Oxford: Capstone.

Cruikshank, Jeffrey L. 1987. *A delicate experiment: The Harvard Business School 1909–1945.* Boston: Harvard Business School Press.

Davenport, D. H., L. Prusak, and H. J. Wilson. 2003. *What's the big idea? Creating and capitalizing on the best new management thinking.* Boston: Harvard Business School Press.

Dos Passos, John. 1938. *U.S.A.* New York: Penguin.

Drucker, Peter F. 1942. *The future of industrial man.* New York: John Day.

———. 1954. *The practice of management.* New York: Harper & Row.

———. 1969. *The age of discontinuity.* New York: Harper & Row.

———. 1980. *Managing in turbulent times.* New York: Harper & Row.

———. 1986. *Managing for results.* New York: Perennial Library.

————. 1988. The coming of the new organization. *Harvard Business Review* January–February: 45–53.

————. 1993. *The concept of the corporation.* New Brunswick, NJ: Transaction Publishers. (Originally published in 1946.)

————. 1995. *Managing in a time of great change.* New York: Truman Talley.

————. 1999. *Management challenges for the 21st century.* New York: HarperBusiness.

————. 2001. *The essential Drucker: Selections from the management works of Peter F. Drucker.* New York: HarperBusiness.

Eccles, Robert G., and Nitin Nohria. 1992. *Beyond the hype: Rediscovering the essence of management.* Boston: Harvard Business School Press.

Follett, Mary Parker. 1995. *Prophet of management: A celebration of writings from the 1920s.* Washington, DC: Beard Books.

Ford, Henry. 2007. *My life and work.* N.p.: NuVision.

Frank, Thomas. 2000. *One market under God: Extreme capitalism, market populism, and the end of economic democracy.* New York: Doubleday.

Ghemawat, Pankaj. 2002. Competition and business strategy in historical perspective. *Business History Review* 76: 37–74.

Gilbreth, Frank B., Jr., and Ernestine Gilbreth Carey. 2005. *Cheaper by the dozen.* New York: HarperCollins.

Gillespie, Richard. 1991. *Manufacturing knowledge: A history of the Hawthorne experiments.* Cambridge: Cambridge University Press.

Gimpl, Martin L., and Stephen R. Dakin. 1984. Management and magic. *California Management Review* 27 (1): 125–136.

Gioia, D. A., and K. G. Corley. 2002. Being good versus looking good: Business school rankings. *Academy of Management Learning and Education* 1: 107–20.

Gordon, Robert, and James Howell. 1959. *Higher education for business.* New York: Columbia University Press.

Grey, Christopher. 2004. Re-inventing business schools. *Academy of Management Learning and Education* 3: 178–189.

Grey, Christopher, and Hugh Willmott, eds. 2005. *Critical management studies: A reader.* Oxford: Oxford University Press.

Hamel, Gary. 2007. *The future of management.* Boston: Harvard Business School Press.

Hamel, Gary, and C. K. Prahalad. 1989. Strategic intent. *Harvard Business Review* May–June: 63–76.

————. 1990. The core competence of the corporation. *Harvard Business Review* May–June: 79–91.

————. 1994. *Competing for the future.* Boston: Harvard Business School Press.

Handy, Charles. 1989. *The age of unreason.* Boston: Harvard Business School Press.

————. 1994. *The empty raincoat.* London: Hutchinson.

Hayes, Robert M., and William J. Abernathy. 1980. Managing our way to economic decline. *Harvard Business Review* July–August: 67–77.

Henderson, Bruce D. 1979. *Henderson on corporate strategy*. Cambridge, MA: Abt Books.

Hill, Napoleon. 2004. *Think and grow rich*. Los Angeles: Highroads Media.

Hofstadter, Richard. 1963. *Anti-intellectualism in American life*. New York: Knopf.

Homans, George Caspar. 1984. *Coming to my senses: The autobiography of a sociologist*. New Brunswick, NJ: Transaction Books.

Hoopes, James. 2003. *False prophets: The gurus who created modern management and why their ideas are bad for business today*. Cambridge, MA: Perseus.

Hoskisson, Robert, Michael A. Hitt, William P. Wan, and Daphne Yiu. 1999. Theory and research in strategy: Swings of pendulum. *Journal of Management* 25: 417–56.

Huczynski, Andrej. 1993. *Management gurus: What makes them and how to become one*. London: Routledge.

Ivanecivich, John M., Robert Konpaske, and Michael J. Matteson. 2005. *Organizational behavior and management*. New York: McGraw-Hill.

Kanigel, Robert. 1997. *The one best way: Frederick Winslow Taylor and the enigma of efficiency*. New York: Viking.

Kanter, Rosabeth Moss. 1984. *The change masters: Innovation and entrepreneurship in the American corporation*. New York: Touchstone.

———. 2003. *On the frontiers of management*. Boston: Harvard Business School Press.

———. 2007. *Confidence: How winning streaks and losing streaks begin and end*. New York: Crown Business.

Khurana, Rakesh. 2007. *From higher aims to hired hands: The social transformation of American business schools and the unfulfilled promise of management as a profession*. Princeton, NJ: Princeton University Press.

Khurana, Rakesh, Nitin Nohria, and Danial Penrice. 2005. Is business management a profession? *Harvard Business School Working Knowledge* February 21, http://hbswk.hbs.edu/archive/4650.html.

Knee, Jonathan A. 2006. *The accidental investment banker: Inside the decade that transformed Wall Street*. Oxford: Oxford University Press.

Koch, Richard. 1998. *The 80/20 principle: The secret of achieving more with less*. New York: Doubleday.

Kreitner, Robert, and Angelo Kinicki. 2007. *Organizational behavior*. New York: McGraw-Hill.

Learned, Edmund P., C. Roland Christensen, Kenneth R. Andrews, and William Guth. 1969. *Business policy: Text and cases*. Homewood, IL: Richard D. Irwin.

Lears, Jackson. 2003. *Something for nothing: Luck in America*. New York: Penguin.

Livingston, J. S. 1971. The myth of the well-educated manager. *Harvard Business Review* 49: 78–89.

Lowell, A. L. 1923. The profession of business. *Harvard Business Review* 1 (2): 129–132.

Mayo, Elton. 1923. Civilized unreason. *Harper's Monthly Magazine* 148: 527–35.

———. 1924. Civilization: The perilous adventure. *Harper's Monthly Magazine* 149: 590–97.

———. 1925a. The great stupidity. *Harper's Monthly Magazine* 151: 225.

———. 1925b. Should marriage be monotonous? *Harper's Monthly Magazine* 151: 420–27.

———. 1926–1927. Sin with a capital "S." *Harper's Monthly Magazine* 154: 537–46.

———. 1930. The human effect of mechanization. *American Economic Review* 20 (1 suppl.): 156–76.

———. 1933. *The human problems of an industrial civilization*. New York: MacMillan.

———. 1945. *The social problems of an industrial civilization*. Boston: Harvard Business School.

McGregor, Douglas. 1960. *The human side of the enterprise*. New York: McGraw-Hill.

———. 1967. *The professional manager*. New York: McGraw-Hill.

McKenna, Christopher D. 2006. *The world's newest profession: Management consulting in the twentieth century*. Cambridge: Cambridge University Press.

Merkle, Judith A. 1980. *Management and ideology*. Berkeley: University of California Press.

Micklethwait, John, and Adrian Wooldridge. 1996. *The witch doctors: Making sense of the management gurus*. New York: Times Books.

Miner, John B. 2002. *Organizational behavior: Foundations, theories, and analysis*. Oxford: Oxford University Press.

Mintzberg, Henry. 1994. *The rise and fall of strategic planning*. New York: Free Press.

———. 2004. *Managers, not MBAs: A hard look at the soft practice of managing and management on development*. San Francisco: Berrett-Koehler.

Mintzberg, Henry, Bruce Ahlstrand, and Joseph Lampel. 2005. *Strategy bites back: It is a lot more, and less, than you ever imagined*. Upper Saddle River, NJ: Pearson Prentice Hall.

Montgomery, David. 1987. *The fall of the house of labor*. Cambridge: Cambridge University Press.

Navarro, Peter. 2008. The MBA core curricula of top-ranked U.S. business schools: A study in failure? *Academy of Management Learning and Education* 7: 108–123.

Nelson, Daniel, ed. 1992. *A mental revolution: Scientific management since Taylor*. Columbus: Ohio State University Press.

O'Shea, James, and Charles Madigan. 1998. *Dangerous company: Management consultants and the businesses they save and ruin*. New York: Penguin.

Parker, Martin. 2002. *Against management*. Cambridge: Polity.

Pattison, Stephen. 1997. *The faith of the managers: When management becomes religion*. London: Cassell.

Penrose, Edith. 1995. *The theory of the growth of the firm.* 3rd ed. Oxford: Oxford University Press.

Peters, Tom. 1987. *Thriving on chaos: Handbook for a management revolution.* New York: Harper & Row.

———. 1992. *Liberation management.* New York: MacMillan.

———. 1994a. *The pursuit of WOW! Every person's guide to topsy-turvy times.* New York: Vintage.

———. 1994b. *The Tom Peters seminar: Crazy times call for crazy organizations.* New York: Vintage.

———. 2001. Tom Peters's true confessions. *Fast Company* 53: 78–89.

———. 2003. *Re-imagine: Business excellence in a disruptive age.* London: Dorling Kindersley.

Peters, Thomas J., and Nancy Austin. 1986. *A passion for excellence: The leadership difference.* New York: Warner.

Peters, Thomas J., and Robert H. Waterman, Jr. 1982. *In search of excellence: Lessons from America's best-run companies.* New York: Warner Books.

Pfeffer, Jeffrey, and Christina T. Fong. 2002. The end of business schools? *Academy of Management Executive* 1 (1): 78–95.

———. 2004. The business school business. *Journal of Management Studies* 41: 1501–20.

Pinault, Lewis. 2001. *Consulting demons: Inside the unscrupulous world of global corporate consulting.* New York: HarperBusiness.

Porter, Michael E. 1979. How competitive forces shape strategy. *Harvard Business Review* March–April: 137–145.

———. 1980. *Competitive strategy. Techniques for analyzing industries and competitors.* New York: Free Press.

———. 1985. *Competitive advantage.* New York: Free Press.

———. 1987. From competitive advantage to corporate strategy. *Harvard Business Review* May–June: 43–59.

———. 1996. What is strategy? *Harvard Business Review* November–December: 61–78.

———. 2008. The five competitive forces that shape strategy. *Harvard Business Review* 86 (1): 78–93.

Porter, Lyman W., and Lawrence E. McKibbin. 1988. *Management education and development: Drift or thrust into the 21st century?* New York: McGraw-Hill.

Powell, Thomas C. 2001. Competitive advantage: Logical and philosophical considerations. *Strategic Management Journal* 22: 875–88.

Rasiel, Ethan M. 1999. *The McKinsey way.* New York: McGraw-Hill.

Scott, William. 1992. *Chester Barnard and the guardians of the managerial state.* Lawrence: University Press of Kansas.

Selznick, Philip. 1957. *Leadership in administration: A sociological interpretation.* Evanston, IL: Row, Peterson and Co.

Simon, Herbert A. 1997. *Administrative behavior.* New York: Free Press.

Sloan, Alfred P., Jr. 1963. *My years with General Motors.* New York: Doubleday.

Spender, J. C. 2007. Management as a regulated profession: An essay. *Journal of Management Inquiry* 16: 32–42.

Spender, J. C., and Hugo Kijne. 1996. *Scientific management: Frederick Winslow Taylor's gift to the world.* Boston: Kluwer.

Starkey, K., A. Hatchard, and S. Tempest. 2004. Re-thinking the business school. *Journal of Management Studies* 41: 1521–1531.

Steiner, George A. 1969. *Top management planning.* New York: MacMillan.

———. 1979. *Strategic planning: What every manager must know.* New York: MacMillan.

Taylor, Frederick Winslow. 1906. *On the art of cutting metals.* New York: American Society of Mechanical Engineers.

———. 1947. *Scientific management.* New York: Harper Brothers.

Townsend, Robert. 2007. *Up the organization.* San Francisco: Jossey-Bass.

Trahair, Richard C. S. 1984. *Elton Mayo: The humanist temper.* New Brunswick, NJ: Transaction Publishers.

Welch, Jack. 2005. *Winning.* New York: Collins.

Wernerfelt, Birger. 1984. A resource based view of the firm. *Strategic Management Journal* 5 (2): 171–80.

———. 1995. Resource based view: Ten years after. *Strategic Management Journal* 16: 171–74.

Wolf, William B. 1974. *The basic Barnard: An introduction to Chester I. Barnard and his theories of organization and management.* Ithaca, NY: Cornell University Press.

Worthy, James C. 1959. *Big business and free men.* New York: Harper.

Wrege, Charles D., and Amedeo G. Perroni. 1974. Taylor's pig-tale: A historical analysis of Frederick W. Taylor's pig-iron experiments. *Academy of Management Journal* 17 (1): 6–27.

Wren, Daniel A. 2005. *The history of management thought.* 5th ed. New York: Wiley.

Bibliographical Appendix

The long-forgotten philosopher George Santayana once said that "a country without a memory is a country of madmen." The land of the management theorists, by this standard, is raving. Even on the respectable, academic side of the discipline, there is an indefensible will to neglect the history of management thought. As a consequence of this neglect, the entire discipline serves as an excellent illustration of the only other saying for which the hapless Santayana is remembered, that "those who cannot learn from history are doomed to repeat it."

There are, however, a number of important exceptions to this historical obliviousness that I have relied upon in writing this book and to which I would like to draw attention in this appendix. Aside from acknowledging some of my debts, I would like to offer suggestions for readers interested in pursuing further some of the topics raised in this book.

Those interested to learn more about the history of management education should turn to Khurana (2007), who provides the most thorough and thoughtful treatment of the subject to date. Khurana argues that the business schools began as a project to create a new profession, but that the drive toward a scientific approach to management, especially in the wake of World War II, crowded out the ethical imperatives of the nascent business profession. "The logic of professionalism that underlay the university-based business school in its formative phase was replaced first by a managerialist logic that emphasized professional knowledge rather than professional ideals, and ultimately by a market logic that, taken to its conclusion, subverts the logic of professionalism altogether," he writes.[1]

Although I find much to admire, as well as much that is useful, in the details of Khurana's account, I remain unpersuaded by his guiding narrative about the business schools' purported fall from grace. The truth is that the business schools, if they fell, did not fall from any great height. In their earliest years, in my view, the schools failed to achieve any great degree of clarity or unity of purpose about their professional mission, and the reasons for this have to do not with malfeasance but with the contradictions lodged in the very idea that business management is a profession. The various pronouncements about professionalism in business in the early part of the twentieth century, which Khurana reads as central to the formation of the schools, are not qualitatively different in this respect from the very similar and, in my view, equally ineffective pronouncements heard today from time to time.

The Gordon and Howell report of 1959 may mark an important inflection point in the development of the schools, as Khurana notes, but its philosophical foundation at bottom amounts to a restatement of the ideology of managerial rationalism that was invoked at the start of the business school project. The rise of shareholder value as the guiding dogma of management thought does represent an important twist in the history of management thought, as Khurana argues, but in my view it should be seen as the continuation of the earlier tradition rather than a departure from it. In short, Khurana seems to have transposed an essentially atemporal flaw in the business schools' professionalization ideology onto a diachronic, historical narrative. Nonetheless, Khurana's criticisms of the contemporary business schools, and in particular his focus on the narrowly financial and individualistic ethic that pervades the schools today, seem very much on the mark to me and should be of interest to anyone concerned about the future of management education.

Readers interested in additional criticism of the existing business school system can now take advantage of a small but growing subgenre of management literature. Mintzberg's *Managers, Not MBAs* (2004) is at the top of the list. Pfeffer and Fong (2002, 2004), and Spender (2007) are also good places to start.

The market for general surveys of the history of management thought seems oddly undeveloped, especially in comparison with that for surveys in the history of philosophy and the history of thought. Daniel Wren (2005) provides perhaps the most serious general effort to date. Hoopes (2003) offers a readable and highly critical survey of a number of key management thinkers, including Taylor and Mayo. Hoopes makes a strong case that, Taylor excepted, most management theorists have preferred to peddle illusory visions of bottom-up management styles than face the reality of top-down management power.

A number of scholars have now turned their attention to the management consulting industry. McKenna (2006), in particular, offers an illuminating history of the business. He argues that the key factor driving the consulting industry in the United States was a change in the regulatory environment in the 1930s. The passage of the Glass-Steagall Act, in particular, prevented banks, law firms, and accounting firms from providing consulting services, and so cleared the competitive space from which consulting firms emerged. McKenna points out that the large consulting firms originated in Chicago because the Windy City lacked a large investment banking community and therefore turned to management consultants for due-diligence activities.

McKenna further argues that consultants have played an important and useful role in disseminating key concepts in managerial practice—notably the decentralized M-Form organizational design. He concludes with a hopeful suggestion that, in the wake of Enron and other corporate scandals, consultants have an opportunity to achieve at long last the professional status to which they have always laid claim. To which I can only add, good luck with that!

McKenna also makes the interesting observation that the genealogy of modern consulting firms can be traced back not to Taylor and the leaders of the scientific management movement, but to their contemporaries in the fields of cost accounting and engineering. This may be true in the detail, but it misses something important in the larger picture. Taylor's contribution both to the consulting industry and to society at large occurred at the level not of individual firms and institutions but of culture and ideology.

The tradition of criticizing the management gurus is almost as old as the management guru business itself. The tradition divides roughly between those who take the gurus' mission seriously on their own terms—even if they find fault with many individual gurus—and those who do not. The most successful representative of the first variety is Micklethwait and Wooldridge's *Witch Doctors* (1996), which, despite its promising title, pulls its punches well short of a general critique of the guru business. Eccles and Nohria (1992) likewise, despite some bold moves at the start, fall into this ameliorative side of the tradition. On the other side of the fence are writers such as, notably, Huczynski (1993), who takes the view that the gurus' success has much less to do with the merits of their ideas than with their salesmanship. Frank (2000) includes an excellent takedown of Peters and offers a perceptive critique that links the ideas of the gurus to "market populism"—the politically powerful and ultimately oppressive idea that free markets represent a democratic ideal and will solve all of our nation's problems.

In the United Kingdom and a few other places outside the United States, a subdiscipline called Critical Management Studies (CMS) has emerged to take on some of the task of analyzing the ideological foundations of management theory. Grey and Willmott (2005), Collins (2000), and Parker (2002) represent notable contributions to the genre. The CMS scholars have an unfortunate tendency, no doubt reinforced by the academic setting of their work, to gaze into their epistemological navels and squander much of their energies debating with themselves what exactly they think they are about to do. Once they clear the postmodern fog and get around to examining the empirical world of management theory and practice from a critical point of view, however, they provide a refreshing break from the heavily ideological cheerleading that characterizes much of the rest of management thought and offer material that should be of interest to all those concerned with the worthy project of developing a critical intellectual apparatus to check the growing power of management in society. Collins (2000), in particular, provides many amusing analyses of the structure and origins of the guru market.

Frederick Winslow Taylor has been the subject of much scholarly interest. The canonical source now is the highly readable and highly recommended biography by Kanigel (1997). Our knowledge of events at Hawthorne is owed to the excellent historical work of Gillespie (1991). In the field of strategy, a book-length, critical survey of the strategy business that might do for the whole discipline what Mintzberg (1994) did for the strategic planning end of things would appear to be lacking. The long article by Ghemawat (2002), however, provides a useful historical survey of the field.

There are many works by management gurus that I neither discuss in this book nor include in the reference list. I neglect, for example, W. E. Deming and the quality movement, and I fail to give Peter Drucker a chapter of his own, as is now the custom among those who comment on the gurus. My excuse is in part that I had to be selective to make this book fit between two covers, and in part that, in my view, the issues that arise in reviewing the work of these neglected schools of thought have already been discussed in the context of those that were included. Deming, for example, who argued for the abolition of merit pay and performance reviews on the grounds that they diminish social solidarity, I view largely as a utopian political philosopher in the style of Mayo. And his interest in applying statistical tools to quality control represents an extension of Taylorism. Although his success in postwar Japan arose out of specific social and political issues in that country that I do not have the space to address, Deming's renown in the United States dates from the 1980s and really belongs to the humanist movement that I discuss in connection with Tom Peters. I should add that there is a large population of gurus on whom no comment should be offered. They are best left in the trash can of history.

Notes

The Accidental Consultant

1. McKenna (2006) uses this expression for the title of his book.
2. Canback (1998), pp. 3–4. Canback puts the number of consultants at 140,000 in 1998, but other sources give a range of estimates up to 300,000 in subsequent years.
3. *Statistical Abstract of the United States*, 1974, 1993, 2008. Note that the 2008 *Statistical Abstract* has 142,000 master's degrees in business for 2005, and I am making the safe assumption that the number did not decline in the subsequent three years. Note also that the Census Bureau does not break out the number of MBAs from the total number of business degrees.
4. David Leonhardt, "A Matter of Degree? Not for Consultants," *New York Times*, October 1, 2000.
5. Pfeffer and Fong (2002), p. 3.
6. H. Mintzberg and J. Lampel, "Do MBAs Make Better CEOs? Sorry, Dubya, It Ain't Necessarily So," *Fortune*, February 19, 2001, p. 244.
7. Anne Fisher, "The Trouble with MBAs," *CNN Fortune*, April 23, 2007, www .money.cnn.com/magazines/fortune.
8. Porter and McKibbin (1988), p. 170.
9. Davenport et al. (2003), p. 81, cited in Pfeffer and Fong (2004), p. 1502.
10. Bennis and O'Toole (2005), p. 96.
11. Ibid., p. 98.
12. Hamel (2007), p. 180.
13. Collins (2001), p. 88.
14. Peters and Waterman (1982), p. xiii.
15. Peters and Austin (1985), p. 7.
16. Scott DeCarlo, "Big Paychecks," *Forbes*, May 3, 2007.

17. Study by the Associated Press, cited by Rachel Beck and Matthew Fordhal, "CEO Pay Rose Higher in '07 despite Economic Woes," *Yahoo! News*, June 15, 2008, www.news.yahoo.com.

18. See Jeanne Sahadi, "CEO Pay," *CNN Money.com*, August 28, 2007, www .money.cnn.com, which puts the number at 364 for 2006, 411 for 2005, and 525 for 2000.

19. Beck and Fordhal, "CEO Pay Rose Higher."

20. Gary Wilson, "How to Rein in the Imperial CEO," *Wall Street Journal*, July 9, 2008.

21. See James K. Galbraith, *The Predator State: How Conservatives Abandoned the Free Market and Why Liberals Should Too* (New York: Free Press, 2008), for discussion of similar questions.

22. Hamel (2007), p. 5.

23. Drucker (2001), p. 3.

24. Friedrich Nietzsche, *Werke*, ed. Karl Schlechta (Frankfurt: Ullstein Materialien, 1984), vol. 2, p. 941.

I. Doing Things with Numbers

1. See the writings of Richard Koch, Vilfredo Pareto, and Joseph Juran.

2. See Joseph M. Juran, *Quality Control Handbook* (New York: McGraw-Hill, 1951).

3. Ryan Lizza, "The Mission: Mitt Romney's Strategies for Success," *New Yorker*, October 29, 2007.

4. I am indebted to Kanigel (1997) as the source for this and most of the Taylor biographical material, supplemented by Copley (1923), Nelson (1992), Hoopes (2003), Khurana (2007), and Spender (2007).

5. Address before the Cleveland Advertising Club, March 3, 1915, cited in Wren (2005), p. 135.

6. Kanigel (1997), p. 380.

7. Birge Harrison, *Recollections*, August 15, 1915; cited in Sudhir Kakar, *Frederick Taylor* (Cambridge, MA: MIT Press, 1970), p. 18.

8. Taylor, *Shop Management*, p. 159, in Taylor (1947).

9. Ibid., p. 189.

10. Ibid., p. 27.

11. Taylor, *Testimony before the Special House Committee*, p. 30, in Taylor (1947).

12. Kanigel (1997), p. 391.

13. Taylor, *Principles of Scientific Management*, pp. 40–41, in Taylor (1947).

14. Taylor, *Shop Management*, p. 18.

15. Taylor, *Testimony*, p. 48.

16. Taylor, *Principles*, p. 8.

17. Taylor, *Testimony*, p. 27.

18. Drucker (1954), p. 280.

19. Hamel (2007), p. 5.

20. Braverman (1974), p. 15.

21. Kanigel (1997) cites these and other religious metaphors throughout his text.

22. Ibid., p. 505.

23. Taylor, *Principles*, p. 5.

24. Morris L. Cooke, "The Spirit and Social Significance of Scientific Management," *Journal of Political Economy*, 21 (1913), p. 481; compare Dwight Waldo, *The Administrative State*, cited in Bendix (1956), p. 275.

25. Khurana (2007), p. 96.

26. V. I. Lenin, "The Immediate Tasks of the Soviet Government," 1918, cited in Braverman (1974), p. 12.

27. J. C. Spender writes on this topic in various places.

28. Cruikshank (1987), p. 54.

29. Ibid., p. 61.

30. Ibid., p. 72.

31. Copley (1923), vol. 2, p. 353.

32. Cruikshank (1987), p. 90.

33. Kanigel (1997), p. 399.

34. For most of the criticisms of the pig-iron tale here, I am indebted to Wrege and Perroni (1974).

35. Taylor used the numbers 20%, 27%, and 225%, but as percentage of stop-watch time added to equal total time—not a deduction from the total as in the pig-iron case.

36. Kanigel (1997), p. 397.

37. Wren (2005), p. 234.

38. Nelson (1992), p. 70.

39. Ibid., p. 59.

40. Cruikshank (1987), p. 54.

41. Follett (1995).

42. Ford (2007), p. 76.

43. Nelson (1992), p. 53.

44. See Merkle (1980), pp. 252–56, for more on the New Machine.

45. Wren (2005), pp. 160–61.

46. Nelson (1992), p. 62.

47. Friedrich Nietzsche, *Werke*, ed. Karl Schlechta (Frankfurt: Ullstein Materialien, 1984), vol. 3, p. 903.

48. See Gimpl and Dakin (1984), passim.

49. O'Shea and Madigan (1998), p. 6.

50. Niccolo Machiavelli, *Il Principe* [The Prince], ed. Laurence Arthur Burd and John Acton (Oxford: Clarendon Press, 1891), p. 352.

51. Hofstadter (1963), p. 247.
52. See Deborah Blum, *Ghost Hunters: William James and the Search for Scientific Proof of Life after Death* (New York: Penguin, 2006).
53. Michael Pollan, "Our National Eating Disorder," *New York Times*, October 17, 2004.
54. Frederick Augustus Baker, *The Coming Age Presaged by an Era of Profounder Research* (Maplewood, NJ, 1933).
55. Norman Vincent Peale, *A Guide to Confident Living* (New York: Simon & Schuster, 2003), p. 113.
56. Van Wyck Brooks, *The Ordeal of Mark Twain* (New York: E. P. Dutton, 1920).
57. Hofstadter (1963), p. 237.
58. Khurana (2007) examines this and other episodes in greater detail.
59. Taylor, *Testimony*, p. 192.
60. Philip Roth, *The Human Stain* (New York: Vintage Books, 2000), p. 147.
61. *The Federalist Papers/Alexander Hamilton, James Madison, John Jay* (New York: Mentor Press, 1999), ch. 51.
62. Hoopes (2003) makes a similar case.
63. Hamel (2007), p. 6.
64. Drucker (1993/1946), p. ix.
65. Gordon and Howell (1959).
66. Andrew Carnegie and John Charles Van Dyke, *Autobiography of Andrew Carnegie* (New York: Houghton Mifflin, 1920), p. 158.

II. Putting People First

1. Baritz (1960), p. 77; for much of the biographical material, I am indebted to Trahair (1984), the only full-length biography of Mayo.
2. Trahair (1984), p. 146.
3. Ibid., p. 199.
4. Baritz (1960), p. 149.
5. Trahair (1984), p. 232.
6. Trahair (1984), p. 349.
7. Ibid., p. 146.
8. Ibid., p. 163.
9. Bourke (1982), p. 229.
10. Mayo (1924), p. 591.
11. Bourke (1982), p. 226.
12. Trahair (1984), p. 135.
13. Ibid., p. 230.
14. Mayo (1924), p. 591.
15. Trahair (1984), p. 221.
16. Gillespie (1991), p. 99.

17. Mayo (1924), p. 597.

18. Vilfredo Pareto and Arthur Livingston, *The Mind and Society: Trattato di Sociologia Generale* (New York: Harcourt, Brace, 1935), p. 1430.

19. Gillespie (1991), p. 187; see also Trahair (1984), pp. 83, 317.

20. Trahair (1984), p. 338.

21. Mayo (1933), p. 185.

22. Homans (1984), p. 139.

23. Trahair (1984), p. 155.

24. Mayo (1923), p. 530.

25. Abraham Zaleznik, in Trahair (1984), p. 11.

26. Homans (1984), p. 135.

27. Gillespie (1991), p. 119.

28. Ibid., p. 18; in this and subsequent accounts of Hawthorne, I rely primarily on Gillespie.

29. Ibid., p. 57.

30. Ibid., p. 61.

31. Ibid., p. 62.

32. Trahair (1984), p. 232.

33. Cruikshank (1987), p. 173.

34. Gillespie (1991), p. 73.

35. Mayo (1933), p. 97.

36. Gillespie (1991), p. 169.

37. Mayo (1945), p. 78.

38. Trahair (1984), p. 247.

39. Ibid., p. 248.

40. Ibid., p. 234.

41. Ibid., p. 235.

42. Mayo (1945), p. 72.

43. Mayo (1933), p. 71.

44. Mayo (1930), p. 176.

45. Fritz Roethlisberger, *Management and Morale* (Cambridge, MA: Harvard University Press, 1941), p. 15.

46. Mayo (1933), p. 46.

47. Mayo (1945), p. 62.

48. Mayo (1933), p. 69.

49. Mayo (1945), p. 78.

50. Gillespie (1991), p. 83.

51. Trahair (1984), p. 258.

52. Gillespie (1991), p. 88.

53. Ibid.

54. Carey (1967), p. 416.

55. Trahair (1984), p. 257.

56. Mayo (1945), p. 119.

57. Drucker (1954), p. 275.

58. Trahair (1984), p. 241.

59. Scott (1992), p. 55.

60. See Henry A. Landsberger, *Hawthorne Revisited* (Ithaca, NY: Cornell University Press, 1958).

61. Scott (1992), p. 84.

62. Barnard (1938).

63. McGregor (1960).

64. Gifford Pinchot, *Intrapreneuring* (New York: HarperCollins, 1986), pp. 247–48, 309–15, 320.

65. William Ouchi, *Theory Z* (Reading, MA: Addison-Wesley, 1981), pp. 4, 165.

66. Gary Hamel, promotional author video on amazon.com (accessed October 27, 2008).

67. Peters and Waterman (1982), pp. 5–6.

68. Robert Owen, *A New View of Society* (New York: Free Press, 1948), p. 73.

69. See Miner (2002), p. 4: "Finally, organizational behavior is not *philosophy*. That, however, is a rather complex story." Indeed!

70. Owen, *New View of Society*, p. 14.

71. Gillespie (1991), p. 122.

72. Peters and Waterman (1982), p. 6.

73. Scott (1992), p. 49.

74. Gordon and Howell (1959), p. 166.

75. Kreitner and Kinicki (2007), p. 13. See also similar comments in Miner (2002), p. 36; and Ivanecivich, Konpaske, and Matteson (2005), p. 13.

76. See Khurana, Noria, and Penrice (2005) and Khurana (2007) for more argument along similar lines.

77. Marty Kihn has a new book out on the topic titled *A$$hole*.

78. Perhaps the best example of the pyramid game at its competitive extreme comes from the Ottoman Empire. The sultans made it a point never to declare which of their many offspring would be heir to the throne. As a result, their children inevitably engaged in a brutal version of the pyramid game. They would form alliances in order to slit the throats of rival siblings, and then they'd turn around and form new alliances to eliminate one another. The last one standing, it was thought, had proved himself both the most ruthless of the brood and, at the same time, the most effective in forming cooperative alliances.

III. Thinking Ahead

1. Steiner (1969), p. 344.

2. Drucker (1986), p. vii.

3. Khurana (2007) p. 39.

4. Antoniou and Sullivan (2006), p. 4.

5. Ibid., p. 11.

6. Robert Grant, quoted in Antoniou and Sullivan (2006), p. 16.

7. Antoniou and Sullivan (2006), p. 97.

8. Ibid., p. 99.

9. Ibid., p. 98.

10. Robert C. Moussetis, in Antoniou and Sullivan (2006), p. 385.

11. Boston Consulting Group website: www.bcg.com/about_bcg/history/1965
    .html (accessed October 27, 2008).

12. O'Shea and Madigan (1998), p. 154.

13. Bruce Henderson, "Why Costs Go Down Forever," cited in Ghemawat
    (2002).

14. "Interview with Michael Porter," *Academy of Management Executive*, 16 (May
    2002), pp. 43–52.

15. Learned et al. (1969), p. 5.

16. Bain (1956), p. 207.

17. Porter (1979).

18. Porter (1980), p. 6.

19. Porter (1979), pp. 137–39.

20. Porter (1980), p. xxii.

21. Ansoff (1988), p. 137.

22. Porter (1980), p. 88.

23. Penrose (1995), p. 10.

24. Selznick (1957), p. 8.

25. Wernerfelt (1984, 1995).

26. Porter (1980), p. xv.

27. Hamel and Prahalad (1994), p. 6.

28. Welch (2005), p. 165.

29. Collins (2001), p. 63.

30. Ansoff (1965), pp. 25–26, 73–74.

31. Steiner (1969), p. 46.

32. Antoniou and Sullivan (2006), p. 99.

33. Richard Rumelt, cited in Mintzberg, Ahlstrand, and Lampel (2005), p. 207.

34. Antoniou and Sullivan (2006), p. 159.

35. Steiner (1969), p. 4.

36. Ibid., p. 26.

37. To muddy the water somewhat, Ansoff is distinct from some of the other plan-
    ners in that he moves a considerable amount of the decision-making task to the
    planners themselves, as a distinct apparatus within the office of the CEO.

38. Michael Porter, "The CEO as Strategist"; cited in Mintzberg, Ahlstrand,
    and Lampel (2005), p. 43.

39. Mintzberg (1994), p. 321.

40. Porter (1987), p. 43.

41. Brian Quinn, cited in Mintzberg (1994) and Peters (1994a).

42. "An Interview with Richard Rumelt," *McKinsey Quarterly*, November 2007, www.mckinseyquarterly.com (accessed November 2007).

43. Richard Rumelt, *Strategy, Structure, and Economic Performance* (Boston: Division of Research, Graduate School of Business Administration, Harvard University, 1974).

44. Porter (1987), p. 43.

45. Antoniou and Sullivan (2006), p. 12.

46. Ibid., p. 360.

47. Ibid.

48. Ghemawat (2002), p. 50; Ghemawat provides a useful general survey of the strategy discipline.

49. Bruce Henderson, "The Origin of Strategy," *Harvard Business Review*, November–December 1989, pp. 139–43.

50. J. Scott Armstrong and Roderick Brodie, "Effects of Portfolio Planning Methods on Decision Making: Experimental Results," *International Journal of Research in Marketing*, 11 (1994), pp. 1–95.

51. Bert Hopwood, *Whatever Happened to the British Motorcycle Industry?*; cited in Mintzberg, Ahlstrand, and Lampel (2005), p. 206.

52. Thomas Hout, "Competing against Time," in *Perspectives on Strategy: From the Boston Consulting Group*, ed. Carl W. Stern and George Stalk, Jr. (New York: Wiley, 1998).

53. See Birnbau (2001), Best (2006), and Carson et al. (2000).

54. Porter (1980), p. xxii.

55. "Interview with Michael Porter," *Academy of Management Executive*, 16 (May 2002), pp. 43–52.

56. Rumelt, *Strategy, Structure, and Economic Performance*.

57. Porter (1996).

58. Hamel and Prahalad (1990), pp. 79–81.

59. "Gates' Law," *Context*, 1 (Winter 1998), 1.

60. Brandenburger and Nalebuff (1996), p. 111.

61. Ibid., p. 116.

62. Ibid., p. 223.

63. Ibid., p. 137.

64. Ibid., p. 146.

65. Ibid., p. 136.

66. Ibid., pp. 185, 191.

67. Ibid., p. 187.

68. Ibid., p. 188.

69. Ibid., p. 192.

70. Ibid., p. 98.
71. Ibid., p. 99.
72. Ibid., p. 195.
73. Ibid., p. 233.
74. Jay Barney, "Michael Porter," *Academy of Management Executive*, 16 (May 2002), pp. 53–57.
75. Cited by Andrew Ferguson, "Back to School, Turning Crimson," *Wall Street Journal*, August 5, 2008.
76. Jon Swartz, "CEO Quits Job over UFO Views," *San Francisco Chronicle*, January 9, 1999.

IV. Striving for Excellence

1. Peters (2001) for this and following interview quotes.
2. Peters (2003), p. 7.
3. Peters and Waterman (1982), pp. 13–15.
4. Ibid., pp. 8, 39.
5. Mark Gimein, "Now That We Live in a Tom Peters World . . . Has He Gone Crazy?" *Fortune*, November 13, 2000.
6. Peters and Austin (1986), p. 265.
7. Micklethwait and Wooldridge (1996), p. 63.
8. Crainer (1997), p. 64.
9. Peter Drucker, *Frontiers of Management: Where Tomorrow's Decisions Are Being Shaped Today* (New York: Truman Talley Books, 1986), p. 187.
10. Stuart Crainer, *The Ultimate Business Library: 50 Books That Shaped Management Thinking* (New York: Amacom, 1997), p. 218.
11. Peters (2003), p. 18.
12. Collins (2001), p. 9.
13. Dan Carroll, "In Search of Excellence," *Harvard Business Review*, November–December 1983.
14. Peters (2001), p. 78.
15. Tompeters.com, posted September 28, 2007.
16. Clayman (1987), p. 54.
17. Peters (1987), p. 3.
18. From a 1997 *Fortune* article; cited in Mintzberg, Ahlstrand, and Lampel (2005).
19. Peters and Waterman (1982), p. 31.
20. Peters (1987), p. 386.
21. Ibid., p. 212.
22. Ibid., p. 398.
23. Hamel and Prahalad (1994), p. x.
24. Pfeffer and Fong (2002).
25. Crainer (1997), p. 230.

26. Drucker (1993/1946), p. ix.

27. Towers Perrin; cited in Hamel (2007), p. 57.

28. Ibid.

29. Hamel and Prahalad (1994), p. ix.

30. Hamel (2007), p. 3.

31. "Innovative Management, A Conversation with Gary Hamel and Lowell Bryan," *McKinsey Quarterly*, October 23, 2007, www.mckinseyquarterly.com.

32. Drucker (2001), p. 347.

33. Drucker (1980), p. 7.

34. Drucker (1969), pp. 9–10.

35. Peter Drucker, *Landmarks of Tomorrow* (New York: Harper, 1959), p. 11.

36. Joseph Schumpeter, *Capitalism, Socialism, and Democracy* (New York: Harper & Brothers, 1942).

37. Karl Marx, *The Communist Manifesto* (Digireads, 2005), p. 33.

38. Peters and Waterman (1982), p. 29.

39. Peters (1992), p. 131.

40. Peters (2003), p. 31.

41. Ibid., p. 203.

42. Ibid., p. 19.

43. Peters (2001), p. 80.

44. Crainer (1997), p. 121.

45. Ibid., p. 184; Tom Peters, "Hot Times Call for Hot Words," *Business Week*, December 11, 1992.

46. Peters (2003), p. 43.

47. Ibid., p. 11.

48. Ibid.

49. Peters (1994a), p. 87.

50. Peters (1987), p. 4.

51. Peters (1994a), p. 7.

52. Hofstadter (1963).

53. Peters (2003), p. 195.

54. Crainer (1997), p. 36.

55. Peters and Waterman (1982).

56. Peters (2003), p. 9.

57. Ibid.

58. Ibid., p. 10.

59. Ibid., p. 26.

60. Drucker (1942), p. 99.

61. Drucker (1988), p. 45.

62. Peter Drucker, "Long Range Planning: Challenges to Management Science," *Management Science* 5(1959), pp. 238–39.

63. Peters (1992), p. 11.

64. Kanter (1984).
65. From a 1996 *Atlantic Monthly* article; cited in Drucker (2001), p. 316.
66. Peters (2003), p. 204.
67. Rhonda Byrne, *The Secret* (New York: Atria Books, 2006).
68. Norman Vincent Peale, *A Guide to Confident Living* (New York: Prentice-Hall, 1948), pp. 46, 55.
69. Peters (2003), 203.
70. Drucker (2001), p. 208.
71. Peters and Waterman (1982), p. 59.
72. *Tom Peters Live—Re-Imagine! Business Excellence in a Disruptive Age*, DVD (Better Life Media, 2004).
73. Crainer (1997), p. 183.
74. Ibid., p. 184.
75. Ibid., p. 131.
76. Peters (1992), p. 758.
77. Peters (2003), p. 168.
78. Ibid., pp. 8, 21.
79. Peters (1987), p. 412.
80. Drucker (1942), p. 99.
81. Drucker (2001), p. 66.
82. Peters (2003), p. 104.
83. Peters and Waterman (1982), p. xii.
84. Peters (1994a), p. 105.
85. Peters (2001), p. 81.
86. Alan Farnham, "In Search of Suckers," *Fortune*, October 14, 1996.

The Future of Management Education

1. Albert Jay Nock, "The Disadvantages of an Education," in *Free Speech and Plain Language* (New York: W. Morrow, 1937), p. 209.
2. Henry Adams, *The Education of Henry Adams: An Autobiography* (Boston: Houghton Mifflin, 1918), p. 297.
3. Livingston (1971), p. 79.
4. Navarro (2008), p. 109.
5. Gioia and Corley (2002).
6. Joseph Stiglitz, *Globalization and Its Discontents* (New York: W. W. Norton, 2003), p. 75.
7. Gary Wilson, "How to Rein in the Imperial CEO," *Wall Street Journal*, July 9, 2008.
8. See Pfeffer and Fong (2004), p. 1506.
9. Mica Schneider and Sheridan Prasso, "How an MBA Can Bend Your Mind," *Business Week*, April 1, 2002.

10. Jennifer Merritt, "You Mean Cheating is Wrong?" *Business Week*, December 9, 2002.
11. Drucker (2001), p. 13.

Bibliographical Appendix

1. Khurana (2007), p. 7.

Acknowledgments

My thanks go to my outstanding editor, Alane Mason; and my indefatigable agent, Andrew Stuart. *The Management Myth* grew out of an essay under the same title published in the *Atlantic Monthly* in June 2006. I am greatly indebted to my excellent editor there, Joy de Menil. For their discussion and comments on early drafts I wish to thank Roger Friedland, Charles Gillispie, Michelle Gittelman, Stephen Murdoch, and Peter Westwick. I was lucky to receive pointed advice on management issues from members of my own family: my brother Robert Stewart, my father James Stewart, my mother Myo Stewart, and my wife Katherine Stewart. I would also like to express my gratitude to the many colleagues and clients with whom I worked as a management consultant. I suspect that they will not object to remaining unnamed.

Index

Page numbers in *italics* refer to illustrations.